JOHN BROWN

"THE THUNDERING VOICE OF JEHOVAH"

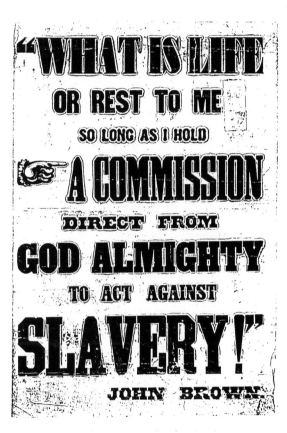

This rare broadside is dated 1860. WVSA

This remarkable photograph belonged to Salmon Brown. It shows five generations of the Brown family. The middle image is Owen Brown, father of John Brown, the abolitionist, pictured at top left. The top right is Salmon, son of John Brown. The bottom right is John, son of Salmon Brown. The bottom left is John, grandson of Salmon.

COURTESY OF JEAN LIBBY

JOHN BROWN
"THE THUNDERING VOICE OF JEHOVAH"

by Stan Cohen

Portrait of John Brown by Helen Tanner Brodt.
OHIO HISTORICAL SOCIETY COLLECTION

PICTORIAL HISTORIES PUBLISHING CO., INC.

LIBRARY OF CONGRESS
CATALOG CARD NUMBER
98-68738

ISBN 1-57510-055-X

First Printing: March 1999
Second Printing: August 2001

Cover artwork is taken from a portion of John Steuart Curry's mural,
Tragic Prelude, *on display in the Kansas Statehouse in Topeka.*
COURTESY KANSAS STATE HISTORICAL SOCIETY

Back cover painting by Col. Charles Waterhouse USMC ret.,
Edison, New Jersey

Note: Some of the geographic name spellings in this book have been changed through the years. At the time of the 1859 raid the spelling of Charles Town, West Virginia, as we know it today, was Charlestown and in the state of Virginia. When the caption or story pertains to the 1850s, the name will be spelled Charlestown. Contemporary information will of course, retain the modern spelling. Harpers Ferry has been spelled both Harpers and Harper's. The more common geographic spelling today is Harpers, so it will remain that way throughout the book.

Original letters, documents and articles have been reproduced as they were written unless otherwise noted.

Cover Graphics: Mike Egeler, Egeler Design
Typography: Leslie Maricelli and Jan Taylor

PICTORIAL HISTORIES PUBLISHING CO., INC.
713 South Third Street West, Missoula, Montana 59801
Phone (406) 549-8488   FAX (406) 728-9280
phpc@montana.com

INTRODUCTION

John Brown was born 24 years after the 13 colonies declared independence and died a tragic death by a hangman's noose, just 16 months before the United States was torn apart by civil war.

His life, which paralleled the rapid growth of the new country, was filled with business reversals, personal tragedies and a fervant moral conviction about the institution of slavery that consumed his later life. It would lead to his and many others' deaths, including several of his sons. Some say he was the spark that ignited the Civil War.

Certainly his act of treason against the existing slave laws of the United States at Harpers Ferry in 1859 pushed the country towards war, but it was only one of many incidents and policies that eventually caused the greatest crisis in our nation's history.

What Brown did by his desire to free the slaves in the Southern States was to go down in history as one of the most controversial figures of his time and his name is forever etched in the pages of American history books.

While his name is most associated with the incident at Harpers Ferry, he was commonly known as "Osawatomie Brown," his 59 years were filled with constant travels and moves around the country trying to make a living for his large family. His passion for freeing the slaves became all-consuming but was only one aspect of his most interesting life.

Brown's life touched an extraordinary number of American government, military, religious and literary figures in the first half of the 19th century. They included: Frederick Douglass, Ralph Waldo Emerson, Henry David Thoreau, Robert E. Lee, J.E.B. Stuart, Gerritt Smith, John Wilkes Booth, Edmund Ruffin, Allen Pinkerton, Samuel Howe, Julia Ward Howe, Gov. Henry Wise, President James Buchanan, Nathanial Hawthorne, John Greenleaf Whittier, Herman Melville, Louisa May Alcott, Henry Ward Beecher, Wendell Phillips, Edward Everett, William Lloyd Garrison, David H. Strother, Oliver Wendell Holmes, Horace Greeley, Harriett Tubman, Abraham Lincoln, Stonewall Jackson and others.

The list of biographies on John Brown is endless, so I have concentrated on his life pictorially following the places he frequented, his associates and the artifacts and objects associated with his life. I have tried to tell his story through his writings and the writings of others of his time as much as possible.

More than any other single event, Brown's raid on Harpers Ferry crystallized and hardened public opinion in both the North and South. The raid and Brown's public execution set in motion a spiral of accusation and counter accusation between northerners and southerners that spun the nation inexorably toward civil war. Soon northerners were marching into Virginia to the tune of "John Brown's Body." Brown's prophecy had been fulfilled, and the man became a northern legend—a symbol of noble idealism and self-sacrifice.

Acknowledgments

Many people throughout the United States helped with research, photographs and critical review: Debbie Piscitelli and Sue Baker of the Harpers Ferry Historical Association; Nancy Hatcher, Bruce J. Noble Jr., and Marsha Stankey of the Harpers Ferry National Historical Park; Susan Collins of the Jefferson County Museum, Charles Town, W.Va.; Debra Basham of the West Virginia State Archives, Charleston; Noah Mehrkam of Charles Town, W.Va.; Becky Ebert of the Handley Library, Winchester, Va.; Ed Edinger of the John Brown Heritage Association, Meadville, Pa.; Jerry Holsworth, Winchester, Va.; Dean Brown, Osawatomie, Kansas; Nancy Sherbert of the Kansas State Historical Society, Topeka; Ted Alexander of the Antietam National Battlefield, Sharpsburg, Md.; Edwin Cotter Jr., Lake Placid, New York; Marilyn Shipley, Osawatomie Chamber of Commerce; Capt. South and Sprigg Lynn of the Kennedy Farm, Md.; Dave Gilbert, Shepherdstown, W.Va.; Jennifer Williams, Tabor Library, Tabor, Iowa; Bob Walker, Cumberland, RI; Gary Kable, Charles Town, W.Va.; Thomas Vince of the Western Reserve Historical Association, Hudson, Ohio; Jim Caccamo of the Hudson Library and Historical Society, Hudson, Ohio; Valerie McQuillan, Springfield Library and Museum Association, Springfield, Mass; Ernest Cedar, Torrington City Historian and the staff of the Torrington Historical Society, Conn.; Morag Boyd, Oberlin Historical Society, Oberlin, Ohio; Jeff Kaeplar, Nebraska City, Ne.; David Shlansky, Cambridge, Mass.; Amy Newell, Put-In-Bay Historical Society, Ohio; Duryea Kemp, Tom House and Melinda Knapp, Ohio Historical Society; Jean Libby, Palo Alto, Ca.; Larry Lawrence, New York City; Sue Talbot and Hays Otoupalik of Missoula, Mont.

The Slavery Question

In 1516, King Charles I of Spain gave colonists and slave traders permission to take slaves into the Spanish colonies in America. By the late 1770s, British ships were carrying about half the slaves brought to America.

In March 1807, the United States prohibited further importation of slaves after Jan. 1, 1808. This act legally ended the overseas trade in slaves.

During the first half of the 19th century, Virginia remained vigilant regarding a genuine fear of "slave insurrection." Between 1800 and 1831, there were two prominent slave revolts, or conspiracies, i.e.: *The Gabriel Uprising of 1800* and *Nat Turner's Insurrection of 1831*. During the Turner Revolt, 55 white men, women and children were murdered by armed slaves.

Because of the nature of Northern farming, slavery was not profitable there. Slavery became concentrated in the South, particularly on the large plantations. A year after the Harpers Ferry raid there were almost four million slaves in the Southern states, nearly one-third of the total population of the 15 slave states.

People of the North and South had completely opposite views of the institution of slavery. Abolitionists branded it as an evil system that led to the ruthless exploitation of labor and the moral degradation of both slaves and masters. Southerners defended slavery as a necessary but kindly labor system which served as a civilizing force for the allegedly barbarous Negro.

The modern abolitionist crusade began to emerge in American society during the 1830s. Abolitionists—who comprised only about two percent of the northern population—condemned slavery as a sin, based on a radical interpretation of evangelical Protestant thought. The abolitionists said that slavery was a sin because it denied slaves free will and free moral agency, blocking peace with God and jeopardizing salvation for both slaves and slaveowners alike. All who were part of a society which allowed human beings to be enslaved were culpable—all were sinners, according to the abolitionists. Of course, millions of other Americans opposed slavery's expansion but not slavery where it already existed.

Most early abolitionists rejected violence as a way to end slavery, opting instead for "moral suasion"—fierce denunciations of slavery in moral and religious terms. They predicted, though, that unless slavery were abolished, an angry God would ultimately visit wrath upon a sinful nation—and this might be violent.

During the 1830s, abolitionists were condemned in the North as well as in the South: anti-abolitionist mobs broke up abolitionist meetings, and northern churches refused to allow their pulpits to be used to denounce slavery.

By the 1850s—abolitionists in increasing numbers began to abandon hopes for a peaceful solution to the question of slavery and began to advocate violence: a holy war to destroy sin. This change from pacifism to advocacy of violence was justified by the Protestant idea of private judgement. Even those abolitionists who continued to advocate peaceful solutions no longer condemned those like John Brown who claimed to have been chosen by God to destroy slavery with violence.

When the Mexican War added nearly a half a million square miles to the Union, a struggle began over the future of slavery in the territories; it ended only with secession and civil war. As a result of the struggles, abolitionists began to gain a more sympathetic hearing. Many feared a slavery power conspiracy which would destroy civil liberties and nationalize slavery.

The slave or non-slave state issue first came before Congress in 1818. The Territory of Missouri, in which slavery was legal, applied for statehood. This would upset the balance of slave and free states. Maine applied in 1820 to be admitted as a free state. So it was worked out to admit both, thus keeping the balance. This was the Missouri Compromise of 1820. The compromise also banned slavery from the Louisiana Purchase north of the southern boundary of Missouri, the line of 36°30' north latitude, except in the state of Missouri.

The Compromise of 1850 was a series of acts by which the United States Congress hoped to settle the strife between opponents and proponents of slavery. One item in the compromise was the Fugitive Slave Law. It imposed heavy penalties upon persons who aided a slave's escape or interfered with his recovery, even free blacks living in the North.

Many Northerners thought the law too harsh, and some states interfered with its enforcement. Many slaves were passed along to Canada via the Underground Railroad.

The Kansas-Nebraska Act of 1854 provided that two new territories, Kansas and Nebraska, were to be made from the Indian land that lay west of the bend of the Missouri River and north of 37° north latitude. The act made slavery legally possible in a vast new area. It also revived the bitter quarrel over the expansion of slavery which had died down after the Compromise of 1850.

This antagonism proved to be fertile ground for John Brown to promote his abolitionist ideas.

Lincoln's Emancipation Proclamation of 1863 declared slaves free in all areas of the Confederate States still in rebellion. Slavery was not abolished in the United States until passage of the 13th Amendment to the Constitution in 1865. The 14th and 15th amendments passed after the war gave former slaves citizenship and civil rights.

Dred Scott Decision

Dred Scott was the slave of an army surgeon, Dr. John Emerson of Missouri. In 1834, Dr. Emerson took Scott to the free state of Illinois and then to that part of Wisconsin territory that later became the state of Minnesota, a region where slavery was forbidden by the Missouri Compromise. In 1838, Scott was taken back to Missouri, a slave state. Scott's master died there, and Scott was sold to John F.A. Sanford.

Scott had been told by interested persons that his residence in a free state and territory made him a free man. He sued for his freedom in 1846, and the state circuit court gave a verdict in his favor. But the state supreme court reversed the decision. The case was transferred to the federal courts, and eventually reached the Supreme Court of the United States. The name Dred Scott Decision refers to this court's decision.

The actual verdict of the Supreme Court was simply that it had no jurisdiction in the Dred Scott case. The court decided that Scott was still a slave. According to ample precedent, his return without protest to Missouri took care of that. As a slave, he was a citizen neither of Missouri nor of the United States, and therefore could not sue in the federal court. The court might well have stopped at this. But seven of the nine justices were Democrats. They seized the chance to record the opinion that the Missouri Compromise was unconstitutional and that slavery could not be excluded from the territories. The two Republicans held that this part of the decision was merely the opinion of a majority of the justices on a matter not before the court, and therefore had no legal force. The announcement of the 7 to 2 decision by Chief Justice Roger B. Taney on Mar. 6, 1857, aroused a violent public reaction. It increased the tension between the North and the South.

William Lloyd Garrison (1805-1879) was an American journalist and reformer who became famous in the 1830s for his denunciations of slavery. He advocated the end of slavery immediately, and criticized anyone who did not agree with him. He edited the *National Philanthropist*, the world's first temperance paper, and became an ardent abolitionist in 1828 after meeting Benjamin Lundy, a pioneer anti-slavery organizer. In 1831, he began publishing *The Liberator* in Boston, which became very influential. He continued to issue it until 1865, when the 13th Amendment ended slavery. He believed that northern states should separate from the South. He refused to vote, and opposed the U.S. Government because it permitted slavery. He eventually supported the government in the Civil War.

☞ The following is a list of the Free Democratic and Anti-Slavery papers published in the United States:

FREE DEMOCRATIC PRESS.

Inquirer, Portland, Me.; A. Willey; $2 per annum.
Ind. Democrat, Concord, N. H.; G. G. Fogg; $2.
News, Keene, N. H.; S. Woodward; $1.25.
Democrat, Manchester, N. H.; J. H. Goodale; $1.50.
Messenger, Portsmouth, N. H.; T. J. Whittam; $1.

Freeman, Montpelier, Vt.; D. P. Thompson; $2.
Observer, Morrisville, Vt.; J. A. Somerby; $1.25.
Telegraph, Springfield, Vt.; L. T. Guernsey; $1.75.
Democrat, Brattleborough, Vt.; W. Nichols; $1.50.
Brandon Post, Brandon, Vt.; P. Welch; $1.
Courier, Burlington, Vt.; G. C. Samson, $1.50.

Commonwealth, Boston, Ms.; J. D. Baldwin; daily $5, weekly $2.
Sentinel, North Adams, Ms.; A. D. Brock; $1.50.
American, Lowell, Ms.; W. S. Robinson; tri-week.; $3.
News, Fitchburg, Mass.; R. F. Rollins; $1.50.
Essex County Freeman, Salem, Ms.; J. Emmett; semi-weekly; $3.50.
Republican, Greenfield, Ms.
Spy, Worcester, Ms.; J. M. Earle; $2.
Standard, New Bedford, Ms.
Courier, Northampton, Ms.
Gazette, Dedham, Ms.; Henry O. Hildreth; $2.
Democrat, Dedham, Ms.; E. G. Robinson; $2.
Sentinel, Lawrence, Ms.; John Ryan & Co.; $2.

Rhode Island Freeman, Providence, R. I.; Crawford & Harris; $1.

Republican, Hartford, Ct.; Bartlett & Hawley; $2.

Herald, Ellington, N. Y.; A. S. Brown.
Evening Chronicle, Syracuse, N. Y.; H. R. Raymond; daily $3, weekly $1.50.
Spirit of the Age, Norwich, N. Y.; J. D. Lawyer; $1.
Wyoming Co. Mirror, Warsaw, N. Y.; A. Holley; $2.
Telegraph, Oneida, N. Y.; D. H. Frost; $1.25.
Banner of the Times, De Ruyter, N. Y.
Free Press, Wellsville, N. Y.; A. N. Cole; $1.50.
Frederick Douglass' Paper, Rochester, N. Y.; Frederick Douglass; $2.
Free Press, Gouverneur, New York; Mitchell & Hulbert; $1.

Herald, Jamestown, N. Y.
Carson League, Syracuse, N. Y.; J. Thomas; $1.50.
Saturday Visiter, Pittsburgh, Pa.; Jane G. & William Swisshelm; $1.50.
Freeman, Mercer, Pa.; W. T. Clark; $1.50.
Weekly Crescent, Erie, Pa.; Caughey & McCreary; $1.50.
The People's Journal, Coudersport, Potter county, Pa.; Dougall, Mann & Haskell; $1.50.
Dispatch, Pittsburg, Pa.; Foster & Fleeson; daily $3, weekly $1.
Clarion of Freedom, Indiana, Pa.; Moorhead & McClaran; $1.
Die Frie Press, Philadelphia, Pa.; F. W. Thomas; daily, $3.
Homestead Journal, Salem, O.; A. Hinksman; $1.50.
Christian Press, Cincinnati, O.; $2.
True Democrat, Cleveland, O.; Thomas Brown; daily $6, weekly $2.
Ashtabula Sentinel, Jefferson and Ashtabula, O.; W. C. Howell; $2.
Mahoning Free Democrat, Youngstown, O.; M. Cullotan; $1.50.
Commercial, Cleveland, O.; H. M. Addison; $1.50.
Journal, Wellington, O.; George Brewster; $1.50.
Western Reserve Chronicle, Warren, O.; E. O. Howard; $2.
Telegraph, Painsville, O.; Gray & Doolittle; $2.
Ohio Times, Mount Vernon, O.; Chapman & Thrall; $1.50.
Independent Democrat, Elyria, O.; Philemon Bliss; $2.
Columbian, Columbus, O.; L. L. Rice.
Free Democrat, Chardon, O.; J. S. Wright; $1.
Star, Ravenna, O.; Lyman W. Hall; $1.50.
Herald of Freedom, Wilmington, O.; J. W. Chaffin; $1.50.
Free Democrat, Detroit, Mich.; S. H. Baker; daily $5, weekly $1.
Free Democrat, Indianapolis, Ind.; R. Vaile; $1.50.
Western Citizen, Chicago, Ill.; Z. C. Eastman; daily and weekly.
Journal, Sparta, Ill.; I. S. Coulter; $1.25.
Western Freeman, Galesburg, Ill.; W. J. Lane; $2.

Free Democrat, Waukesha, Wis.; S. M. Booth; daily $4, weekly $2.
Telegraph, Kenosha, Wis.; Sholes & Frank; $2.
Free Press, Janesville, Wis.; Joseph Baker; $1.50.
Free Press, Sheboygan Falls, Wis.; J. A. Smith; $2.
Advocate, Racine, Wis.; C. Clements; $2.

Kentucky News, Newport, Ky.; W. S. Bailey; $1.

True Democrat, Mount Pleasant, Iowa; J. W. Howe; $1.50.
Der Demokrat, Davenport, Iowa; Th. Gulich; $2.

Pacific Statesman, San Francisco, Cal.; J. H. Purdy.

Der National Demokrat, Washington, D. C.; Fred. Schmidt, editor; Buell & Blanchard, publishers; $2.

ANTI-SLAVERY PRESS.

Liberator, Boston, Ms.; Wm. Lloyd Garrison; $2.50.
Pennsylvania Freeman, Philadelphia, Pa.; C. M. Burleigh; $2.
National Anti-Slavery Standard, New York, N. Y.; S. H. Gay & E. Quincy; $2.
Anti-Slavery Bugle, Salem, O.; M. R. Robinson; $1.50.
Voice of the Fugitive.

☞ Persons desiring the FACTS FOR THE PEOPLE are informed that we printed a large edition of the first number, and are still able to supply it to those who may wish it from the commencement. Orders should be sent without delay.

FACTS FOR THE PEOPLE.

A Monthly Newspaper, published by G. BAILEY, Washington, D. C., designed for preservation as a document for reference, or for general circulation especially among those not yet familiar with the Anti-Slavery movement, composed chiefly of articles from the National Era.

TERMS.

6 copies to one address		$1
20 do. do.		3
100 do. do.		12

☞ Payments strictly in advance.

Slaves working on a plantation on Edisto Island, South Carolina.

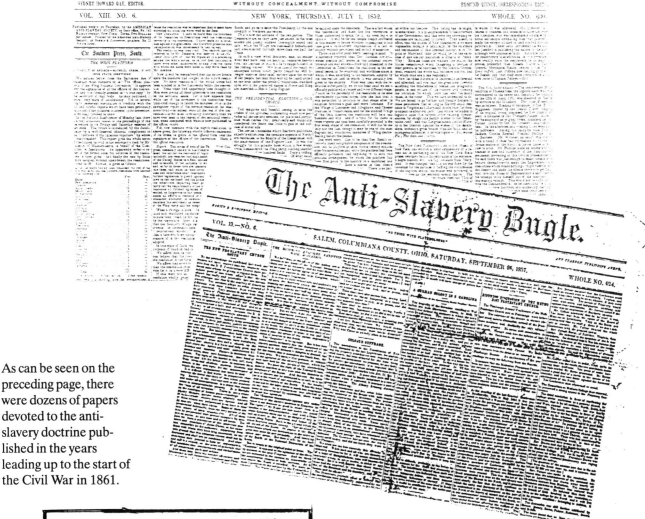

As can be seen on the preceding page, there were dozens of papers devoted to the anti-slavery doctrine published in the years leading up to the start of the Civil War in 1861.

Uncle Tom's Cabin, first published in 1851, is one of the most famous novels in American literature. It analyzes the issue of slavery in the Middle West, New England and the South during the days of the Fugitive Slave Law. The book intensified the disagreement between North and South and, along with John Brown's raid on Harpers Ferry, pushed the country toward war. Its author Harriet Beecher Stowe's (1811-1896) name became hated in the South. She wrote the novel in Brunswick, Maine, and also published many other works throughout her life.

Frederick Douglass (1817-1895) was born a slave in Maryland and escaped to Massachusetts in 1838. He became one of the speakers for the Massachusetts Anti-Slavery Society and became a national leader in the antislavery movement. John Brown met him in Springfield, Mass., and later in Franklin County, Pa. He tried to persuade Brown from his plans to attack Harpers Ferry and to try more peaceful means to end slavery. During the Civil War, Douglass organized two Black regiments in Massachusetts and discussed the slavery problem with President Lincoln several times. After the war, he was a government official for the District of Columbia and the U.S. minister to Haiti.

Underground Railroad

The underground railroad was a system for helping Negro slaves escape to the northern states and Canada in the days before the Civil War. It was really neither underground nor a railroad. It was called the underground railroad because of the swift, secret way in which Negroes seemed to escape.

The underground railroad had no formal organization. A large part of its work was done by southern slaves who, though unable to escape themselves, helped runaways with food, clothing, and directions. Free Negroes in both the South and the North fre-

quently assisted the runaways. The most famous Negro "railroader" was Harriet "Moses" Tubman (1820-1913). She was a fugitive herself, but returned to the South 19 times and helped about 300 Negroes escape. A $40,000 reward was offered for her capture.

The work of northern white abolitionists in manning the *stations* (hiding places) of the underground railroad, and in helping the slaves move from one refuge to another, has often been exaggerated. There were few such "agents" and there was little organized activity. But many Quakers and persons of other faiths who felt that slavery was evil were involved in the underground railroad.

About 50,000 slaves escaped between 1830 and 1860. The underground railroad was most active in Ohio and Pennsylvania. But by the outbreak of the Civil War, runaways were being helped in every northern state from New England to Kansas.

Many fugitive slaves settled in the northern free states. But when Congress passed a strict fugitive slave law as part of the Compromise of 1850, thousands of these settled Negroes fled to Canada for safety.

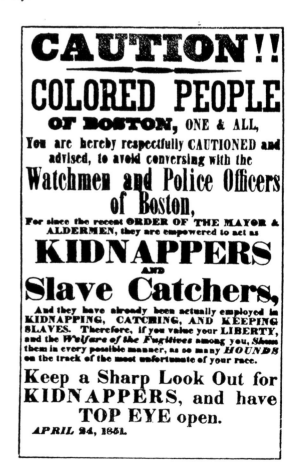

Table of Contents

Photo Credits

WVSA – West Virginia State Archives, Boyd B. Stutler Collection, Charleston, W.Va.
LC – Library of Congress, Washington, D.C.
NPS (with negative number) – National Park Service Archives, Harpers Ferry National Historical Park
JCM – Jefferson County Museum, Charles Town, W.Va.
Uncredited photos are from the Pictorial Histories Archive.
Other photos are acknowledged by their source.

DEDICATION

This book is dedicated to Boyd Stutler from my hometown of Charleston, West Virginia. He was an ardent collector of John Brown and Civil War material. Without his collection, this book would not have been possible.

John Brown - one of the earliest photographs, made at Springfield, Mass., in 1846. It was claimed by Brown to have been made by a Black photographer named Washington. Two other portraits were made at the same time, one a half-length single portrait and a second with Thomas Thomas, a Black, sitting and Brown standing with his hand on Thomas' shoulder. Thomas holds a banner with the letters S.P.W. on it, the initials of Brown's own underground railroad the Subterranean Pass Way. The banner held by Brown here may be the same one with the letters concealed by the fold. No copy of the photo with Thomas and Brown is known to exist. WVSA

John Brown-His Life, Family, Business & Travels

John Brown's life began in Torrington, Connecticut, on May 9, 1800, the son of Owen and Ruth Brown. Owen's father was Capt. John Brown, a Revolutionary War soldier who died in 1776. Owen and Ruth Mills were married in 1793 and had six sons, two daughters and one adopted son. Ruth died in childbirth in 1808 and Owen married Sally Root in 1809. From that marriage four sons and five daughters were born. Sally died in 1840 and Owen married Lucy Hinsdale in 1841. Owen died in 1856.

Owen and Ruth taught their children that slavery was a sin against God, not to hate Negroes and to oppose their enslavement. As a youth, John saw a Negro boy with whom he had become friendly badly beaten and harshly treated. This and his religious beliefs influenced his thoughts and actions throughout his life.

In 1805, the family moved to Hudson in the Western Reserve area of the new state of Ohio. Hudson was founded by a New Englander who hated slavery and it was a perfect place for the family to move to pursue their moral convictions and to farm new fertile ground.

Owen started a tannery in Hudson and John started working there possibly as early as 1810. Two years later, he joined the Congregational Church and hoped to become a minister. He attended several religious schools in Massachusetts and Connecticut, but lack of funds and a serious eye infection forced him to return home to Ohio in 1817. By the time John married Dianthe Lusk in 1820, he was a capable farmer, leather tanner and cattleman. Dianthe bore seven children but only four sons, John, Jr., Jason, Owen, Frederick and one daughter, Ruth, survived.

The family moved again in 1826 to a largely unsettled wilderness near Meadville, Pennsylvania. This was one of many moves Brown would make in his 59 years. He built a tannery and became a leading figure in the community. But in 1832 tragedy struck the family when Dianthe died in childbirth. By this time, Brown was helping runaway slaves on the Underground Railroad, a mission which would consume the rest of his life.

With five children to raise, Brown married again in 1833 to 17-year-old Mary Ann Day. They had 13 children but only six attained adulthood—Anne, Sarah, Ellen, Watson, Salmon and Oliver.

In 1835 the family moved back to the Western Reserve area in Franklin Township. They spent the next 20 years off and on living on farms at Franklin Mills (now Kent) Hudson, Richfield and Akron. At an abolitionist meeting in Hudson in 1837, Brown stood up, raised his right hand and declared, "Here, before God, in the presence of these witnesses, I consecrate my life to the destruction of slavery." His entire family would be involved and three of his sons would give their lives for the cause.

In the next few years, Brown had to fight business reversals and eventually bankruptcy in 1842. He lost his farm and had to go to work for one of his creditors in Richfield. Four of his children died within a few days of each other from dysentery in September 1843.

Owen Brown was John Brown's father. He was born in 1771, the son of John and Hannah Brown. Owen married Ruth Mills in 1793 and they had eight children; Salmon I, Anna, John, Salmon II, Oliver, Fredrick, Sally and an adopted son, Levi Blakeslee. The Brown family lived in Connecticut at the time of John's birth, but moved to Hudson, Ohio, in 1805. Owen was very religious and hated slavery throughout his life. On Dec. 9, 1808, his wife, Ruth died in childbirth. A year later Owen married Sally Root and they had eight children; Sally Marian, Watson Hughes, Florilla, Jermiah Root, Edward, Martha I, Lucien and Martha II. Sally died in 1840 and Owen remarried the next year to Lucy Hinsdale. Owen died in 1856. WVSA

Children of Owen Brown

First wife, **Ruth Mills Brown** married February 13, 1793
Died December 9, 1808, a few hours after their infant daughter.

Levi Blakeslee	adopted son
Salmon Brown I	Born June 29, 1794 Died February 18, 1796
Infant son	Died at birth 1796
Anna Brown	Born July 5, 1798 Died June 12, 1838
John Brown	Born May 9, 1800 Died December 2, 1859
Salmon Brown II	Born April 30, 1802 Died September 6, 1833
Oliver C. Brown	Born October 20, 1804 Died September 20, 1858
Frederick Brown	Born February 13, 1807 Died July 15, 1877
Sally	Born December 9, 1808 Died shortly after birth

Second wife, **Sally Root** married November 8, 1809
Died August 11, 1840

Sally Marian	Born April 19, 1811 Died 1894
Watson Hughs	Born July 22, 1813 Died January 29, 1832
Florilla	Born May 19, 1816 Died February 6, 1865
Jermiah Root	Born November 7, 1819 Died February 22, 1874
Edward	Born July 13, 1823 Died March 23, 1883
Martha I	Born September 21, 1825 Died September 18, 1826
Lucien	Born September 18, 1829 Died December 1, 1847
Martha II	Born June 18, 1832 Died June 28, 1910

Third wife, **Lucy Hinsdale** married April 1841.

Children of John Brown

First wife, **Dianthe Lusk**, Married June 21, 1820
Born January 12, 1801
Died August 10, 1832, New Richmond, PA.

John Jr.	Born July 25, 1821, Hudson, OH Died May 2, 1895

John Brown's children, cont.

Jason	Born January 19, 1823, Hudson Died December 24, 1912
Owen	Born November 4, 1824, Hudson Died January 8, 1889
Frederick I	Born January 9, 1827, New Richmond Died March 31, 1831
Ruth	Born February 18, 1829, New Richmond Died January 18, 1904
Frederick II	Born December 21, 1830, New Richmond Died August 30, 1856
Infant son	Died at birth August 7, 1832, New Richmond

Second wife, **Mary Ann Day**, Born April 15, 1816
Died February 29, 1884, Saratoga, CA

Sarah I	Born May 11, 1834, New Richmond Died September 23, 1843
Watson	Born October 7, 1835, Franklin Mills, OH Died October 19, 1859
Salmon	Born October 2, 1836, Hudson Died May 10, 1919
Charles	Born November 3, 1837, Hudson Died September 11, 1843
Oliver	Born March 9, 1839, Franklin Mills Died October 18, 1859
Peter	Born December 7, 1840, Hudson Died September 22, 1843
Austin	Born September 14, 1842, Richfield, OH Died September 21, 1843
Anne	Born December 23, 1843, Richfield Died October 3, 1926
Amelia	Born June 22, 1845, Akron, OH Died October 30, 1846
Sarah II	Born September 11, 1846, Akron Died June 30, 1916
Ellen I	Born May 20, 1848, Springfield, MA Died April 30, 1849
Infant son	Born April 26, 1852, Akron Died May 17, 1852
Ellen II	Born September 25, 1854, Akron, OH Died July 15, 1916

Brown's second wife was Mary Ann Day. She was born on April 15, 1816, near Granville, New York. She was a selfless and dedicated wife and mother, who gave birth to 13 children. Mary visited her husband a day before his execution at the Charlestown jail. The next day she took his body back to North Elba for burial. Only six of her 13 children lived until adulthood. In 1863, because of the harshness of life at North Elba, she set out for California with her son, Salmon, and his wife and two children, and three of her daughters, Annie, Sarah and Ellen. They ended up in Red Bluff. The citizens of the town built her a house in 1866 and she lived there until 1870 when she and her family followed Salmon to Rhonerville in Humboldt County. She later moved to Saratoga in Santa Clara County with her daughters, Sarah and Ellen. Mary died in 1884 and is buried in the Madronia Cemetery in Saratoga.

Brown's fortunes changed somewhat when he met a rich merchant named Simon Perkins, Jr., in 1844. They decided to go into the wool business together and Brown traveled widely buying sheep and selling wool. He and John Jr. moved to Springfield, Mass., to establish an eastern wool business. Jason and Owen Brown stayed in Akron to run the business in the west.

About this time, John first met with Frederick Douglass, the well-known Black activist, in Springfield. From 1847 until the Harpers Ferry raid, Brown and Douglass would be in contact. Brown was determined to free the slaves in the South by whatever means possible. The country at this time was heading for a sharp division between slave and non-slave states. Wool prices were dropping in 1848 and after leaving his sons in charge of both businesses, Brown once again made a major decision.

Gerrit Smith, a wealthy landowner in New York and a noted abolitionist and philanthropist, had established a colony in the Adirondack Mountains for Blacks. It was named Timbucto. The area's weather was harsh in winter, not conducive to profitable farming. Brown offered to go there and teach the Blacks how to farm. One hundred thousand acres of wilderness were set up for Blacks from New York state. In 1849, the Brown family moved onto a several hundred acre tract in this wilderness and eventually bought land from Smith.

Brown's business in Springfield was about to go under because the price of wool was so low, so he set sail for England in August 1849 to try and sell his wool in Europe. This did not work out and upon his return home, he was again deep in debt.

With the passing of the Fugitive Slave Act of 1850, the Black communities in the North and South were in turmoil. The Underground Railroad was active in the states north of the Mason-Dixon Line transporting escaped slaves towards Canada. In January 1851, Brown formed an antislavery organization called the League of Gileadites in Springfield. He was now fully committed to the liberation of all Blacks in the United States.

The family moved again in 1851, this time back to Akron, and stayed for four years. His older sons had married and moved to farms of their own. The wool partnership with Perkins was dissolved after many lawsuits and Brown was again almost penniless.

The new territory of Kansas was opening to settlers after the passage of the Kansas-Nebraska Act of 1854. Brown's brother-in-law Rev. Samuel Adair had moved to Osawatomie, Kansas, and soon John Jr., Jason, Owen, Frederick and Salmon followed. "Bleeding Kansas" was soon to occur and the Brown sons were caught up in the civil strife. John Brown answered the call from his sons in 1855 to help keep the state free of slaves. At this point he became nationally known for his violent antislavery views and actions.

A final move had been made back to North Elba in 1855. The family moved into a farmhouse built by a son-in-law and Brown returned here only sporadically during the following years. When absent, he sent money and supplies to assist his family.

As a base for his Kansas operations, Brown selected Tabor, Iowa, a Quaker community 20 miles from the Kansas border. He stored guns and ammunition here for the fighting in Kansas. He also made trips back to Massachusetts and New York to solicit money from wealthy individuals to keep his arsenal and ideals alive. Six of these men, who were Brown's main backers, became known as the "Secret Six."

The issue of slavery in Kansas was basically solved by October 1857 and Brown's attention turned to a new strategy—an attack on a site in a mountainous region of the upper South where he could establish a base of operations to rally the slaves to join him. The location picked would be the United States Armory and Arsenal at Harpers Ferry, Virginia.

He started recruiting members of his provisional army, first in Tabor and later in Ontario, Canada, where he drafted his "Provisional Constitution for the People of the United States."

The arms stored in Iowa were now being shipped to Ashtabula county in Ohio (where his son John Jr. lived) for storage until needed for the "invasion" of the South. Brown met with Frederick Douglass again to gain his support for his invasion plans but Douglass thought the idea was impractical. He wanted to ac-

complish the goal of freeing the slaves by peaceful means.

Spring of 1858 found Brown again in Kansas, and in December of that year, he escorted a number of slaves from Missouri on a journey that ended in Canada. After two more trips home to North Elba, he spent the remaining months of his life planning and executing his invasion of Harpers Ferry.

He spent months in the Franklin County, Pennsylvania area staying for a time in Chambersburg under the assumed name of Isaac Smith. He was building his arms supply, recruiting raiders and scouting out the area. He met again with Frederick Douglass in August 1859 and attended his lecture in Chambersburg on Aug. 20. Brown was also consulting with the Secret Six members to obtain adequate funds for his invasion plans.

The great adventure was about to begin. John Brown's life was at a climax. The years of struggle and disappointment were behind him. He was set to fulfill what he believed God had put him on the earth to do—free the Black people who had been held in bondage for hundreds of years.

John Brown's birthplace in Torrington, Ct., on John Brown Road off Route 4. He was born in this house on May 9, 1800. The house-turned-museum burned down in 1918. The property is now maintained by the John Brown Association. NPS HF-189

This is a 1940 view of the house John Brown owned in Hudson, Ohio. It has been extensively remodeled since its construction in 1825 and is now a private residence.(see page 192). WVSA

Ashtabula County, Ohio

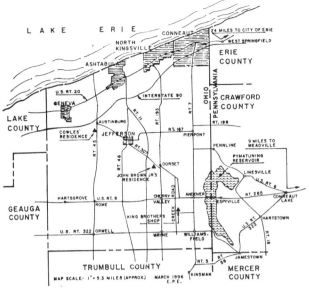

Crawford County, Pennsylvania

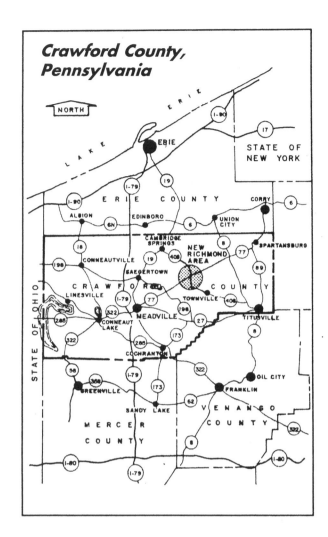

New Richmond Area

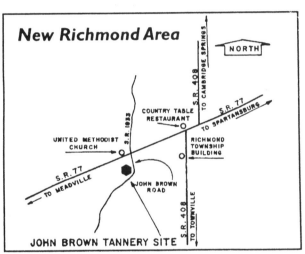

John Brown's tannery in New Richmond, Crawford County, Pennsylvania, as it appeared in 1885 (circa). It was originally built in 1826. He operated it until moving to Ohio in 1835. The building became a creamery, jelly factory and gristmill over the years. In 1907, fire destroyed the second story, a dwelling at the time. A volunteer group began preservation work in 1916. The property went through a succession of owners. From 1924 to 1949 the John Brown Memorial Association had responsibility for the site. Dr. Charles Olsen bought the site in 1949. The John Brown Amphitheater Association was formed in 1974 and today the John Brown Heritage Association is steward of the site, maintaining it for public visitation. Only the first floor stone walls remain. NPS HF-199

Portraits of John Brown

A daguerreotype taken about 1857 when Brown was in Kansas. Photographer John Bowles took this photo along with the one on page 22. WVSA

This photo was taken in either 1846 or 47. NPS HF-104

This portrait was probably taken just prior to growing his beard, sometime in 1857. NPS HF-789

From an Engraving after a daguerreotype made in Boston in 1857.

The Real John Brown, as he appeared, when fighting in Kansas. From "The Beacon Biographies," by permission, Copyright 1899 by Small, Maynard & Co.

The well known picture representing him in his last year. He wore the beard only in the last two years of his life. From the life and letters of John Brown, by F. B. Sanborn.

THREE PORTRAITS OF JOHN BROWN

One of the most well-known photos of Brown was taken in Boston by J.W. Black in May 1859. Brown was clean-shaven most of his life and grew his beard as a disguise before the Harpers Ferry raid. WVSA

A daguerreotype taken in Kansas in 1856.

An 1882 color painting by Selden J. Woodman commissioned by A.J. Hawes, who served with Brown in Kansas, on display at the West Virginia State Museum, Charleston.
PHOTO BY MICHAEL KELLER

OSSAWATTAMIE BROWN.—FROM A SKETCH BY OUR SPECIAL ARTIST, TAKEN IMMEDIATELY AFTER HE WAS MADE PRISONER, SHOWING THE WOUNDS IN HIS FOREHEAD.

This sketch was made by David Hunter Strother (Porte Crayon) for *Frank Leslie's Illustrated Newspaper*, October 29, 1859. NPS
HF-335

John Brown's Children

John Brown Jr. NPS HF-174

The Black Strings

In 1859 about 500 men who were residents of Ashtabula County, Ohio, formed the Independent Sons of Liberty, known locally as The Black Strings. They were called this because of their secret insignia—a small piece of black thread sewn into the neck buttonhole of their shirts.

Their purpose was to prevent the removal of anyone from the county as a witness or conspirator in connection with the U.S. Senate hearings on the Harpers Ferry attack.

John Brown Jr. lived in a farmhouse southeast of Jefferson in the county at the time. The Black Strings hid him in various places in the county along with his brother Owen, who escaped the raid. Also hidden was James Redpath, an abolitionist newspaper correspondent and Brown's first biographer, who was also under a federal subpoena from the senate hearings.

Federal authorities thought that if they sent in U.S. Marshals to try and arrest these men armed resistance would ensue, so they backed away from confrontations and no arrests were made.

John Brown Jr. (1821-1895) was born in Hudson, Ohio. He worked for his father in the wool business before moving to Kansas with his brothers in 1855. He participated in the border conflict and was captured by pro-slavery forces. From this he suffered a mental breakdown and carried the scars of Kansas throughout his life. He was later set free and moved to a farm near Jefferson, Ohio, with his wife, Wealthy and their children. From his farm, he routed weapons and supplies to his father's followers before the Harpers Ferry raid and was their contact with the outside world. He did not participate directly in the raid. He served briefly in the Union army but poor health forced him to resign after a year. In 1862 the family settled on a farm at Put-in-Bay, Ohio. He and his brother Owen, who also moved there after the raid, wanted to escape the animosity that their family name engendered among many Americans. Brown was a respected member of his community and lived there the rest of his life. He died in 1895 at age 73 and is buried at Put-In-Bay, South Bass Island, Lake Erie, Ohio.

Jason Brown (1823-1912) was born at Hudson, Ohio. He worked with his father in the wool business. He married Ellen Sherbondy in 1847 and the family moved to Kansas in 1854. The family moved back to Ohio in 1855. Jason did not participate in the Harpers Ferry attack. He later moved to California. He died at the age of 89 in 1912 and is buried at Akron, Ohio.

Owen Brown (1824-1889) was born in Hudson, Ohio. He worked with his father in the wool business. He had been crippled by an injury to his right arm as a child. He never married. In 1854, he moved with his brothers to settle in Kansas where he took part in the warfare there. He participated in the Harpers Ferry attack but escaped. He lived for more than 20 years at Put-in-Bay, Ohio, before moving to Altadina, California, in the 1880s. He lived there with his brother, Jason, until he died in 1889. He is buried on a hill above his home near Pasadena.

Frederick Brown I (1827-1831) was born in New Richmond, Pennsylvania, but lived only four years. He is buried in New Richmond.

Ruth Brown (1829-1904) was born in New Richmond, Pennsylvania. She married Henry Thompson in 1850 and settled on a farm at North Elba, New York. In 1884 the Thompsons followed other family members to California, eventually to the Pasadenaarea. She died in 1904 at age 74 and is buried in Mountain View Cemetery in Pasadena.

Frederick Brown II (1830-1856) was born in New Richmond, Pennsylvania. He went west to Kansas with his father and was killed at age 25. He is buried in Osawatomie, Kansas.

Infant son, born in New Richmond, Pennsylvania, in 1832, but died three days later. He is buried with his mother, Dianthe, in New Richmond.

Sarah Brown I (1834-1843) was born in New Richmond, Pennsylvania. She died of dysentery at age nine in 1843. She is buried in Richfield, Ohio.

Watson Brown (1835-1859) was born in Franklin Mills, now Kent, Ohio. He married Isabella M. Thompson in 1856. Watson died of wounds received during the Harpers Ferry attack. His remains were taken to the Winchester, Virginia, Medical College for anatomical use. During the Civil War, his bones were seized by Union troops and they were later used in various lodge initiation ceremonies. His remains were returned to the family in 1882 and interred in North Elba.

Salmon Brown (1836-1919) was born in Hudson, Ohio. He worked with his father in the wool business but moved to Kansas with his brothers in 1855 where he participated in the warfare there. He was not at Harpers Ferry. He married Abbie C. Hinckley in 1857. After failing in his attempt to raise a company for the Union Army in the Civil War, he moved with his family to California in 1864. He had a long life as a cattle and sheep rancher. In the early 1890s, his family moved to Portland, Oregon, after suffering business losses in California. Salmon committed suicide in 1919 after suffering serious medical problems. He is buried in Portland.

Charles Brown (1837-1843) was born in Hudson, Ohio, and died at age five of dysentery. He is buried in Richfield, Ohio.

Oliver Brown (1839-1859) was born in Franklin Mills, Ohio. He married Martha Evelyn Brewster in 1858. Oliver traveled to Kansas with his father and was involved in the warfare there. He died of wounds received during the raid on Harpers Ferry and was buried on the banks of the Shenandoah River. His remains were exhumed along with those of the other raiders and reinterred in North Elba in 1899.

Peter Brown (1840-1843) was born in Hudson, Ohio, and died of dysentery at age two. He is buried in Richfield, Ohio.

Austin Brown (1842-1843) was born in Richfield, Ohio. He died of dysentery at age one and is buried in Richfield.

Anne(Annie)Brown (1843-1926) was born in Richfield, Ohio. Annie spent time at the Kennedy Farm, before the raid on Harpers Ferry, cooking for the raiders. She moved to California in 1864 with her mother and married Samuel Adams in Red Bluff in 1869. They settled in Humboldt County where she died in 1926. She is buried in Shively, California.

Amelia Brown (1845-1846) was born in Akron, Ohio. She died in 1846 at age one when her sister, Ruth, accidentally scalded her with hot water. She is buried in Akron.

Sarah Brown II (1846-1916) was born in Akron, Ohio. She moved to California with her mother in 1864. She never married but became a prominent figure in several California communities in which she lived. She died at age 70 and is buried in Saratoga, California.

Ellen Brown I (1848-1849) was born in Springfield, Massachusetts. She died in 1849 at age one. She is buried in Springfield, Mass.

Infant son (1852) was born in Akron, Ohio. He died of whooping cough 21 days after birth. He is buried in Akron.

Ellen Brown II (1854-1916) was born in Akron, Ohio. She moved to California with her mother in 1864. She married James Fablinger in 1876 and they lived in various communities in California. The Fablinger's had 11 children. She died in 1916 at 62 and is buried in Saratoga, California.

John Brown's Children

Oliver Brown and his wife Martha Brewster Brown. Martha was at the Kennedy farm before the Harpers Ferry raid. She died in March of 1860.

Watson Brown. NPS HF-519

Jason Brown. NPS HF-156

Owen Brown. NPS HF-244

Owen Brown in his later years. WVSA

Salmon Brown. NPS HF-148

Salmon Brown in his later years in California. WVSA

Ellen Brown. WVSA

Sarah Brown. NPS HF-159

Ruth Brown. NPS

Anne (Annie) Brown. NPS HF-150

Mary Brown Hand, sister of John Brown. NPS HF-211

Martha Brown Davis, the youngest sister of John Brown. NPS HF-270

Three of John Brown's children pose for this rare photo with members of John Brown Jr.'s militia unit. At left is John Brown Jr., in the middle either Salmon or Frederick, and at right Jason.
OHIO HISTORICAL SOCIETY

John Brown Jr. lived on South Bass Island at Put-in-Bay, Ohio, in Lake Erie during the Civil War. On Johnson's Island in Sandusky Baywas located a large prison camp for captive Confederate soldiers. In 1864 Confederate agents, operating from Canada, planned to seize merchant vessels on Lake Erie, steam into the Bay at night and commandeer a heavily armed Federal warship, blast down the stockade and liberate the prisoners. Brown saw the *Island Queen* taken by Confederates on the night of Sept. 19, 1864, and sprung into action. He gathered a few men and rowed to the mainland and walked eight miles to the prison camp to warn them of the impending attack. Brown and his men volunteered to help defend the prison but the rebel attack never came. Several months later Brown organized the "Captain Brown's Independent Company of Militia" at Put-in-Bay to counter any future rebel attacks, but none occurred.

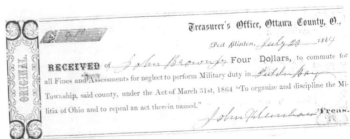

John Brown Jr.'s receipt for $4 for a fine paid for neglect to perform military duty.

The gravesite of Owen Brown who died in 1889 is on the summit of "Little Round Top" off of a fire lane which is an extension of El Prieto Road in the Angeles National Forest north of Altadena. Only a wooden slab marked his resting place until 1898 when this boulder replaced it. It reads: "Owen Brown, son of John Brown the liberator, Died January 9, 1889, aged 64 years." WVSA

Graves of Salmon Brown and his wife, Abbie, in the G.A.R. Division, Greenwood Cemetery, Portland, Oregon. WVSA

Graves of Charles, Austin, Peter and Sarah Brown in Ridgefield, Ohio. All these children died of dysentery within days of each other. WVSA

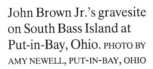

John Brown Jr.'s gravesite on South Bass Island at Put-in-Bay, Ohio. PHOTO BY AMY NEWELL, PUT-IN-BAY, OHIO

Mary Ann Brown and her two daughters, Sarah and Ellen, along with Ellen's husband and grandchildren, are all buried in the family plot in Madronia Cemetery in Saratoga, California. WVSA

Surviving sons of John Brown pose for a photo in front of Owen and Jason's cabin on their small ranch above Pasadena, Calif., in the 1880s. Jason is on the left, John Jr., who was visiting is in the center, and Owen is on the right. NPS HF-188

Three of John Brown's children pose in front of a log cabin somewhere in California, from left, Owen, Ruth and Jason. WVSA

Historical Sketches of Springfield . . . No. 65

JOHN BROWN'S HOUSE
31 FRANKLIN ST.

JOHN BROWN
AT A MEETING
OF THE
SPRINGFIELD
NEGROES

ROBERT
HOLCOMB

During the long years of bitter controversy, before the Civil War, over the slavery issue, Springfield was the scene of many episodes of stirring interest. John Brown, one of the town's most famous residents, was in the thick of many of them. It was during this time that Brown organized the Springfield Negroes into "The Springfield Gileadites," a branch of the national organization. The purpose was to arm the Negroes with pikes, to resist the capture of fugitive slaves, and eventually to fight against slavery itself. About 50 local Negroes joined, although the record shows that only 44 actually signed up. They met in Brown's house on Franklin St., some coming in working clothes because they were poor laborers, while others were members of the Negro clergy. One was the sexton of the South Church, J.N. Howard, and the name of B.C. Dowling heads the list.

This house at 31 Frankin Street in Springfield, Mass., was the home of John Brown and his family from 1846-1849. The house, which was considerably altered many years after Brown moved, was torn down in 1962. When the family moved into the house, Brown took a vote....to see if they would furnish the parlor or use the money to buy clothing for fugitive Negroes in the North Elba, NY area. The vote went for the Negroes. WVSA

The Secret Six

John Brown had the drive and conviction to try and free the slaves, but he did not have the financial resources to do it on his own. In 1857, after his forays in Kansas his plan for a larger thrust into freeing the slaves was formulated. For this he needed funds to recruit volunteers, to feed and arm them and to travel around the country.

A committee had previously been established called the Massachusetts State Kansas Committee to further the aims of the Free-state settlers. Brown met with its secretary Franklin Sanborn in Boston to try and gain funding for further actions in Kansas.

Brown was also introduced to some wealthy and influential Bostonians including Rev. Theodore Parker, George Stearns, Dr. Samuel G. Howe and Pastor Thomas W. Higginson. These fine men along with Gerrit Smith a wealthy landowner from Peterboro, New York, would later be the primary financiers of Brown's adventures up to and including the Harpers Ferry attack. They would be known as the "Secret Six."

Their first goal was to send arms and pikes to Kansas but by 1857 the battle between pro- and anti-slavery forces was coming to an end. Brown's grand plans was to strike a federal site in the mountains of Virginia and to rally the slaves of the South to his cause.

The men of the "Secret Six" were like-minded as to the opposition to slavery but at varying degrees as to how to proceed. Brown convinced them, some reluctantly, that a military operation was the only solution to the problem.

The "Secret Six" were a distinguished but diverse group of individuals:

Francis Sanborn

Sanborn was 26 in 1857 when he first met Brown. A graduate of Harvard, he soon moved to Concord and opened a college preparatory school. Sanborn introduced Brown to other influential men in Boston and later wrote a biography of him in 1885. He fled to Canada after the raid and was later arrested along with other members of the "Secret Six" but was released in an altercation with marshals. Sanborn became a prominent public figure after the Civil War, even offering to help care for Brown's widow. He died in 1917.

Dr. Samuel Gridley Howe

Howe was born in Boston in 1801 to a family tradition rich in Revolutionary history. He graduated from Brown University in 1821 and Harvard Medical School in 1824. He was a champion of revolutionary causes, especially freeing the slaves, but he was also nationally known for his work with the blind. He founded the first industrial training shop and first braille circulating library for the blind. He became the first in the world to teach language to a blind-deaf mute. His marriage to poetess Julia Ward was noted for his infidelities, insults and desertions. He fled to Canada after the raid and along with the other "Secret Six" members was never indicted for helping with the Harpers Ferry raid. He served in the federal government both during after the Civil War, dying in 1876.

Theodore Parker

Parker, born in 1810, was the grandson of Captain Parker who commanded the Minutemen at Lexington, Mass., in 1775. The younger Parker, a graduate of Harvard Divinity School, became a leading transcendentalist and an outspoken abolitionist. In 1860, soon after Brown's execution, Parker died in Italy of tuberculosis.

Thomas Wentworth Higginson

Born in 1823 to a distinguished New England family, Higginson entered Harvard in 1837 and later its divinity school where he was ordained a Unitarian minister in 1847. He was a member of the Boston vigilance committee that opposed the Fugitive Slave Law. After losing his 1848 election bid for Congress, running on the Free Soil Party ticket, he was forced to resign his pulpit. After the Harpers Ferry raid he plotted the rescue of two of the raiders, but no action was taken. During the Civil War Higginson commanded a black regiment.

George Luther Stearns

Stearns was born in Medford, Mass., in 1809. He had a modest upbringing but, through shrewd investments, became a wealthy businessman and a Boston philanthropist. He was very methodical but became an ardent abolitionist and advocated violence if necessary to resist the Fugitive Slave Law. He died in the late 1860's.

Gerrit Smith

Smith inherited vast tracts of New York land from his father, who made his fortune in the fur business with John Jacob Astor. From his mansion at Peterboro, New York, Smith doled out his money to charity. He set aside 120,000 acres of land in the Adirondack mountains as homesteads for free Blacks from New York. Brown moved to this area to farm. Smith donated money to Brown's cause. After the raid, Smith suffered a nervous breakdown which possibly had its start when he was defeated in New York's 1858 gubernatorial race. He eventually recovered after spending months in an asylum but died suddenly in December of 1874.

The U.S. Senate selected a committee on Dec. 14, 1859, to investigate the Harpers Ferry raid and any involvement by others. Senator James Mason was the chairman. Stearns and Howe testified, Sanborn and Higginson refused, Parker was in Europe and Smith was sick. The committee closed its investigation in June 1860, chastising the members of the "Secret Six" for supporting Brown. There was a minority opinion, however, that the six plus other people had were found not to have had "any complicity with this conspiracy, or its purposes in the year 1859, through Richard Realf, Hugh Forbes and some very few may have understood it in 1858, when it failed of execution."

GEORGE L. STEARNS

GERRIT SMITH

FRANK B. SANBORN

T. W. HIGGINSON

THEODORE PARKER

SAMUEL G. HOWE

Drawing of the schoolhouse in Chatham, Ontario, Canada used by John Brown for his Constitutional Convention in 1858.

Historical marker at the First Baptist Church in Chatham, Ontario. WVSA

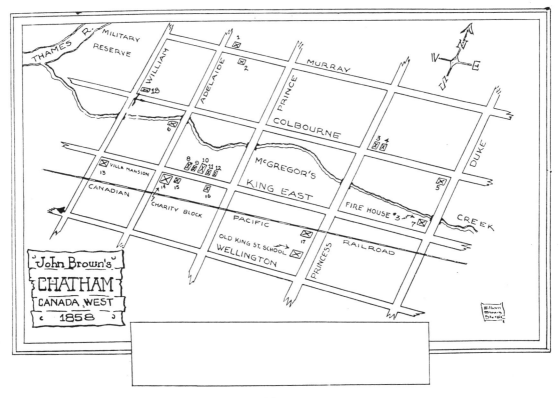

Sites associated with John Brown 1800 - 1859

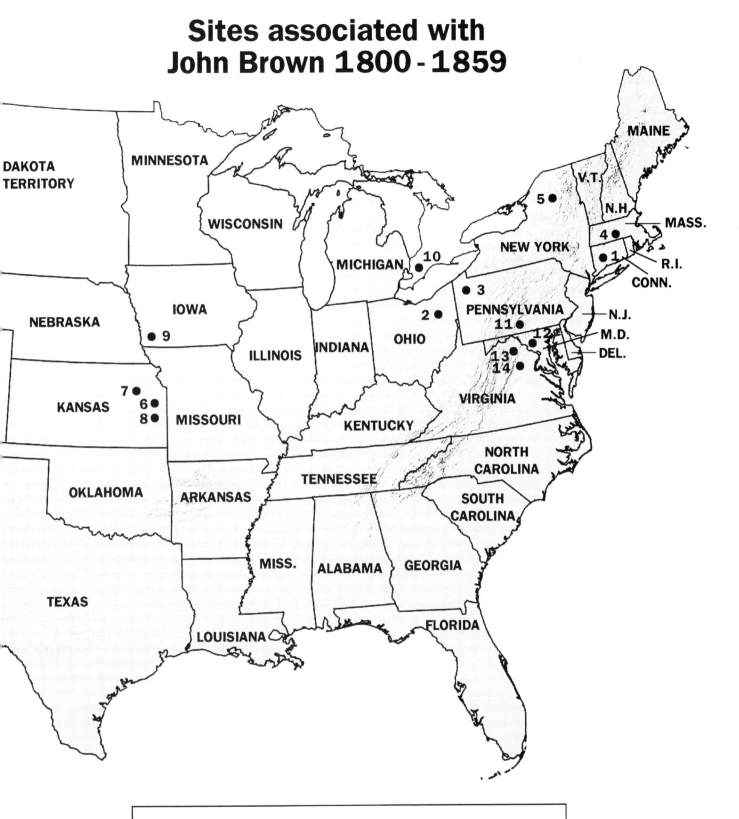

1.	Torrington, CT	8.	Osawatomie, KS
2.	Hudson, Akron OH area	9.	Tabor, IA
3.	Crawford Co., PA	10.	Chatham, Ontario
4.	Springfield, MA	11.	Franklin Co., PA
5.	North Elba, NY	12.	Kennedy Farm, MD
6.	Black Jack Springs, KS	13.	Harpers Ferry, VA
7.	Lawrence, KS	14.	Charlestown, VA

Interior of the Adair
Cabin as it looked in
1944.

John Brown and Bleeding Kansas

On Oct. 6, 1855, John Brown arrived in Kansas. It was at the urging of his son, John Jr., who had moved west with his family and four of his brothers, Owen, Jason, Frederick and Salmon, in 1855.

Brown's sons had pleaded with him for some time to join them in their abolitionist cause. John Jr. wrote his father in 1855:

"I tell you the truth when I say that while the interest of despotism has secured to its cause hundreds of thousands of the meanest and most desperate of men, armed to the teeth with Revolvers, Bowie Knives, Rifles & Cannon—while they are not only thoroughly organized, but under pay from Slaveholders—the friends of freedom are *not one fourth* of them *half armed*, and as to *military organization* among them *it no where exists in this territory* unless they have recently done something in Lawrence. The result of this is that the people here exhibit the most abject and cowardly spirit, whenever their dearest rights are invaded and trampled down by the lawless band of miscreants which Missouri has ready at a moment's call to pour in upon them. This is the *general* effect upon the people here so far as I have noticed; there are a few, and but a few exceptions. . . . CONTINUED ON THE NEXT PAGE ·

Rev. Samuel Adair and the Adair Cabin

One of Osawatomie's most prominent pre-Civil War citizens was the Rev. Samuel Adair, who married John Brown's half-sister, Florilla.

The Adairs were graduates of co-ed, biracial Oberlin College in Ohio. They moved to Osawatomie in 1854, and became the intellectual and spiritual foundation of the Free-State movement in this part of Kansas.

Their log cabin, inside a stone pergola, is now the Adair Cabin State Historic Site, located in the John Brown Memorial Park. It was used by Brown when he lived in the area. Many escaped slaves were hidden in the cabin before being sent north on the underground railroad. The cabin, originally one mile west of town, was purchased by the Adairs in March 1854 for $200. Six months later, Brown moved in and built an addition, which he used for free-state meetings.

The Adairs were devoted servants to the Abolitionist cause but were opposed to the violent actions of John Brown.

Adair was a chaplain in the Union Army during the Civil War and was the first chaplain of the State Asylum in Osawatomie. This view is circa 1893. WVSA

Now the remedy we propose is that the Anti-Slavery portion of the inhabitants should *immediately, thoroughly arm*, and *organize themselves* in *military companies*. In order to effect this, some persons must begin and lead off in the matter."

As early as 1837 Brown, in the midst of his failed business dealings, became an ardent abolitionist. He devoted his life to the overthrow of slavery after attending a public meeting concerning the murder of abolitionist editor, Elijah Lovejoy, at Alton, Illinois.

Kansas would be the first bloody test of the conflict between slave and non-slave state residents. The Fugitive Slave Law of 1850 reinforced the northern view of the division between the United States and the individual states.

The passage of the Kansas-Nebraska Act of 1854 legislated that the citizens of a territory would be allowed to vote on whether to allow slavery in the region. Both Free-Soilers and pro-slavery advocates flocked to Kansas to press their views in non-violent and violent means.

This was a ready-made situation for Brown who came to Kansas ready for a battle. En route he gathered arms for himself and his sons. This would be the start of his journey to Harpers Ferry.

On May 21 and 22, 1856, a force of pro-slavery men sacked the free-state town of Lawrence. Two men were killed, buildings burned and newspaper presses destroyed. Two days later, Brown, with four of his sons, a son-in-law and two others, attacked the settlement of Pottawatomie and brutally murdered five pro-slavery men. The massacre occurred just north of Lane, at Dutch Henry's crossing in Miami County.

This event gave Brown a reputation which would sicken even some of his staunchest supporters. He was shunned by Free-state friends and hunted by enemies. John Jr. and Jason, who had nothing to do with the murders, were captured by posses, beaten and put in jail, narrowly escaping the hangman's noose. They were eventually released.

Eight days after the massacre, word was received that a group of pro-slavery Missourians, commanded by Henry Clay Pate, was camped on the Santa Fe Trail at Black Jack Springs. Warrants had been issued for Brown's gang and Pate was anxious to apprehend them. On June 2, Brown surrounded Pate's troops and forced their surrender after killing four men, wounding several others and capturing horses, arms and Pate, himself.

Soon after the battle, a troop of United States Cavalry advanced on Brown's camp, ordering his men to disband and to free Pate and the other prisoners. No attempt was made to arrest Brown raising ques-

Six members of the Kansas Free State battery stand ready with the Mexican War-era cannon "Old Sacramento" in Lawrence in September 1856. From left: Owen, showing his withered right arm; George B. Gill, an officer in Brown's Provincial Government and a participant in the Chatham Convention; John T. "Ottawa" Jones, a Chippewa Indian whose house Brown and his men used after the Missouri rescue; Augustus Wattles, a Kansas freestate leader and associate editor of the *Herald of Freedom* in Lawrence; August Bondi, a Jewish emigrant from Austria and an associate of Brown in Kansas; and James Redpath, with cannon swab, an abolitionist journalist. The cannon is now on display at the Watkins Community Museum in Lawrence.

tions about whether the officers feared him, sympathized with him or saw it their duty to only restore order by breaking up pro-slavery and Free-state parties alike.

In the following months, Brown and his followers were active the area along the Missouri-Kansas border. On Aug. 30, 1856, a heated battle took place at the small settlement of Osawatomie. The Free-state force clashed with pro-slavery Missourians led by John Ried. Five of Brown's men were killed, including son Frederick, who is buried at the site. Osawatomie was subsequently burned to the ground. The action earned Brown the nickname "Osawatomie" and hardened his stand against slavery. He stated afterwards, "I have only a short time to live—only one death to die, and I will die fighting for this cause. There will be no peace in this land until slavery is done for. I will give them something else to do than to extend slave territory. I will carry this war into Africa." He would carry out his prophecy three years later in Virginia.

The pro-slavery forces in the territory wrote a constitution favoring slavery, but a vote of the people defeated it. Finally Free-staters gained control of the legislature and repealed the pro-slavery laws. A new constitution was written that forbid slavery and Congress was petitioned to admit Kansas as a free state. It would not happen until Jan. 29, 1861, after several southern states had left the Union, tipping the balance of votes for free-state admittance.

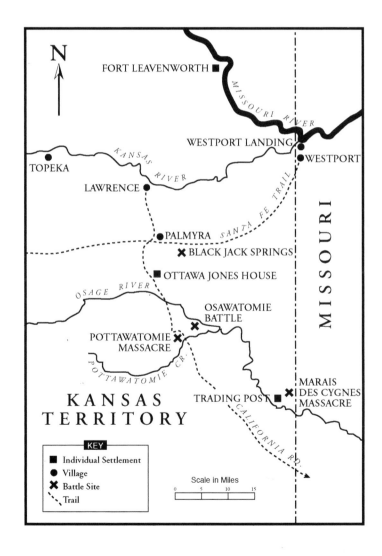

Col. Henry Clay Pate was defeated and captured by Brown at the Battle of Black Jack Springs. During the Civil War he formed the 5th Virginia Cavalry and was killed at the Battle of Yellow Tavern in Virginia on May 11, 1864. In 1863 Pate was held for court martial by Gen. J.E.B. Stuart, but charges were eventually dropped. wvsa

Soon after he left Springfield, Mass. for Kansas, John Brown sent an order to T.W. Carter of Chicopee for a consignment of muskets with which to carry on his ill-starred campaign against slavery.

The accompanying letter affords an interesting sidelight on the intensity of his devotion to the cause he championed.

Osawatomie, Kansas Territory, 20th Feby 1856

T.W. Carter Esqr Agt
Chicopee Falls
• Mass

Dear Sir

Your kind favour of the 5th Jany was received a few days since mentioning receipt of Draft & offering a further supply of arms. I would again immediately take the responsibility of ordering another lot: but I am not at this moment prepared to say how I would <u>dare</u> to have them directed. The other lot I came on with myself; bringing with the other Arms contributed by the friends of freedom in Mass & other parts I cannot just now name any one who is coming on: suitable to take charge of them. Hen Pomeroy went East lately, but I do not know where a letter would find him. I now think I shall immediately make a <u>further & more earnest</u> appeal to the lovers of Freedom in New England for the means of procuring Arms & Amunition for the maintainance of that cause in Kansas; as I think the Crisis <u>has not yet come</u>. I firmly believe that the Administration intends to drive the people here to an abject submission; or to fight the Government troops (now in the Territory ostensibly to remove intruders from certain Indian lands) Bow in submission to the vilest tyrany or be guilty of what <u>will be called</u> treason; will I believe be the next, & only alternative for the Free State men of Kansas. O God must this thing be? Must the people here shoot down the poor Soldier with whom they have no quarrel? Can you not through your extensive acquaintance aid me in this work; if you can be satisfied that I am <u>trustworthy</u>. I am well known by many at Springfield. I very much want a lot of the Carbines as soon as I can see any <u>way clear</u> to pay for them; & then to get them through safe. Please write me the lowest terms at wholesale for just such Carbines as you furnish the Government. I may write you further within few days.

Very Respectfully Your Friend
John Brown

John Brown and his men on their arrival in Lawrence, Kansas, October, 1855. WVSA

Tabor, Iowa

Tabor is a small town in Fremont County in the southwestern corner of Iowa. It was founded by deeply religious people from Oberlin, Ohio. Brown first came to this town in 1856 seeking help in establishing his Underground Railroad across Iowa. Several prominent citizens of Tabor, including George Gaston, founder of the town, and the Rev. John Todd, hid runaway slaves in their homes.

Homes became storehouses for arms and ammunitions. Haystacks concealed brass cannons and the town park became a drill field for Brown's army. From August to November 1857, Brown and Hugh Forbes, his military advisor, were in Tabor practicing target shooting with Sharp's rifles. They also studied Forbes manual on military science entitled *The Patriotic Volunteer*.

Brown next appeared in Tabor on Feb. 5, 1859, after he and his men had freed 11 slaves in Missouri. They had killed one slave-holder and stole his belongings. The local citizens felt Brown was inviting an armed invasion by Missourians bent on vengeance and asked him to leave town. Gathering his men and cache of arms he left town. He led the group through Iowa to Springdale and then put the slaves on a train to Chicago, Detroit and finally to safety in Canada.

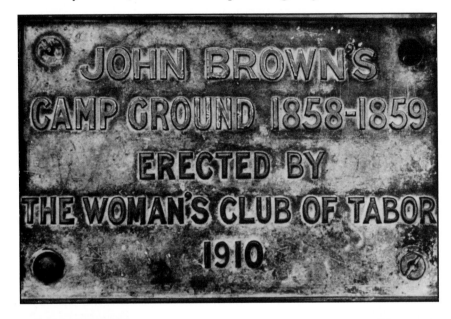

This marker was erected in the Town Park in 1910. A year later someone tried to blow it up with dynamite. The park was a drill field for Brown's "army" which made raids into Missouri and Kansas. WVSA

The Todd House in Tabor was built in 1853 by Rev. John Todd, Tabor's first Congregational minister. The house's cellar was filled with boxes of clothing, ammunition, muskets, sabers and 20 boxes of Sharp's rifles. The house was repaired in 1890. The old cottonwood siding was replaced by pine, and a porch in front and a bay window on the south were added. The Tabor Historical Society maintains it as a museum. The Todd House is listed in the National Register of Historic Places. PHOTOS BY JENNIFER WILLIAMS OF TABOR, IOWA.

A letter in the George W. Brown Papers of the Kansas State Historical Society, Topeka, Kansas

Fort Scott, Kans.
Aug. 4, 1879

Hon. Eli Thayer
Worcester, Mass.

My Dear Sir: Yours of the 28th ult recd asking for facts in my possession in regard to John Brown's participation in what is known as the Pottawatomie massacre and the raid into Missouri.... I was in John Brown's camp at the Trading Post in Linn Co. Kansas early in January A.D. 1859 and had conversations with him in regard to both transactions.

As to the Massacre he said he would not say that he was not engaged in it, but he would say that he advised it and justified it and was willing to take a full share of the responsibility of it. He said that the death of those pro-slavery men had been determined upon at a meeting of free-state settlers the day before — that he was present at that meeting and, I think, presided, and that the executioners were then and there appointed. He said he would not say that he was one of them, but...that if it was wrong he was as much to blame as any.

He gave a reason for the deed that the men were carriers of news to Missourians, that they kept a grape-vine telegraph with Missourians and were endangering the settlements by bringing in the invaders. He said it became necessary to make an example, and so strike terror and put an end to that sort of thing.

As to the raid into Missouri — it was made on the 20th Dec. 1858....It was led by Capt. Brown in person...and proceeded into Vernon Co. Mo., a distance of three or four miles. The Missouri Democrat of Dec 30th 1858 gave the Missouri statement of the losses....It states that they murdered David Crews (or Cruise), kidnapped a negro woman, took wagon, horses &c. & robbed Mr. Martin and family of a fine mule — took from the estate of James Lawrence, in possession of his son-in-law five negroes, 2 horses, 1 yoke of cattle and ox-wagon, double-barrel shotgun, saddle and clothing. From Isaac B. La Rue, five negroes, six horses, 1 yoke of cattle, clothing — and took prisoners who they released. In the conversation to which I have alluded Capt. Brown said he had sent the slaves on to their freedom — that they had earned the property of their masters — and that his young men were entitled to forage to the extent of their subsistence. He denied the current rumor that the slaves had been taken away by violence and against their will. As to the killing of Cruise, he said that he had given strict orders...that there should be no firing unless resistance was offered.... Cruise was a...plain, unoffending farmer. It was reported that he had no weapons on his person. The killing of him was regarded as an unjustifiable outrage — and it subjected our settlements to great danger from retaliatory measures.

I protested to the Captain against this violence. We were settlers — he was not. He could strike a blow and leave. The retaliatory blow would fall on us. Being a free state man, I myself was held personally responsible by pro-slavery ruffians in Ft. Scott for the acts of Capt. Brown. One of these ruffians — Brockett — when they gave me notice to leave the town, said, "When a snake bites me I don't go hunting for that particular snake. I kill the first snake I come to."

I called Capt. Brown's attention to the facts that we were at peace with Missouri — that our Legislature was then in the hands of free state men to make the law — that even in our disturbed Counties of Bourbon and Linn they were in a majority and had elected the officers both to make and execute the laws — that without peace we could have no immigration — that no southern immigration was coming — that agitation such as his was only keeping our northern friends away &c. &c.

The old man replied that it was no pleasure to him — an old man — to be living in the saddle — away from home and family and exposing his life — and if the free state men in Kansas felt that they no longer needed him he would be glad to go.

He seemed very erratic — at war with all our accustomed ideas on the slavery question — but very earnest.

I think the conversation made an impression on him — for he soon after went to his self-sacrifice at Harper's Ferry.

Yours,/   George A. Crawford

P.S....Let me say for Capt. Brown that if alive he would allow no man to apologize for that Pottawatomie affair,

The Daily Journal (Lawrence, Kans.) Dec. 10, 1879

I am a native of...Maryland...a painter by trade.... [On] October 20, 1855,...I emigrated to Kansas with my family and settled in Anderson County, on the Pottawatomie Creek, about one mile west of Greeley. I joined the Pottawatomie rifle company at its reorganization in May, 1856, at which time John Brown Jr. was elected captain.... About noon [on May] 23d, old John Brown came to me and said he had just received information that trouble was expected on the Pottawatomie, and wanted to know if I would take my team and take him and his boys back so that they could keep watch of what was going on.... The party, consisting of old John Brown, Frederick Brown, Owen Brown, Watson Brown, Oliver Brown, Henry Thompson (John Brown's son-in-law), and Mr. Winer...started...about two o'clock p.m. All of the party, except Mr. Winer, who rode a pony, rode with me in my wagon. When within two or three miles of the Pottawatomie creek we turned off the main road to the right, drove down into the edge of the timber between the two deep ravines and camped about one mile above Dutch Henry's crossing.

After my team was fed and the party had taken supper, John Brown told me for the first time what he proposed to do. He said he wanted me to pilot the company up to the forks of the creek some five or six miles above, into the neighborhood in which I lived, and show them where all the pro-slavery men resided; that he proposed to sweep the creek as he came down of all the pro-slavery men living on it. I positively refused.... He insisted..., but when he found out I would not go he decided to postpone the expedition until the following night. I then wanted to take my team and go home, but he refused...and said I should remain.... We remained in camp that night, and all day the next day. Sometime after dark we were ordered to march.

We started, the whole company, in a northerly direction, crossing Mosquito creek above the residence of the Doyles. Soon after crossing the creek someone of the party knocked at the door of a cabin but received no reply.... The next place we came to was the residence of the Doyles.... The old man Doyle and two sons were called out and marched...toward Dutch Henry's in the road, where a halt was made. Old John Brown drew his revolver and shot the old man Doyle in the forehead, and Brown's two youngest sons immediately fell upon the younger Doyles with their short two-edged swords.

One of the young Doyles was stricken down in an instant, but the other attempted to escape, and was pursued a short distance...and cut down. The company then proceeded down Mosquito creek to the house of Allen Wilkinson. Here the old man Brown, three of his sons, and son-in-law...went to the door and ordered Wilkinson to come out, leaving Frederick Brown, Winer, and myself standing in the road.... Wilkinson was taken and marched some distance...and slain in the road with a short sword by one of the younger Browns....

We then crossed the Pottawatomie and came to the house of Henry Sherman, generally known as Dutch Henry. Here John Brown and the party, excepting Frederick Brown, Winer, and myself...went into the house and brought out one or two persons, talked with them some, and then took them in again. They afterward brought out William Sherman, Dutch Henry's brother, marched him down into the Pottawatomie Creek, where he was slain with swords by Brown's two youngest sons....

I desire...to say that I did not then approve of the killing of those men, but Brown said it must be done for the protection of the Free State settlers; that the pro-slavery party must be terrified, and that it was better that a score of bad men should die than that one man who came here to make Kansas a free State should be driven out.... That night and the acts then perpetrated are vividly fixed in my memory, and I have thought of them many times since.

I then thought that the transaction was terrible, and have mentioned it to but few persons since. In after time, however, I became satisfied that it resulted in good to the Free State cause, and was especially beneficial to Free State settlers on Pottawatomie Creek. The pro-slavery men *were dreadfully* terrified, and large numbers of them soon left the Territory. It was afterwards said that one Free State man could scare a company of them. I always understood that Geo. W. Grant came to our camp on Ottawa Creek, near Captain Shore's, with a message from his father...to John Brown, asking for protection from threatened assaults of the Shermans and other pro-slavery ruffians. But I did not know Geo. W. Grant at the time and do not remember of seeing him. I frequently heard the circumstance mentioned as a fact....

After several days...while John Brown was cooking breakfast for the company, James Redpath came into our camp and had some conversation with Captain Brown. I saw Redpath again after the battle of Black Jack..., and I desire to say, in this connection, that I never told Redpath at any time that John Brown was not present at the Pottawatomie tragedy. His statement, which has been read to me, to the effect that two squatters, who aided in the execution, gave him such information, is totally false, so far as I am concerned. As Winer and myself were the only settlers in the neighborhood not members of Brown's family, who were present at the tragedy, I can only conclude he referred to us....

Lane, Kansas, Dec. 6, 1879

JAMES TOWNSLEY

John Brown after his capture at Harpers Ferry. An oil painting used by Elijah Avey in his lectures on John Brown. Captioned "The Imprisonment of John Brown," copyrighted 1904 and 1906 by Elijah Avey, originator and proprioter. The artist was H. Webb Keedy who painted this for the 1904 St. Louis World's Fair. It apparently was painted from a sketch by Alfred Berghaus for the Oct.29,1859, issue of *Frank Leslie's Illustrated Newspaper*. People identified, left to right: soldier, Lt. J.E.B.Stuart; Sen. James M. Mason of Virginia; Gov. Henry A. Wise of Virginia; county officers and reporters. The original is in the West Virginia State Museum collection.
WVSA

The Harpers Ferry Incident

After Brown's convention in Ontario and his one last trip to Kansas to bring slaves to freedom in the winter of 1858-59, he moved to Chambersburg, Pennsylvania, in May 1859 to set up a weapons cache and to make plans for his raid on Harpers Ferry. He rented a house on East King Street owned by Mary Ritner and used the name Isaac Smith to conceal his real identity.

Brown and some of his followers were in and out of the area during the summer and fall of 1859. John Kagi stayed in Chambersburg most of the time until going to the Kennedy farm in October. The Cumberland Valley Railroad was used to transport the weapons from Ohio to Chambersburg. From there they were hauled to the Kennedy farm by wagon. John Brown Jr., who would not take part in the October raid on Harpers Ferry, supervised a lot of this arms shipping from his home in Ashtabula County, Ohio.

Brown would also spend some time at the iron furnace at Mont Alto, 15 miles north of Chambersburg. It is thought he was employed as a tie contractor for the South Mountain Railroad and set up Sunday school classes for Negro children at the local Emmanuel Chapel.

CONTINUED ON PAGE 45

The Oakes and Caufman warehouse was one of several sites in Chambersburg that John Brown used to store his weapons until transporting them to the Kennedy farm.

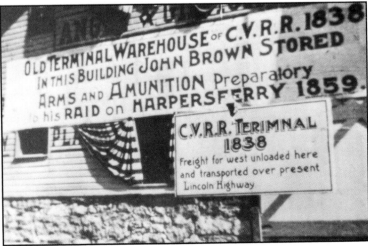

- 29 -

U.S. ARMORY IN HARPERS FERRY.
JEFFERSON COUNTY VA

This view of Harpers Ferry was painted by German-born artist, Edward Beyer in the late 1850s. His *Album of Virginia*; or *Illustration of the Old Dominion* was composed of 40 color lithographs in 1858. In the album's accompanying booklet, the following introduction was included:

The Artist [Edward Beyer], a Graduate of the Dusseldorf Academy, has been for three years engaged in painting some of the most remarkable Scenery of Virginia; and the writer feels he has copied Nature with such striking fidelity as to recommend his Sketches to every true lover of the beautiful in Nature, and especially to those who bear in their hearts the Home Scenes of the Old Dominion.

A VIRGINIAN
Richmond, May 12, 1857

Harpers Ferry

In 1733, Peter Stephens settled at "The Hole" where the Shenandoah and Potomac rivers met in Virginia. Robert Harper purchased the site in 1747 and operated a ferry across the Potomac River. The Virginia General Assembly established the town of Shenandoah Falls at Mr. Harper's Ferry in 1763 and George Washington toured the area in 1786 as the president of the Patowmack Company. The U.S. Government purchased 118 acres at what is now called Harpers Ferry in 1796 and began construction of an armory and arsenal in 1799. In 1863, this area became part of the new state of West Virginia. In 1944 a Congressional Act established the Harpers Ferry National Monument and it is now a national historical park.

This photo of Harpers Ferry was taken prior to 1968 as John Brown's fort has not yet been moved to Lower Town. The obelisk at the fort's original site can be seen.

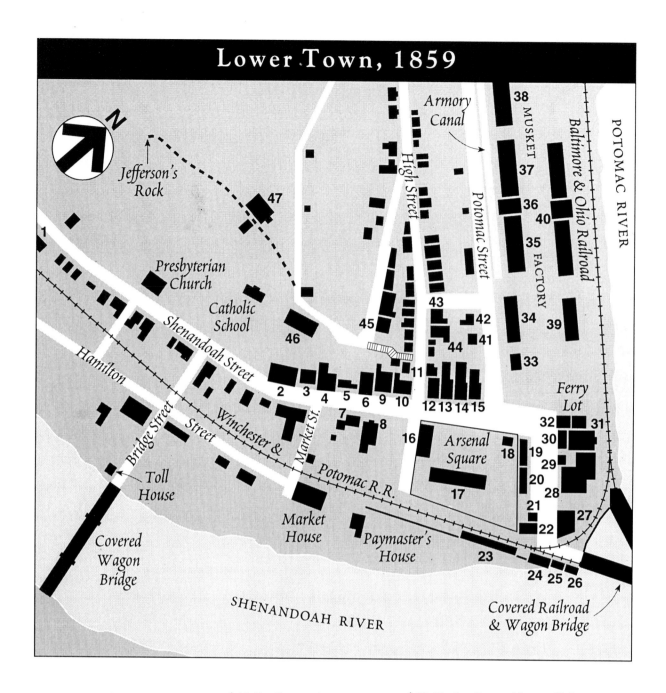

Lower Town, 1859

Jefferson's Rock

Armory Canal

38

MUSKET

37

Baltimore & Ohio Railroad

POTOMAC RIVER

36

40

35

Presbyterian Church

47

High Street

FACTORY

Catholic School

Potomac Street

43

45

42

34

39

46

44

41

Shenandoah Street

11

33

Hamilton

Winchester &

2 3 4 5 9 10

12 13 14 15

Ferry Lot

Street

Market St.

7

6

32

31

Bridge Street

8

16

Arsenal Square

18

30

19

29

Toll House

Potomac R.R.

17

20

28

21

27

22

Covered Wagon Bridge

Market House

Paymaster's House

23

24 25 26

Covered Railroad & Wagon Bridge

SHENANDOAH RIVER

1. Armory Stable
2. Shops
3. Bakery
4. Shops and boardinghouse
5. Grocery and liquor store
6. Philip Frankel & Co's Ready-Made Clothing Store
7. Old Master Armorer's quarters
8. New Master Armorer's quarters (vacant)
9. Butcher and grocery store
10. Dry goods store
11. John T. Rieley's Boot & Shoe Manufactory
12. Dry goods store
13. The Charles Johnson Dry Goods Store
14. Great Southern Clothing Hall
15. Dry goods store

16. Small arsenal
17. Large arsenal
18. Old superintendent's office
19. Clothing store and shoe store
20. Tobacco shop
21. Barber shop
22. Jewelry store
23. Winchester & Potomac Railroad depot
24. The Gault House Saloon
25. B&O Railroad office
26. Toll house
27. B&O Railroad depot
28. The Wager House Hotel
29. John Strauss & Co. Ready-Made Clothing Store
30. Drug store
31. Potomac Restaurant
32. Dry goods store

33. Engine & guard house (John Brown's Fort)
34. Armory offices
35. "Bell" or finishing shop
36. Polishing shop and washhouse
37. Boring mill
38. Stocking and machine shop
39. Warehouse
40. Smith and forging shop
41. White Hall
42. Tavern
43. Confectionery
44. Shoemaker's shop
45. Harper House
46. St. Peter's Roman Catholic Church
47. St. John's Protestant Episcopal Church

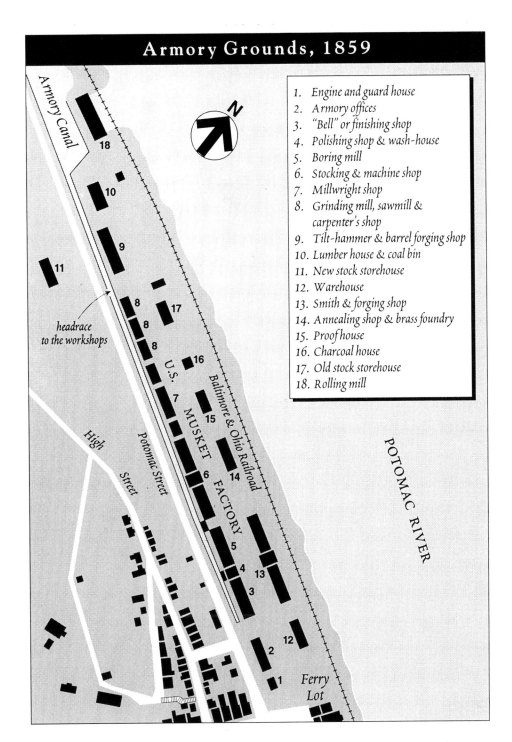

Armory Grounds, 1859

1. Engine and guard house
2. Armory offices
3. "Bell" or finishing shop
4. Polishing shop & wash-house
5. Boring mill
6. Stocking & machine shop
7. Millwright shop
8. Grinding mill, sawmill & carpenter's shop
9. Tilt-hammer & barrel forging shop
10. Lumber house & coal bin
11. New stock storehouse
12. Warehouse
13. Smith & forging shop
14. Annealing shop & brass foundry
15. Proof house
16. Charcoal house
17. Old stock storehouse
18. Rolling mill

An armory was established at Harpers Ferry in 1799 at the insistence of George Washington. The site was a safe distance farther up the Potomac from the new capitol. Many believed the Potomac would be a major transportation artery westward. The site also had abundant water power.

Rifles, tomahawks and knives were made at the armory for the 1803-06 Lewis and Clark Expedition. The Model 1803 Harpers Ferry became the first standard military rifle. The first military pistols were also produced here.

The Hall Rifle Works was established here in 1819 to manufacture breech-loading rifles. The company developed the system of interchangable parts, making possible the basis for modern industrialism.

In its 63 years of operation, from 1798 to 1861, nearly 600,000 muskets and rifle-muskets, over 4,000 pistols, bayonets and spare parts were manufactured.

On April 18, 1861, the U.S. Army destroyed the armory and arsenal at the approach of troops from Virginia. The armory was saved by local townspeople but retreating Confederate troops set the armory buildings on fire two months later. BOTH MAPS BY DAVE GILBERT, SHEPHERDSTOWN, W.VA.

The Kennedy Farm

The Kennedy farm was the headquarters for John Brown and his raiders before their historic raid on Harpers Ferry. The nondescript house was built in 1840 and was originally used to house colliers working at an iron furnace at the mouth of Antietam Creek in western Maryland.

Sometime later the house was purchased by Booth Kennedy, a Virginia doctor. Brown rented the house for eight months in the summer of 1859 from Kennedy's heirs for a total of $35. The farmhouse had a half-basement kitchen and storeroom, a living room, two bedrooms on the second floor and a small attic. Another smaller cabin was across the road that connected Harpers Ferry and Boonsboro, Maryland.

The farm went through a series of owners and alterations until the late 1940s when it was purchased by the Improved Benevolent Protective Order of Elks, a black fraternal organization. They used the property as an antislavery memorial and a recreational retreat. By the 1960s, it had gone through a succession of owners and had deteriorated to the point that it was to be demolished and the farm subdivided.

In 1973, South Trimble Lynn, a local man, purchased the property and started the historical restoration which has brought the farmhouse back to its 1859 look. Lynn received help and grants from the Maryland Historical Trust, the Hagerstown Trust and Archie W. Franzen, an historical architect from Harpers Ferry. The interior is historically furnished and is complete with the figures of John Brown and some of his raiders. The property, now a National Historic Landmark, is open most weekends.

THE CABIN ACROSS THE ROAD
FROM THE FARMHOUSE

The Kennedy farmhouse as photographed on July 11, 1930, by Dr. Clarence Gee, scholar and collector of John Brown material. WSVA

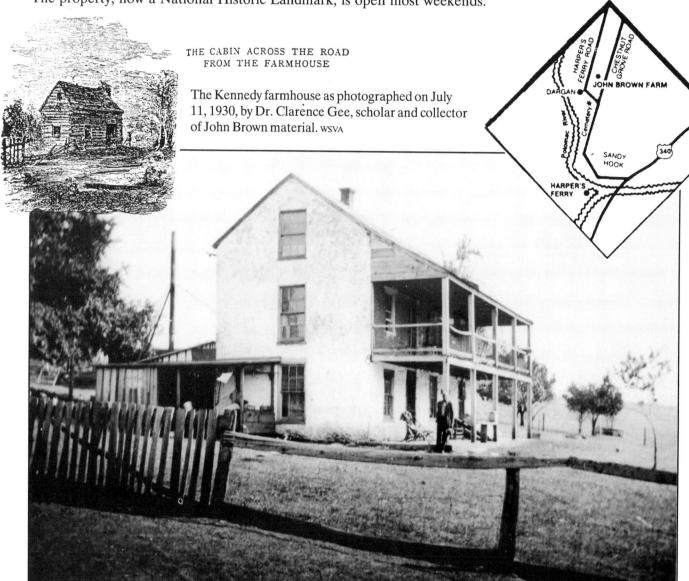

I RODE WITH STONEWALL

The following was published in Henry Kyd Douglas' book, *I Rode With Stonewall*, published by the University of North Carolina Press in 1940. Douglas lived at Ferry Hill Plantation overlooking the Potomac River and Shepherdstown, W.Va., not too far from Brown's headquarters at the Kennedy Farm. The plantation is now headquarters for the Chesapeake & Ohio Canal National Historical Park. *

John Brown lived for a little while, before his attempted insurrection, at the Kennedy Farm among the hills, about three miles down the river from my father's place, five miles from Harper's Ferry, and near the Antietam Iron Works. He seemed a hermit and only attracted attention because of his apparent eccentricity of manner and life, and went by the name of Isaac Smith. Although, it was reported, he had occasional unknown visitors, I never saw but one person at his humble home, an old Negro woman of most uncomely aspect, who seemed to be his housekeeper and companion. He professed to be prospecting for minerals, which he said were hidden in these wooded hills. In this as in all other respects his life proved to be a lie.

One wet day, not long before his attack, I was crossing from Shepherdstown, when I found him at the foot of the hill which rises from the river, with an overloaded two-horse wagon. He told me he was hauling miner's tools for prospecting and needed help. I went up home (Ferry Hill Plantation), got my father's carriage horses and their driver, Enoch, and with their aid Mr. Smith's wagon was taken a mile over the hills toward Sharpsburg, his best route home. Being very young, I was much impressed with the grateful simplicity of the venerable actor as we parted in the rain and mud, with many dignified expressions of thanks on his part. I had not a suspicion that he was other than he seemed. But it was not very long until I found out that the rickety wagon contained boxes of "John Brown's pikes" and that I was an innocent *particeps criminis* in their introduction into Maryland. He had brought them from a station on the Baltimore and Ohio Railroad in Virginia, to which they had been shipped from New England. (The pikes were actually shipped from Chambersburg, Pa.)

It is an historical regret that John Brown, *alias* Isaac Smith, had not fallen among a more curious people, who might have watched and made record of his movements. Our people took little notice of him for they did not like him. As he was leading a life of deception, preparatory to crime, he of course did not seek acquaintances of friends. Not a kindly or creditable act is told of his life during these days. With a previous record as a horse thief and a murderer, he was now playing the new role of a conspirator. Full of cunning, with much experience and with no intelligence, cruel, bloodthirsty, and altogether unscrupulous, he seemed singularly ignorant not only of the white people among whom he had camped, but of the characteristics of the race for whom he was about to raise the standard of insurrection. His cause, when the time cam, frightened but did not attract the Negroes, and only made them keep quiet and remain closer to their quarters. Five of them joined him in his Raid: one of these was killed, and the others deserted him.

There is nothing in all the history of fanaticism, its crimes and follies, so strange and inexplicable as that the people of New England, with all their shrewdness and general sense of justice, should have attempted to lift up the sordid name of that old wretch and, by a political apotheosis, to exalt him among the heroes and benefactors of this land. I can understand why enthusiasts and fanatics in the cause of the abolition of slavery might have sent him to Kansas and aided him with their means to keep that from becoming a slave state; but why they should have sent him money and arms to encourage him to murder the white people of Virginia is beyond my comprehension.

Personally I had no feeling of resentment against the people of the North because of their desire for the emancipation of the slave, for I believed Negro slavery was a curse to the people of the Middle States. As a boy I had determined never to own one. Whether I would have followed the example of shrewd New Englanders in compromising with philanthropy by selling my slaves for a valuable consideration before I became and abolitionist, I will not pretend to say. But I do not think I could have followed that example so far as to drag the banner of freedom into the mire of deception and insurrection that Brown prepared for it and then glory in the falsification of his true character. John Brown closed a life of vice and cruelty by flagrantly violating the laws of God and his country; if "his soul is marching on" it is to be hoped it will confine its wanderings to the people who exalt and glorify it.

I never saw John Brown again until the morning of the 19th (actually the 18th) of October 1859, when I witnessed the attack of the United States Marines under Lieutenant Israel Green on the engine house at Harper's Ferry and saw him brought out of it.

* Douglas' account has never been substantiated in the historical record so is presented here as his words only. During the Civil War Douglas became the youngest member of Stonwall Jackson's staff. He was wounded and captured at Gettysburg but was exchanged after nine months imprisonment. After the war he practiced law and became a circuit judge in Maryland. He died in 1903 and is buried in Shepherdstown, W. Va.

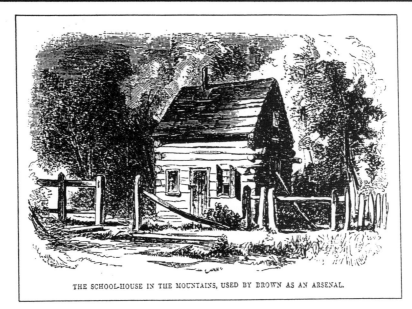

THE SCHOOL-HOUSE IN THE MOUNTAINS, USED BY BROWN AS AN ARSENAL.

This schoolhouse, near the Kennedy farm, was used by some of the raiders to store arms during the raid. About 30 children and the schoolmaster, Lind F. Currie, were in the school when several raiders entered. Currie had to dismiss school when some of the younger children started to cry. NPS HF

Casualties of the Harpers Ferry Raid

Raiders killed Oct. 16-18, 1859
Jeremiah Anderson
Oliver Brown
Watson Brown
John Henry Kagi
Lewis Leary
William H. Leeman
Dangerfield Newby
Dauphin Thompson
William Thompson
Stewart Taylor

U.S. Marines
Pvt. Luke Quinn – killed
Pvt. Mathew Ruppert – wounded

Civilian Deaths
Mr. Fontaine Beckham,
    mayor of Harpers Ferry
Mr. Thomas Boerly
Mr. George W. Turner
Heyward Shepherd

Raiders executed by the State of Virginia
John Brown
John A. Copeland
Edwin Coppoc
John E. Cook
Shields Green
Albert Hazlett
Aaron D. Stevens

Quinn's gravestone in St. Peter's Catholic Cemetery, Harpers Ferry.

The Raiders

John E. Cook (27) was from a wealthy Connecticut family and, attended Yale University and studied law in New York City. In 1855, he moved to Kansas and took part in the conflict there. Brown's son, Salmon characterized Cook as "highly erratic in temperament" and "not overly stocked with morality. He was the best pistol shot I ever saw...[and] just as much of an expert in getting into the good graces of the girls. He loved to talk and rattle on about himself." Cook escaped after the raid but was captured at Mont Alto, Pa., a few days later and taken to Charlestown to stand trial. On Dec. 15, 1859 he and Edwin Coppoc attempted to escape from the Charlestown jail but were caught and hanged the next day. NPS HF-169

Aaron D. Stevens (26) was a native of Connecticut. At 16, he ran away from home to join the Massachusetts Volunteer Regiment fighting in the Mexican War. He left the army at the end of the war but soon rejoined and became a bugler in a dragoon regiment in the West. He took part in campaigns against the Navaho and Apache Indians. In the mid-1850s at Taos, New Mexico, he nearly killed an officer in a drunken brawl and was sentenced to death. His sentence was commuted to three years hard labor at Fort Leavenworth, Kansas, where he escaped in January 1856. He joined the Free-State cause and fought in some of the bloodiest battles in Kansas as a colonel of the Second Kansas Volunteer Regiment. He was totally dedicated to the overthrow of slavery and was in charge of military training for the raiders at the Kennedy farm. Stevens was captured at Harpers Ferry and hanged on Dec. 16, 1859. NPS HF-1114

John H. Kagi (22) was self-educated and had taught school in Virginia, close to the Harpers Ferry area. His abolitionist views got him in trouble with local officials and he fled the state. He became a lawyer in Nebraska City, Nebraska, in 1856 and was a correspondent for several Eastern newspapers. He joined the Second Kansas Volunteer Regiment in 1856 and was soon taken prisoner by Federal troops. He served four months in jail before being released on bail. In January 1857, he was shot by a pro-slavery judge during a disagreement and joined Brown's group while still suffering from his wounds. An Iowa youth wrote that, "his fertility of resources made him a tower of strength to John Brown." He was a logician of more than ordinary ability. He was full of wonderful vitality and all things were fit food for his brain." Kagi was one of Brown's most trusted lieutenants. He was killed trying to escape from Harpers Ferry in the middle os the Shenandoah River on Oct. 18. 1859. NPS HF-181

Oliver, Watson and Owen Brown have been described previously.

Stewart Taylor was born in Canada. He was sent to capture Colonel Washington. Taylor was shot in the forehead in the enginehouse. NPS HF-1105

Albert Hazlett (22). Before joining Brown in 1859, he worked on his brother's farm in Pennsylvania. He stated, "I am willing to die in the cause of liberty. If I had 10,000 lives, I would willingly lay them all down for the same cause." Hazlett escaped from Harpers Ferry but was later caught and hanged. NPS HF-1111

Dauphin (20) and **William** (26) **Thompson.** The brothers lived in North Elba, N.Y. They were dedicated abolitionists but had taken no part in previous battles. William had started for Kansas in 1856 but had turned back and Dauphin had never been away from home before. Both died at Harpers Ferry. NPS HF-1112

Jeremiah Anderson was from Indiana. He died at
Harpers Ferry, and his body was turned over to the
Winchester Medical College. NPS HF-1110

Francis Jackson Merriam (22) was the grandson of
Francis Jackson, a Boston historian and abolitionist.
He was very unstable and troublesome to the other
raiders. He remained behind at the Kennedy farm
and escaped to Canada after the raid. NPS HF-1116

William H. Leeman (20) was born in Maine, and
worked in a shoe factory before moving to Kansas in
1856. He served with Brown's "Liberty Guards" and
was described as "only a boy, who smoked a great deal
and drank a little...very handsome and very attrac-
tive." On Oct. 17, he dashed across the armory
compound, leaped over the railroad line and jumped
into the Potomac River. A couple of townsfolk
rowed out in the river and shot Leeman in the head.
NPS HF-1117

Charles Plummer Tidd (25) was a former Maine
woods- man and had been with Brown since meeting
him in Tabor, Iowa, in 1857. Quick-tempered, a fine
singer and of "strong family affections," he was
"hungry for action" and anxious to confront slavery
face-to-face. Tidd was sent to capture Col. Washington and bring him to Harpers Ferry, then sent to the
schoolhouse to get more arms. He was one of the
five raiders to escape from the area. NPS HF-1108

Shields Green (23) was an escaped slave from Charleston, South Carolina, whom Brown had met at Frederick Douglass' house in Chambersburg, Pennslyvania. Green was sent to capture Colonel Washington and then brought him to Harpers Ferry. He was captured and hanged on Dec. 16, 1859. NPS HF-520

Dangerfield Newby (48) was the oldest of the raiders. Born into slavery and freed by his white father, Newby had a very personal reason to join Brown. He had moved north seeking employment so he could purchase his wife and six children. After securing the funds, he tried several times to purchase his family but was unsuccessful. Joining Brown was his last hope of freeing his loved ones. On Oct. 17, Newby was shot and killed, the first raider to die. A letter, dated Aug. 16, 1859, was found in his pocket. It read in part:

Dear Husband:

It is said Master is in want of money. If so, I know not what time he may sell me, and then all my bright hopes of the future are blasted, for their has been one bright hope to cheer me in all my troubles, that is to be with you. If I thought I should never see you this earth would have no charms for me. Come this fall without fail money or no money, Do all you can for me, witch [sic] I have no doubt you will. The children are all well. The baby cannot walk yet. You must write soon and say when you think you can come.

—Your affectionate wife,
Harriet Newby

After this letter was found Harriet was sold to a Louisiana slave dealer. NPS HF-263

Osborn P. Anderson (33), one of five black raiders, was a free Negro who had worked as a printer before joining Brown in Canada. He escaped with Hazlett from Harpers Ferry by paddling across the Potomac River in a stolen boat and disappearing into the Maryland woods. He later wrote a book about the raid. NPS HF-264

Lewis Leary was one of Brown's five black followers. He was killed at Harpers Ferry. NPS HF-265

John Copeland was also one of the five blacks. He tried to escape by running into the Shenandoah River but was captured. He was hanged on Dec. 16, 1857. NPS HF-1107

Another set of brothers were **Edwin** (24) and **Barclay** (20) **Coppoc**. Both were Quakers and were in Kansas during the conflict but took no part in the fighting. Both had joined Brown in 1858 at Springdale, Iowa, their hometown. Edwin was captured and hanged on Dec. 16, 1859. Barclay escaped after the raid. NPS HF-1109

WESTERN INDEPENDENT TELEGRAPH LINE,
FROM
BALTIMORE
TO CINCINNATI,
VIA
Baltimore and Ohio R. R. & Marietta and Cincinnati R. R.

THIS LINE WORKS
DIRECTLY THROUGH TO CINCINNATI,
Sun Iron Building, Corner of Baltimore and South Streets,
BALTIMORE.
FIRE-FLY SUN BUILDING

Dated, Richmond 17th 1859.
Col John Thos Gibson
55th Regiment
Charlestown
Jefferson Co Va

Sir. the commander
in chief calls your
attention to the
provisions of the first
sections of chapter
twenty nine of the Code
& directs that you call
out immediately. a

WESTERN INDEPENDENT TELEGRAPH LINE,
FROM
BALTIMORE
TO CINCINNATI,
VIA
Baltimore and Ohio R. R. & Marietta and Cincinnati R. R.

THIS LINE WORKS
DIRECTLY THROUGH TO CINCINNATI,
Sun Iron Building, Corner of Baltimore and South Streets,
BALTIMORE.
FIRE-FLY SUN BUILDING

2/

Dated, 1859.
sufficient force from
your Regiment to put
down the Riotors at
Harpers Ferry the
Commander in Chief
is informed that the
Arsenal & Government
property at that
place are in
possession of a Band
of Riotors. you will
act promptly & fully
in this emergency

WESTERN INDEPENDENT TELEGRAPH LINE,
FROM
BALTIMORE
TO CINCINNATI,
VIA
Baltimore and Ohio R. R. & Marietta and Cincinnati R. R.

THIS LINE WORKS
DIRECTLY THROUGH TO CINCINNATI,
Sun Iron Building, Corner of Baltimore and South Streets,
BALTIMORE.
FIRE-FLY SUN BUILDING

3/

Dated, 1859.
and command the
troops called out in
person. By command
Wm H. Richardson
Adjutant General

Richmond 17th 1859
Col. John Thos Gibson
55th Regiment
Charlestown
Jefferson Co. Va.

Sir. The Commander in Chief calls your attention to the provisions of the first section of chapter twenty nine of the Code & directs that you call out immediately. A sufficient force from your Regiment to put down the Riotors at Harpers Ferry. The Commander in Chief is informed that the Arsenal & Government property at that place are in possession of a Band of Riotors. You will act promptly & fully in the emergency and command the troops called out in person. By command

Wm H. Richardson
Adjutant General

Richmond 17 1859
L.W. Yuott
Prest B&O RR

The Governor requests that you will send the above order to Col. Gibson, three good companies from that Regiment can be immediately called out.

Wm. H. Richardson
Adjutant General

This is the telegraph message sent by Governor Wise in Richmond to Col. Gibson on Oct. 17, 1859. The original is in the Gibson papers at the Jefferson County Museum.

Col. John T. Gibson (1825-1904) was the commander of the 55th Regiment Virginia Militia and the first on the scene to counter Brown's men. He was credited with cutting off Brown's escape from town. Late on Oct. 17, he was relieved of command by Col. Robert W. Baylor. At the start of the Civil War he joined the Confederate Army and was paroled at Appomattox. He later built a house on the site of Brown's execution in Charles Town. After the war, he became a farmer, served as mayor of Charles Town and was a member of the county court. He died in 1904. WVSA

"En Route for Harpers Ferry," sketched by Porte Crayon. Reproduced in *Harper's Weekly*, it depicts "old and young" from all parts of Virginia excited and hurrying to Harpers Ferry at the news of the raid. NPS HF-513

Dr. John D. Starry of Harpers Ferry lived near the armory. He was there when the raid started. After trying to help the dying Heywood Shepherd, he mounted his horse and rode to the home of A.M. Kitzmiller, acting superintendent of the arsenal to spread the alarm. Next, he tried to gather arms for the townspeople, sent a messenger to Charlestown and eventually rode there himself. Arriving back at Harpers Ferry, he organized a group of citizens to counter the raiders actions. After John Copeland was captured in the Shenandoah River, Starry saved him from a lynch mob until a policeman came to take him away. Dr. Starry is the unsung hero of the abortive invasion.
WVSA

Gov. Henry A. Wise (1806-1876) shown here as a Confederate general. He was governor of Virginia at the time of John Brown's raid and called out the troops to repel it. After Brown was captured, Wise came up from Richmond to interview him. During the Civil War, he was in command of Confederate forces in the Kanawha Valley, Virginia (now West Virginia) in July 1861 and under General Lee in his western Virginia campaign until relieved of command in September 1861.

On August 20, Frederick Douglass gave a lecture at Franklin Hall in Chambersburg and Brown later met with him at a local stone quarry in an effort to persuade him to join in the attack on Harpers Ferry. Douglass tried to talk Brown out of it and suggested he direct his actions in a more nonviolent effort, but to no avail. Shields Green, a friend of Douglass, who was with him, decided to go with Brown to the Kennedy farm.

Brown had brought his daughter, Annie and his daughter-in-law, Martha Evelyn Brown, Oliver's wife, to the farm. They were there to do the housekeeping, cooking and to quiet neighborhood suspicions as to the true nature of the group. Brown again took the name of Isaac Smith to conceal his identity. By the end of September Annie and Martha were sent back to New York.

On Sunday evening, Oct. 16, 1859, at 8:00 p.m., John Brown and 18 of his followers left the farm and headed toward their destiny at Harpers Ferry. Three of his men, headed by Owen Brown, stayed behind with weapons and supplies ready to bring to a schoolhouse near the Potomac River when called for.

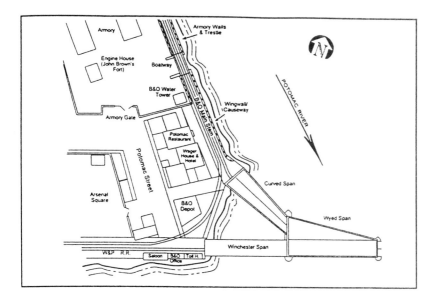

This map depicts the area at the west end of the B&O railroad bridge in 1859. DRAWING BY MICHAEL W. CAPLINGER, INSTITUTE FOR THE HISTORY OF TECHNOLOGY AND INDUSTRIAL ARCHAEOLOGY, MORGANTOWN, W.VA.

Photo of the B&O railroad bridge across the Potomac River in 1859. Brown's men captured the bridge on the night of Oct. 16 along with the bridge watchman, William Williams. Soon an eastbound train arrived and was stopped by Brown. He ordered the train to proceed, but the conductor waited until daylight fearing the bridge had been sabotaged. Brown then walked across the bridge to show it was safe. Fontaine Beckham, Mayor of Harpers Ferry, was killed while peering around the corner of Bollman's water tower in the lower left corner. On July 14, 1861, Confederate troops burned the Wyed and Curved spans which had been built in 1842. The Winchester Span, completed in 1851, was also damaged. NPS

Richard Realf was a 23-year-old Englishman, a poet and former lover of Lady Noell Byron, widow of Lord Byron. He moved to the United States and became a radical abolitionist. He wound up in Lawrence, Kansas, in 1857 as a correspondent for the *Illinois State Gazette*. He met Brown and became one of his recruits. At the Chatham convention, Brown made Realf his secretary of state. He went to England on the pretense of raising money for Brown's cause but raised no money. Upon his return in early 1859, he went to New Orleans and took no further part in Brown's activities. After the raid he gave some damaging testimony in Washington against members of the Secret Six. In 1862, he joined the Union Army and fought with distinction. After the war, he was an officer in a Negro regiment. Realf married three times, joined several religions, had prolonged psychic blackouts, was a lecturer and journalist and finally committed suicide.

NPS HF-172

Beallair, located on County Route 24 near Halltown in Jefferson County, was the home of Lewis W. Washington. The original part of the house was built by Thomas Beall before 1800. It passed out of the Washington family in 1877 and fell into disrepair. It is now in private hands. NPS HF-197

Col. Lewis W. Washington (1812-1871) was a great-grand-nephew of George Washington. He lived in his mansion called Beallair, four miles from Harpers Ferry in Halltown. He was a retired cavalry officer, farmer and assistant to Governor Wise. He also owned a pair of pistols given to General Washington by Lafayette and a sword presented by Frederick The Great. He also was a slave owner. Five of the raiders took him prisoner at his home on the morning of the 17th, loaded him and several of his slaves in his carriage and took them to Harpers Ferry. Washington was held as a hostage in the ensuing struggle and was rescued at the end of the battle. NPS HF-161

Terrence Byrne was a Maryland farmer and slave-owner who lived between the Kennedy farm and Sharpsburg, Maryland. He was taken prisoner by four of Brown's raiders and taken to Harpers Ferry. Some of his slaves helped Owen Brown move arms and ammunition. He was released with the other prisoners at the end of hostilities. NPS HF-212

Thomas Allstadt was the son of plantation owner John H. Allstadt. The Allstadts and their slaves were taken prisoners by the raiders and released with the others at the end of hostilities. NPS HF-267

The home of Terrence Byrne. NPS

The action at the Baltimore & Ohio bridge on Oct. 17. Sketch by Alfred Berghaus for *Leslie's Weekly*, Oct. 29, 1859. WVSA

Citizens of the area attacked the raiders in the armory grounds on Oct. 17. Drawn are the musket factory, armory, fire enginehouse, commercial structures, Loudoun Heights, the armory gate, B&O railroad trestle and Maryland Heights. WVSA

THE STORMING OF THE ENGINE-HOUSE BY THE UNITED STATES MARINES.—[SKETCHED BY PORTE CRAYON.]

U.S. Marines storming the enginehouse. Sketch by Porte Crayon for *Harpers Weekly*, Nov. 5, 1859. WVSA

The final moments of the battle at the engine-house. Brown would soon fall victim to Lieutenant Greene's sword.

Marines at Harpers Ferry

First Lt. Israel Greene was the senior line officer on duty at the Washington Navy Yard the day of the attack on Harpers Ferry. Temporarily in command of the Marine Barracks there, he organized the unit to Harpers Ferry. At the enginehouse, Greene and his assistant, Maj. William W. Russell and 27 Marines gathered (a total of 90 Marines had been brought to Harpers Ferry), but out of the insurgents' line of fire. Greene ordered his men to use a ladder to batter down the front door. Armed only with his light dress sword, Greene jumped from the cover of the abutment and bounded through the opening with three other Marines. He slashed at Brown with his sword which left a deep cut across the back of Brown's neck. The blade bent double on Brown's ammo belt when Greene thrust it at his heart, so Brown was spared for the hangman.

Greene was born in New York, raised in Wisconsin, and moved to Virginia when he married. He declined appointments as a Lieutenant Colonel in the Virginia Infantry and Colonel in the Wisconsin Militia and became a Captain in the Confederate States Marine Corps at the beginning of the Civil War. He was a Major, Adjutant and Inspector of the Corps throughout the war at Confederate Marine headquarters in Richmond. He was captured and paroled at Farmville, Virginia, in April 1865. He later settled in Mitchell, South Dakota, and died there in 1909, 50 years after the Harpers Ferry raid.

Lieutenant Greene and the Marines enter the enginehouse.

Portrait of Lt. Israel Greene, USMC, when he commanded the Marines at Harpers Ferry. NPS HF-257

Photo of Israel Greene late in his life. NPS HF-528

Robert E. Lee (1807-1870). Secretary of War John B. Floyd called on his old friend Col. Robert E. Lee to take command of Federal forces that were being sent to Harpers Ferry. Lee, a former superintendent of West Point, was from a famous Virginia family, and lived in a mansion at Arlington, Va. At the beginning of the Civil War, Lee kept his allegiance to this native state and became the most beloved leader in the Confederate Army. After the war, he was appointed president of Washington College in Lexington, Virginia, where he died in 1870.

First Lt. J.E.B. "Jeb" Stuart (1833-64) was on a six-month leave from his frontier post at Fort Riley, Kansas, when he was called to accompany Col. Robert E. Lee to Harpers Ferry. At the enginehouse, Stuart went to the door to deliver a message to Brown under a flag of truce. Brown was to surrender immediately and unconditionally. This he would not do and the final battle commenced. During the Civil War, Stuart commanded the cavalry under Lee's Army of Northern Virginia and was killed at the Battle of Yellow Tavern in 1864.

"With one son dead by his side, and another dying, he felt the pulse of his dying son with one hand and held his rifle with the other."

From James Redpath's, *The Life, Trial and Execution of John Brown*.

Interior of the enginehouse just before the Marines broke down the front door. The captors, including Colonel Washington, are standing at the left. Sketch by Alfred Berghaus for *Leslie's Weekly*, Nov. 5, 1859.

Drawing of the aftermath of Brown's raid showing him lying wounded on the ground outside the enginehouse. Also lying dazed is Pvt. Luke Quinn with other Marines holding onto Brown. NPS HF-496

Governor Wise (tall hat, third from left) and D.A. Ould (second from right) examining the prisoners after the October 18 battle. Sketch by Alfred Berghaus for *Leslie's Weekly*, Oct. 29, 1859.

Recollections of the John Brown Raid by a Virginian Who Witnessed the Fight

By Alexander Boteler *
This account originally appeared in the *Century Magazine* 26, (July 1883)

On the morning of the raid, Monday, Oct. 17, 1859, I was at my home near Shepherdstown (ten miles west of Harper's Ferry), and had hardly finished breakfast when a carriage came to the door with one of my daughters, who told me that a messenger had arrived at Shepherdstown, a few minutes before, with the startling intelligence of a negro insurrection at Harper's Ferry!

She could give no particulars, except that a number of armed abolitionists from the North—supposed to be some hundreds—had stolen into "the Ferry" during the previous night, and, having taken possession of the national armories and arsenal, were issuing guns to the negroes and shooting down unarmed citizens in the streets. Ordering my horse, I started at once for Harper's Ferry, by way of Shepherdstown, where I found the people very much excited. Their first feeling, on hearing the news, had naturally been one of amazed and, with some, of amused incredulity, which, however, soon gave place to an intense and pardonable indignation.

The only military organization of the precinct—a rifle company, called "The Hamtramck Guards"—had been ordered out, and as I rode through town the command was nearly ready to take up its line of march for the Ferry, while a goodly number of volunteers, with every sort of fire-arm, from old Tower muskets which had done service in colonial days to modern bird-guns, were joining them. I observed, in passing the farms along my route, that the negroes were at work as usual.

It is necessary here to give a summary of the day's doings up to the time of my arrival at the Ferry, together with a preliminary explanation of Brown's plans and preparations. From facts which are fully admitted by his friends, it is now known that for more than five and twenty years Brown had cherished the idea of making slavery "insecure" in the States where it existed by a preconcerted series of hostile raids and servile insurrections, and that at least two years previous to his raid on Harper's Ferry he had selected it as a suitable place for the initial attack. His three principal reasons for choosing the Ferry as his *point d'appui* were: (1) The presence of a large slave population in what is known as "the Lower Valley," which is that fair and fertile portion of the great valley of Virginia embraces within the angle formed by the Potomac and Shenandoah rivers before their confluence at Harper's Ferry; (2) the proximity of the Blue Ridge range of mountains, where, in their rocky recesses and along their densely wooded slopes, he would be comparatively safe from pursuit and better able to protect himself from attack; (3) because of the location at Harper's Ferry of the United States armories and arsenal, in which were always stored many thousand stands of arms without sufficient guard to protect them.

His plan was to make the Blue Ridge Mountains his base of operations and, descending from them at night with his armed marauders, to attack the unprotected villages and isolated farm-houses within his reach, wherever and whenever his incursions would probably be least expected.

These raids were to be made on the Piedmont side of the Blue Ridge, as well as in the Valley,—"his forces acting as infantry or cavalry," according to circumstances, and to have no scruples against taking the horses of the slave-holders and other needed property.

As many of the slaves as could be induced to abandon their homes were to be armed and drilled, and, by recruiting his "army of occupation" in this way, he expected soon to raise a large body of blacks, reinforced by such white men as he could enlist, with which he believed he could maintain himself successfully in the mountains, and, by a predatory war, so harass and paralyze the people along the Blue Ridge, through Virginia and Tennessee into Alabama, that the whole South would become alarmed and slavery be made so insecure that the slave-holders themselves, for their own safety and that of their families, would be compelled to emancipate their negroes. It was, also, a part of his plan to seize the prominent slave-owners and hold them prisoners either "for the purposes of retaliation," or as hostages for the safety of himself and his band, to be ransomed only Upon the surrender of a specified number of their slaves, who were to be given their freedom in exchange for that of their masters.

He allowed few of his friends besides his immediate followers to know his plans; but there were certain pseudo-philanthropists in the North who knew all about them, and who now boast that, with a full knowledge of his intentions, they "were indifferent to the reproach of having aided him" with means for their execution. While the self-sacrificing bravery of Brown has a claim to our respect and admiration, however, much we may condemn his unlawful and treacherous attack, Southern people can feel only abhorrence and contempt for the cowardly conspirators who encouraged his design without having the manliness to share its dangers.

John Brown's first appearance south of Mason and Dixon's line was on June 30th, 1859, at Hagerstown, in Maryland. Coming from Chambersburg, in company with a man named Anderson, who was one of his "lieutenants," they remained over night there, "passing themselves off for Yankees going through the mountains in search of minerals."

On July 3, he appeared at Harper's Ferry, under the assumed name of Smith, with his two sons—Watson and Oliver—and "Lieutenant" Anderson, passing that night at a small tavern in Sandy Hook, a hamlet on the left, or Maryland, bank of the Potomac, about a mile below the Ferry. The next day, July 4, a farmer, whom I knew very well, met them on a mountain road above the Ferry, when, in reply to his remark: "Well, gentlemen, I suppose you are out hunting minerals?" Brown said, "No, we are not; we are looking for land." He said they were "farmers from the western part of New York," whose crops had been so "cut off" by the frosts, that they had concluded to settle farther south.

Subsequent conversations directed Brown's attention to a small tract further up the road, about five miles from the Ferry, belonging to the heirs of Dr. Booth Kennedy, and a few weeks later he rented a portion of it, including "the improvements," which consisted of a plain two-storied log-house with a high basement, and a small outhouse or shop, which was also of logs; for which, with the right to fire-wood and pasture for a horse and cow, he paid, in-advance, thirty-five dollars, taking the property until the first of March following. The place was admirably adapted to the purposes of concealment, being somewhat remote from other settlements, surrounded by dense forests, with its houses some distance back from the rarely traveled public road in front of them, and almost entirely hidden from view by undergrowth.

Having thus secured a suitable hiding-place, his men began to gather there, — coming from the North, one or two at a time, at intervals, and generally in the night. Meanwhile, there also arrived quietly from the same quarter — great precautions being used to conceal their destination as well as their contents — a number of boxes filled with guns, pistols, pikes, powder, and percussion caps, together with fixed ammunition, swords, bayonets, blankets, canvas for tents, tools of all kinds, maps and stationery; so that few camps were ever more fully supplied for an active campaign than was Old John Brown's mountain aerie.

Sunday night, October 16th, was fixed for the foray; and at eight o'clock that evening, Brown said to his companions: "Come, men, get on your arms; we will proceed to the Ferry." They took with them a one-horse wagon, in which were placed a parcel of pikes, torches, and some tools, including a crowbar and sledge-hammer, and in which also Brown himself rode as far as the Ferry.

Brown's actual force, all told, consisted of only twenty-two men including himself, three of whom never crossed the Potomac. Five of those who did cross were negroes, of whom three were fugitive slaves. Ten of them were killed in Virginia; seven were hanged there, and five are said to have escaped, viz., two of those who crossed the river, and the three who did not cross. Six of the white men were members of Brown's family, or connected with it by marriage, and five of these paid the forfeit of their lives to the Virginians.

When Brown's party arrived opposite the Ferry at the entrance to the Baltimore and Ohio Railroad bridge over the Potomac, — along the side of which there was, as now, a wagon road, — two of the number (Cook and Tidd) were detailed to tear down the telegraph wires, while two more (Kagi and Stevens), crossing the bridge in advance of the others, captured the nightwatchman, whose name was Williams, and who was entirely too old to make any effective resistance. Leaving Watson Brown and Stewart Taylor as a guard at the Virginia end of the bridge, and taking old Williams, the watchman, with them, the rest of the company proceeded with Brown and his one-horse wagon to the gate of the United States armory, which was not more than sixty yards distant from the bridge.

Finding it locked, they peremptorily ordered the armory watchman, Daniel Whelan, who was on the inner side of the gate, to open it, which he as peremptorily refused to do. In his testimony before the U.S. Senate committee, of which Mr. Mason of Virginia was chairman, Whelan described this scene so graphically that I here quote a part of it, as follows:

"'Open the gate!' said they. I said 'I could not if I was stuck,' and one of them jumped up on the pier of the gate over my head, and another fellow ran and put his hand on me and caught me by the coat and held me. I was inside and they were outside, and the fellow standing over my head upon the pier. And then, when I would not open the gate for them, five or six ran from the wagon, clapped their guns against my breast, and told me I should deliver up the key. I told them I could not, and another fellow said they had not time now to be waiting for a key, but to go to the wagon and bring out a crowbar and a large hammer and they would soon get in."

After telling how, with their crowbar and sledge, they broke the fastenings of the gate, Whelan went on to testify:

"They told me to be very still and make no noise, or else they would put me to eternity.***After that, the head man of them, Brown, said to me: 'I came here from Kansas, and this is a slave State. I want to free all the negroes in this State; I have possession now of the United States armory, and if the citizens interfere with me I must only burn the town and have blood.'"

Edwin Coppic and Hazlett were next sent across the street to break into the United States arsenal, which stood within another inclosure and where there was no guard whatever; while, at the same time, Oliver Brown and William Thompson occupied the bridge over the Shenandoah near the arsenal, and Kagi, with John Copeland, went up the Shenandoah to the Government rifle-works, about half a mile above, where there was another superannuated and unarmed watchman to encounter, whom they likewise captured, and then they took possession of "the works."

It was now near midnight. Brown's next step was to dispatch Stevens, Cook, and others, six in all, to the country to capture my life-long friend and college-mate Colonel Lewis N. Washington, and also to kidnap his negroes. In capturing Colonel Washington, they also seized the historic dress-sword which had been given by Frederick the Great to George Washington, with the memorable words: "From the oldest soldier to the greatest" together with one of a pair of pistols presented by Lafayette to General Washington, and some other valuable arms. They brought Colonel Washington to Harper's Ferry in his own carriage, and his negro men in his four-horse farm-wagon, — stopping on their way at the house of another farmer, Mr. Alstadt, whom they likewise took prisoner, together with his son and men-servants, all of whom were taken under guard to Brown at the armory, arriving there before daylight.

In the meantime, the eastern-bound passenger train on

the Baltimore and Ohio Railroad arrived at the Ferry after midnight, and was detained there until daylight by Brown's order, his son Watson stopping the train as it approached the station. The passengers were at a loss to comprehend the cause of the delay, some of them supposing it to be a strike of railroad hands, and others thinking it was an emeute among the armorers. While they were yet in ignorance of the real cause, an incident occurred at about half-past one o'clock which served sufficiently to show, at least, the murderous character of the insurgents.

Shepherd Haywood [sic.], one of the most respectable free negroes in the county and the regular railroad porter, employed to look after the luggage of passengers, had occasion to see the night-watchman, Williams, whose post of duty was on the bridge.

This was the first victim of the foray, and there is a suggestive significance in the fact that it was an inoffensive free negro, and that his assassination was as cowardly as it was cruel and uncalled for. This firing was the first intimation that any of the citizens of the Ferry had—except, of course, the captured watchman—that there was an enemy in their midst. Several persons living near the bridge were awakened by it, some of whom got up and looked out of their windows to ascertain the cause. But as they heard nothing more, and it was took dark to distinguish objects a few feet from them, they concluded that the noise had been occasioned by midnight revelers shooting off their pistols in sport, and they returned to their beds.

One of these awakened citizens, however, Dr. Starry, was not so easily contented to lie down again without looking a little further into the matter, as he had heard a cry of distress following the shots, and his professional instincts prompted him to go to the relief of the sufferer. The wounded negro had managed to make his way back to the office of Mr. Beckham, the railroad agent, where the Doctor found him lying upon the floor, writhing in agony. After doing what he could to make him more comfortable, and having learned from him the circumstances under which he had been shot, the Doctor started out to investigate more fully the situation.

When he had watched the movements of the raiders for some time and from different points of observation, he was enabled to form an idea of what they had done and were then doing, though not of their ulterior designs; for he thought that their only object was robbery. With this idea in his mind he determined to arouse Mr. Kitzmiller, the chief clerk, who, in the absence of Colonel Alfred H. Barbour, the superintendent, had official charge of the armories. So, getting out his horse, he made his way to Kitzmiller's house, which was in quite a different part of the town; and having informed him of the condition of things at the armory, he rode on to Bolivar and elsewhere, arousing the people as he went. By this time it was broad daylight, and some of the citizens were appearing in the streets. Such of them, in the lower part of the town near the Government works, as had occasion to pass down Shenandoah and High streets, were surprised to see them picketed near their intersection, and, as may be supposed, their surprise was not diminished on being rudely told they were

prisoners and being unceremoniously marched to a building in the armory yard which Brown had appropriated as headquarters for himself and as a "calaboose" for his captives, of whom some thirty or forty altogether were thus taken and held by him.

One of the citizens by the name of Boerley,—a well-to-do grocer, and an Irishman by birth,—when walking quietly along not far from his residence, happened to get within range of a picket,—a black fellow who called himself Dangerfield Newby,—whereupon the negro raised his rifle and without a word of warning shot him dead, with as little compunction as if he had been a mad dog.

It was now about seven o'clock, by which time most of the people of the town had been warned of the raid and its real object. Accordingly, messengers were sent for assistance to the neighboring towns, while prompt and effective steps were taken by the citizens of the Ferry to resist the insurgents, whose force was supposed to be far greater than it really was, from the fact of Brown's making an ostentatious display of sentinels outside of the armory buildings while keeping up from their interiors a desultory fire upon the citizens, when any of them appeared in sight.

There was unavoidable delay in the preparations for a fight, because of the scarcity of weapons; for only a few squirrel guns and fowling-pieces could be found. There were then at Harper's Ferry thousands and tens of thousands of muskets and rifles of the most approved patterns, but they were all boxed up in the arsenal, and the arsenal was in the hands of the enemy. And such, too, was the scarcity of ammunition that, after using up the limited supply of lead found in the village stores, pewter plates and spoons had to be melted and molded into bullets for the occasion.

By nine o'clock a number of indifferently armed citizens assembled on Camp Hill and decided that the party, consisting of half a dozen men, should cross the Potomac a short distance above the Ferry, and, going down the tow-path of the Chesapeake and Ohio canal as far as the railway bridge, should attack the two sentinels stationed there, who, by the way, had been reinforced by four more of Brown's party. Another small party under Captain Medler was to cross the Shenandoah and take position opposite the rifle works, while Captain Avis, with a sufficient force, should take possession of the Shenandoah Bridge, and Captain Roderick, with some of the armorers, should post themselves on the Baltimore and Ohio Railway west of the Ferry just above the armories.

These movements and dispositions were made with commendable promptness under the general direction of Colonels Robert W. Baylor and John T. Gibson—the former being the ranking officer by right of seniority. Thus was cut off Brown's retreat to the mountains in Maryland across the Potomac, or to those in Virginia across the Shenandoah. Shortly after the first of the above-mentioned parties had crossed the Potomac and driven the enemy's sentinels from the Maryland end of the bridge to its Virginia entrance, the "Jefferson Guards," under Captain Moore, and the "Botts Greys," under Captain Lawson Botts, arrived at the Ferry from Charlestown; and the former company being immediately sent over the river at the "Old

Furnace," to reinforce those who had crossed before them into Maryland, as soon as they had reached the railway bridge charged across it, killing one of the insurgent sentinels and capturing another (William Thompson), whom they confined in the railway hotel facing the bridge.

Cook and Tidd, of Brown's party, were at this time in Maryland, having been sent early in the morning to the Kennedy farm with Colonel Washington's farm-wagon and some of his servants to bring down the boxes of Sharp rifles, Ames pistols, pikes, etc., to a school-house about a mile above the Ferry, which was intended to be a convenient depot of supplies for the raiders in the event of their falling back into Maryland. So, of course, as the bridge was no longer in possession of the insurgents, they were unable to rejoin their companions now cooped up in the armories and rifle works. Just after the Botts Greys reached the Ferry, a man reported to its captain that he had come from the "Gault House" (a small tavern situated near the arsenal at the junction of the two rivers commanding the mouth of the bridge and a view of the armory yard), where there was but one man, its proprietor (George Chambers), who was maintaining an unequal skirmish with the raiders, had but one load left for his gun, and wanted reinforcements.

Captain Botts called for twenty volunteers to go with him, and more than twice the number stepped out from the ranks. They had great difficulty in getting to the tavern, being obliged, in order to avoid a raking fire from the raiders, to make a detour around the base of the hill under "Jefferson's Rock," and along the bank of the Shenandoah, and then to climb up a wall thirty feet high so as to enter the house by a cellar window, reaching their destination just as Chambers fired his last shot, which wounded the insurgent Stevens.

About the same time, Mr. George Turner, who had the respect and esteem of the entire community, was killed. He was a graduate of West Point. When he heard that his friend, Colonel Lewis Washington, had been forcibly abducted by a band of ruffians, and was a prisoner in their hands, he started at once for the Ferry. As he rode into the upper part of the town, some one handed him a shotgun for his protection. Dismounting from his horse, he walked down High Street, which runs parallel with and only a few paces from the long range of buildings in the armory grounds. When he had approached within some fifty yards of the corner of High and Shenandoah streets, the same negro—Dangerfield Newby—who had killed Boerley, saw him coming, and, taking deliberate aim, shot him dead. But the assassin himself was soon made to bite the dust. For one of the armorers, by the name of Bogert, a few minutes afterward got the opportunity of a shot at him from an upper window of Mrs. Stephenson's house at the corner of High and Shenandoah streets, and killed him on the spot. I saw his body while it was yet warm as it lay on the pavement in front of the arsenal yard, and I never saw, on any battle-field, a more hideous musket-wound than his. For his throat was cut literally from ear to ear, which was afterward accounted for by the fact that the armorer, having no bullets, had charged his musket with a six-inch iron spike.

As already mentioned, it was a little before noon when I reached Harper's Ferry on the day of the raid. By that time Brown and those of his party who were with him in the armory buildings were completely hemmed in. The bridges over both rivers, north and east, together with the western or upper end of the armory grounds, were in possession of the citizens. Who occupied every "coign of vantage" from which they could get a fair shot at the insurgents, who, on their part, fighting from under cover of the buildings, were equally on the alert to retaliate in kind, so that there was a lively little skirmish going on when I got there, which I watched for some time from an open space on High street overlooking the lower part of the armory yard. Seeing that there was no probability of the escape of the insurgents, surrounded as they were on all sides,—with the volunteer citizens on both flanks, the Potomac in their front, and in their rear the town, which was becoming rapidly filled with people from every portion of the county, and ascertaining, also, that no attempt would be made to take the armories by assault before the arrival of the volunteers from Martinsburg and Shepherdstown,—I returned to the upper part of the town, where I had left my horse, and rode around toward the rifle-works, getting there in time to see the assault made on them which drove Kagi and his party pell-mell out of the rear of the building into the Shenandoah River, where a very exciting scene occurred; for, as soon as the insurgents were recognized attempting to cross the river, there was a shout among the citizens, who opened a hot fire upon them from both banks.

The river at that point runs rippling over a rocky bed, and at ordinary stages of the water is easily forded. The raiders, finding their retreat to the opposite shore intercepted by Medler's men, made for a large flat rock near the middle of the stream. Before reaching it, however, Kagi fell and died in the water, apparently without a struggle. Four others reached the rock, where, for a while, they made an ineffectual stand, returning the fire of the citizens. But it was not long before two of them were killed outright and another prostrated by a mortal wound, leaving Copeland, a mulatto, standing alone and unharmed upon their rock of refuge.

Thereupon, a Harper's Ferry man, James H. Holt, dashed into the river, gun in hand, to capture Copeland, who, as he approached him, made a show of fight by pointing his gun at Holt, who halted and leveled his; but, to the surprise of the lookers-on, neither of their weapons were discharged, both having been rendered temporarily useless, as I afterward learned, from being wet. Holt, however, as he again advanced, continued to snap his gun, while Copeland did the same.

Reaching the rock, Holt clubbed his gun and we expected to see a hand to hand fight between them; but the mulatto, showing the white feather, flung down his weapon and surrendered. Copeland, when he was brought ashore, was badly frightened, and well he might be in the midst of the excited crowd who surrounded him, some of whom began to knot their handkerchiefs together, with ominous threats of "Lynch law." But better counsels prevailed, and he was taken before a magistrate, who committed him to jail to await his trial.

When I returned to my former place of observation on High street, the expected reinforcements from Martinsburg and Shepherdstown had arrived, as also a small body of cavalry under Lieutenant Hess, the latter of whom (dismounted) were, with the Shepherdstown company, posted on Shenandoah street near the armory gate at the lower or eastern end of the grounds, while the men from Martinsburg and those under Roderick prepared to charge the raiders from the upper or western end.

The charge, which I witnessed, was spirited and made in the face of the concentrated fire of Brown's party, who were forced to retreat into the engine-house near the armory gate, where nine or ten of the most prominent of the prisoners had been previously placed by Brown as hostages for his own safely and that of his companions. Watson Brown was wounded when this charge was made, also several of the citizens, among whom was a gallant young man by the name of George Wollet, whom I particularly noticed among the foremost of the Martinsburg men until he was disabled by a shot in his wrist. A young lawyer, also from Martinsburg, George Murphy, was wounded in the leg, and an old gentleman of the county, Mr. Watson, who was seventy-five years of age, had the stock of his gun shattered as he raised it to his shoulder to shoot. Thomas P. Young, of Charlestown, who was permanently disabled during this day, got his wound, too, I think, in this charge; but of this I am not so certain.

Brown, having now barricaded himself and prisoners in the engine-house, — a small but substantial building of brick, still standing, — said to "Phil," one of Alstadt's kidnapped servants, "You're a pretty stout-looking fellow; can't you knock a hole through there for me?" at the same time handing him some mason's tools with which he compelled him to make several loopholes in the walls through which to shoot. He also fastened, with ropes, the large double door of the house so as to permit its folding leaves (which opened in-ward) to be partly separated so that he might fire through that opening.

These arrangements having been hurriedly made, Brown and his men opened an indiscriminate fire upon the citizens. While they were thus shooting at every one they saw without regard to his being armed or not, Mr. Fountain Beckham, station agent, who was then mayor of the town, happened to walk out upon the depot platform near his office; when, incautiously exposing himself, he was instantly shot down, though it was evident he was unarmed, as he had his hands in his pockets at the time. This was the fourth victim of the foray.

When Mr. Beckham's friends upon the platform saw him fall dead in their presence, — shot throught the heart without a word of warning, — killed without having taken any part in the fight, notwithstanding the special provocation he had received that morning in having his favorite servant murdered by the men who had now caused his own death, — their rage became uncontrollable, and they impulsively rushed into the railroad hotel to take summary vengeance on the prisoner, Thompson, who was confined there. But the lady of the house, Miss Christine C. Fouke, a most estimable woman, placing herself in front of the prisoner, declared that as long as he was under the shelter of her roof she would protect him, with her life, from harm, — which for a time saves the prisoner from death. But the respite was a brief one, for the maddened crowd soon brought him forth upon the platform where he was immediately shot, and his body thrown over the parapet of the bridge into the river below.

One of the raiders, Leeman, was discovered trying to escape across the river; and having been fired on and wounded, an excited volunteer from Martinsburg waded out to where he was in the water and killed him, it was said, after he had surrendered.

Shortly after, the charge was made which brought Brown to bay in the engine-house; and while I was yet standing at the point on High street whence I had witnessed the fight, where there was an unobstructed view across the river, I heard the hum of a ball as it went singing by me, and presently it was followed by another which passed in unpleasant proximity to my head. There were several persons with me at the time who were armed and who, discovering by the smoke that the shots, so evidently meant for ourselves, had come from a clump of small trees on the mountain side across the river, fired a volley in that direction which silenced the unseen marksman. I refer to this triffling incident only because it was mentioned by Cook in his "Confession," as follows:

"I saw," said he, "that our party were completely surrounded, and as I saw a body of men on High street firing down upon them, though they were about half a mile distant from me, I thought I would draw their fire — upon myself; I therefore raised my rifle and — took the best aim I could and fired. It had the desired effect, for the very instant the party returned it. Several shots were exchanged. The last one they fired at me cut a small limb I had hold of just below my hand, and gave me a fall of about fifteen feet, by which I was severely bruised, and my flesh somewhat lacerated."

It was now near nightfall, and the gathering gloom of a drizzly evening began to obscure surrounding objects, making it so difficult to distinguish them that, as if by common consent on both sides, active operations were suspended.

At this time a conference was held by three or four of the principal officers in command, to which two or three civilians, including myself, were invited, — the object of the consultation being to determine whether or not to take the engine-house by assault at once, or to wait until morning.

It was represented to us by the prisoners whom Brown had released, when he selected out of their number nine or ten to be held as hostages in the engine-house, that, if an attempt should be made to carry it by storm at night, it would be impossible to distinguish the hostages from the insurgents; and that Brown would probably place the former in front of his own party as a protection, and thereby cause them to receive the brunt of the attack.

It was also urged that the raiders were then as securely imprisoned in their place of refuge as if incarcerated in the county jail and could be taken in the morning without much risk to our friends. Before deciding the question under consideration, it was thought proper, at any rate, to send Brown a summons to surrender, and a respectable farmer of the neighborhood, Mr. Samuel S----- was selected to make the demand, — a duty which he undertook very willingly, although it was not unattended with danger, as the usages of ordinary warfare had been more than once disregarded, during the day, by the belligerents on both sides. Mr. S. was man of indomitable energy, undoubted courage, and of such a genial disposition as to make him a general favorite; but he was somewhat eccentric and so fond of using *sesquipedalia verba* that, occasionally, he was betrayed thereby into those peculiarities of speech which characterized the conversation of Mrs. Malaprop.

Tying a white handkerchief to the ferrule of a faded umbrella, he went forth upon his mission with a self-imposed gravity becoming his own appreciation of its importance.

Marching up to the door of the enginehouse, he called out in stentorian tones. "Who commands this fortification?"

"Captain Brown, of Kansas," was the answer, from within the building. "Well, Captain Brown, of Kansas," continued Mr. S., with his voice pitched in the same high key, "I am sent here, sir, by the authorities in command, for to summon you to surrender; and, sir, I do it in the name of the Commonwealth of old Virginia—God bless her!

"What terms do you offer?" inquired Brown. "Terms!" exclaimed S. "I heard nothing said about them, sir, by those who sent me. What terms do you want?"

"I want to be allowed," said Brown, "to take my men and prisoners across the bridge to Maryland and as far up the river as the lock-house (which was about a mile above) where I will release the prisoners unharmed, provided no pursuit shall be made until I get beyond that point." To which S. replied by saying: "Captain, you"ll have to put that down in writing."

"It's too dark to write," answered Brown. "Pshaw!" said S.; "that's nonsense,—for you needn't tell me that an old soldier like you hasn't got all the modern conveniences. So, if you don't write your terms down, in black and white, I won't take 'em back to those who sent me."

Thereupon, a light was struck in the engine-house, and presently a piece of paper was handed out to S., on which Brown had written what he wished to have accorded him. The proposed terms were, of course, inadmissible; and after the paper containing them had been read by two or three of us it was handed to Lawson Botts, who threw it contemptuously upon the floor, and placing his foot on it, said: "Gentlemen, this is adding insult to injury. I think we ought to storm the engine-house, and take those fellows without further delay." But the representations of the released prisoners, already mentioned, caused the contemplated assault to be postponed for the night.

The next morning the first thing I learned was that Colonel Robert E. Lee and Lieutenant J.E.B. Stuart had arrived about midnight with a small body of marines from Washington, and that Colonel Lee had assumed command of all the forces assembled in the place. Having the pleasure of his acquaintance, I lost no time in calling upon him, when he informed me that he intended at once to take Brown and his party. Accordingly, at about seven o'clock, a detachment of marines—three of whom had heavy sledge-hammers—were marched up to the west end of the "watch-house" which hid them from the insurgents, and which was under the same roof as the engine-house, being separated from it only by a brick partition. Colonel Lee himself (who was not in uniform) took a position outside of the armory gate, within thirty paces of the engine-house, but protected from those within it by one of the heavy brick pillars of the railing that surrounded the inclosure.

All now being in readiness, Colonel Lee beckoned to Stuart, who, accompanied by a citizen displaying a flag of truce, approached the engine-house. A parley then ensued between Stuart and Brown, which was watched with breathless interest by the crowd.

Although from the position I occupied (which was, probably, some sixty paces from the engine-house) I could not hear the conversation between them, I often afterward heard it detailed by Stuart, when sharing his tent or sitting with him by his camp fire, and therefore am enabled to confirm the correctness of the report of it, made by my friend and former comrade, Major John Esten Cooke, in a graphic account given by him. Stuart began by saying:

"You are Ossawattomie Brown, of Kansas?"

"Well, they do call me that sometimes, Lieutenant," said Brown. "I thought I remembered meeting you in Kansas, " continued Stuart. "This is a bad business you are engaged in, Captain. The United States troops have arrived, and I am sent to demand your surrender."

"Upon what terms?" asked Brown.

"The terms," replied Stuart, "are that you shall surrender to the officer commanding the troops, who will protect you and your men from the crowd, and guarantee you a fair trial by the civil authorities."

"I can't surrender on such terms," said Brown, "you must allow me to leave this place with my party and prisoners for the lock-house on the Maryland side. There I will release the prisoners, and as soon as this is done, you and your troops may fire on us and pursue us."

"I have no authority to agree to such an arrangemen," said Stuart, "my orders being to demand your surrender on the terms I have stated."

"Well, Lieutenant," replied Brown, "I see we can't agree. You have the numbers on me, but you know we soldiers are not afraid of death. I would as leave die by a bullet as on the gallows."

"Is that your final answer, Captain?" inquired Stuart. "Yes," said Brown.

This closed the interview. Thereupon Stuart bowed, and as he turned to leave made a sign, previously agreed upon, to Colonel Lee, who immediately raised his hand, which was the signal of assault. Instantly the storming party under Lieutenant Green, consisting of a dozen marines, sprang forward from behind the angle of the wall that had concealed them, and for perhaps two minutes or more the blows of the sledge-hammers on the door of the engine-house sounded with startling distinctness, and were reechoed from the rocky sides of the lofty mountains that rose in all their rugged majesty around us.

As yet, to our surprise, there was no shot fired by the insurgents, nor any sound heard from within the engine-house. Unable to batter down its doors, the men with the sledges threw them aside, at a sign from Stuart, and withdrew behind the adjoining building. Then there was a brief pause of oppressive silence, as some twenty-five or thirty more marines were seen coming down the yard with a long ladder that had been leaning against one of the shops. Nearing the engine-house they started into a run, and dashed their improvised battering ram against the door with a crashing sound, but not with sufficient force to effect an entrance.

Falling back a short distance they made another run, delivering another blow, and as they did so a volley was fired by the conspirators, and two of the marines let go the ladder—both wounded and one of them mortally. Two others quickly took their places, and the third blow, splintering the right-hand leaf of the door, caused it to lean inward sufficiently to admit a man. Just then Lieutenant Green, who had been standing close to the wall, sword in hand, leaped upon the inclining door-leaf, which, yielding to his weight, fell inside and he himself disappeared from our view in the interior of the building. There was a shot, some inarticulate exclamations, and a short struggle inside the engine-house, and then, as our rescued friends emerged from the smoke that filled it, followed by marines bringing out the prisoners, the pent-up feelings of the spectators found appropriate expression in a general shout.

As Colonel Lewis Washington came out I hastened to him with my congratulations, and to my inquiry: "Lewis, old fellow, how do you feel?"

He replied, with characteristic emphasis: "Feel! Why, I feel as hungry as a hound and as dry as a powder-horn; for, only think of it, I've not had anything to eat for forty odd hours, and nothing better to drink than water out of a horse-bucket!"

He told me that when Lieutenant Green leaped into the engine-house, he greeted him with the exclamation: "God bless you, Green! There's Brown!" at the same time pointing out to him the brave but unscrupulous old fanatic, who, having discharged his rifle, had seized a spear, and was yet in the half-kneeling position he had assumed when he fired his last shot. He said, also, that the cut which Green made at Brown would undoubtedly have cleft his skull, if the point of the sword had not caught on a rope, which or course weakened the force of the blow; but it was sufficient to cause him to fall to the floor and relax his hold upon the spear, which, by the way, I took possession of as a relic of the raid.

Within the engine-house one of Brown's party was found lying dead on the floor, and another (Watson Brown) was stretched out on a bench at the right-hand side of the door, and seemed to be in a dying condition. John Brown himself had been brought out and was then lying on the grass; but so great was the curiosity to see him that the soldiers found some difficulty in keeping back the crowd, and Colonel Lee consequently had him removed to a room in an adjoining building, strictly guarded by sentinels, where, shortly afterward, I had an interview with him, the particulars of which have remained distinctly impressed upon my memory.

On entering the room where he was I found him alone, lying on the floor on his left side, and with his back turned toward me. The right side of his face was smeared with blood from the sword-cut on his head, causing his grim and grizzly countenance to look like that of some aboriginal savage with his war-paint on. Approaching him, I began the conversation with the inquiry:

"Captain Brown, are you hurt anywhere except on your head?"

"Yes, in my side, here," said he, indicating the place with his hand. I then told him that a surgeon would be in presently to attend to his wounds, and expressed the hope that they were not very serious. Thereupon he asked me who I was, and on giving him my name as if speaking to himself: "Yes, yes, I know now, member of Congress, this district."

I then asked the question: "Captain, what brought you here?"

"To free your slaves," was the reply.

"How did you expect to accomplish it with the small force you brought with you?"

"I expected help," said he.

"Where, whence, and from whom, Captain, did you expect it?"

"Here and from elsewhere," he answered.

"Did you expect to get assistance from whites here as well as from the blacks?" was my next question.

"I did," he replied.

"Then," said I, "you have been disappointed in not getting it from either?"

"Yes," he muttered, "I have been disappointed."

I then asked him who planned his movement on Harper's Ferry, to which he replied, "I planned it all myself," and upon my remarking that it was a sad affair to him and the country, and that I trusted no one would follow his example by undertaking a similar raid, he made no response. I next inquired if he had any family besides the sons who had accompanied him on his incursion, to which he replied by telling me he had a wife and children in the State of New York at North Elba, and on my then asking if he would like to write to them and let them know how he was, he quickly responded: "Yes, I would like to send them a letter."

"Very well," said I, "you will doubtless be permitted to do so. But, Captain," I added, "probably you understand that, being in the hands of the civil authorities of the State, your letters will have to be seen by them before they can be sent."

"Certainly," said he. "Then, with that understanding," continued I, "there will, I'm sure, be no objections to your writing home; and although I myself have no authority on the premises, I promise to do what I can to have your wishes in that respect complied with."

"Thank you—thank you, sir," said he, repeating his acknowledgment for the proffered favor and, for the first time, turning his face toward me.

In my desire to hear him distinctly I had placed myself by his side, with one knee resting on the floor, so that when he turned, it brought his face quite close to mine, and I remember well the earnest gaze of the gray eye that looked straight into mine. I then remarked:

"Captain, we too have wives and children This attempt of yours to interfere with our slaves has created great excitement, and naturally causes anxiety on account of our families. Now, let me ask you: Is this failure of yours likely to be followed by similar attempts to create disaffection among our servants and bring upon our homes the horrors of a servile war?"

"Time will show," was his significant reply. Just then a Catholic priest appeared at the door of the room. He had been administering the last consolations of religion to Quinn the marine, who was dying in the adjoining office; and the moment Brown saw him he became violently angry, and plainly showed, by the expression of his countenance, how capable he was of feeling "hatred, malice, and all uncharitableness."

"Go out of here—I don't want you about me—go out!" was the salutation he gave the priest, who, bowing gravely, immediately retired. Whereupon I arose from the floor, and bidding Brown good-morning, likewise left him.

In the entry leading to the room where Brown was, I met Major Russell, of the marine corps, who was going in to see him, and I detailed to him the conversation I had just had. Meeting the major subsequently he told me that when he entered the apartment Brown was standing up—with his clothes unfastened—examining the wound in his side, and that as soon as he saw him he forthwith resumed his former position on the floor; which incident tended to confirm the impression I had already formed, that there was a good deal of vitality left in the old man, notwithstanding his wounds—a fact more fully developed that evening after I had left Harper's Ferry for home, when he had his spirited and historic talk with Wise, Hunter and Vallandigham.

*Boteler was born near Shepherdstown in 1815. He graduated from Princeton College in 1835 and devoted his time to literary and agricultural pursuits. He won a seat in Congress in 1859 and resigned in 1861 to join the Confederate Congress. He helped design the Confederate flag and designed the Confederate seal. During the war he served on the staffs of Stonewall Jackson and Jeb Stuart. After the war he held several government positions before retiring to Shepherdstown where he died in 1892.

Alexander Boteler sketched John Brown just after his capture at Harpers Ferry in October, 1859. This pencil sketch, showing the bearded Brown with a bandaged head, his eyes level and unapologetic, was one of two Boteler made of Brown. This excerpt from an interview of Boteler by George Alfred Townsend (pen name, Gath), the great Civil War correspondent, tells the story of the two Boteler sketches of Brown. The words are Boteler's as quoted by Townsend:

"I not only saw him (Brown) hauled out of the engine-house, but while he was yet freshly wounded Colonel Robert Lee allowed me to pass in and talk to him as he lay on the bare floor in one of the army buildings. There is a singular circumstance about that. Some time before Brown's descent on Harpers Ferry I took to my wife one day a sketch that I made with a pencil in the cars coming from Point of Rocks to Harpers Ferry. Said I: 'My dear, here is a genuine picture of the Wandering Jew.' 'Who is it' said she. 'I don't know. It was a strange old man with fingers like the talons of a bird that I saw talking to two young men. He had the most remarkable head I have looked at for years. His hair went up like spikes, his jaw and mouth were very strong, and he had an eye that would look you through and through. His nose was like an eagle's, and there was something very fascinating about him, yet superstitious; and I made that sketch of him and called it the Wandering Jew. He was talking about sheep-raising and talked very intelligently, too, and I was interested in what he said, because I thought he might be going to buy land in our parts.' Well, my wife put that picture away and forgot about it. Suddenly the descent on Harpers Ferry was made. It did not then occur to me that Brown was the same man I had seen. But when he was tried at Charlestown and stood up to make the speech before sentence was passed upon him, I took the opportunity to draw another sketch of him. By that time he had somewhat recovered from his wounds. I took the sketch home, and said 'There, Mrs. Boteler, you see old John Brown.' 'Why,' said she, 'I have seen this man before.' 'Oh, I guess not,' said I. 'Yes, I have.' She thought about it awhile, and then turned to the drawer where she had put my sketch of the Wandering Jew and drew it out. 'Yes,' said she, 'here is the very man.' I had made the sketch of John Brown unwittingly."

The first Boteler sketch of Brown, the one which he made without knowing that he was sketching Brown, was the one that was sold to the Military Historical Society of Massachusetts in the late 1800's, along with six oil sketches of important Confederate figures, and which has since disappeared. The six oil sketches remain.

Beneath this sketch of Brown are written the words, "Old John Brown after his capture."

This drawing by Porte Crayon shows the death of William Leeman who had swum to a rock in the Potomac River and Jeremiah Anderson who was thrown off the B&O trestle. NPS HF-337

Of the 21 raiders, seven escaped from the Harpers Ferry area: John Cook, Albert Hazlett, Francis Jackson Merriam, Charles Plummer Tidd, Osborn Anderson, Barclay Coppoc and Owen Brown. Cook was captured at Mont Alto, Pa., a few days after the raid and Hazlett soon afterwards in Carlisle, Penna. They were taken back to Charlestown and hanged. The other five stayed together eight days in the Pennsylvania woods before Merriam left for Philadelphia. The rest stayed together three or four weeks until Coppoc went on to Ohio. Brown and Tidd made their way to Crawford County, Penn., John Brown's old homestead. Anderson, Coppoc and eventually Merriam, all traveled separately and eventually wound up in the St. Catharines area of Ontario, Canada. John Brown Jr., who did not participate directly at Harpers Ferry, was holed up in Ashtabula, Ohio. The last five were never brought to justice for their part in the Harpers Ferry affair.

Supplies in John Brown's cabin Maryland.

102 Sharpe's Rifles.	1 Pair Linen Pants.
12 Mass. Arms Company's Pistols.	Canvas for Tent.
56 " " " Powder	1 Old Porte-monnaie.
4 Large Powder Flasks. [Flasks.	625 Envelopes.
10 Kegs Gunpowder.	1 Pocket Map of Kentucky.
23,000 Percussion Rifle Caps.	1 Pocket Map of Delaware.
100,000 Percussion Pistol Caps	3 Gross Steel Pens.
13,000 Sharpe's Rifle Cartridges, slightly	5 Inkstands.
damaged by water.	21 Lead Pencils.
160 Sharpe's Primers.	34 Pen Holders.
14 lbs. Lead Balls.	2 Boxes Wafers.
1 Old Percussion Pistol.	47 Small Blank Books.
1 Major General's Sword.	2 Papers Pins.
55 Old Bayonets.	5 Pocket Small Tooth Combs.*
12 Old Artillery Swords.	1 Ball Hemp Twine.
483 Pikes.	1 Ball Cotton Twine.
150 Broken Handles for Pikes.	50 Leather Water Caps.
16 Picks.	1 Emery.
40 Shovels.	2 Yards Cotton Flannel.
[The railroad way bill called for several	1 Roll Sticking Plaster for Wounds
dozen, showing that more were to come.]	12 Reams Cartridge Paper.
1 Tin Powder Case.	2 Bottles Medicine.
1 Sack Coat.	1 Large Trunk.
1 Pair Cloth Pants.	1 Horse Wagon.

* The discovery of these "deadly" implements of domestic warfare, it has been argued, proved incontestably the intention of the Liberators to make war upon the "peculiar institutions" of Virginia.

EMPEROR AND COPPICK, AS THEY APPEARED IN THE ENGINE-HOUSE, AFTER SURRENDERING TO THE U. S.

Roadside historical sign at Mount Alto, Pa.

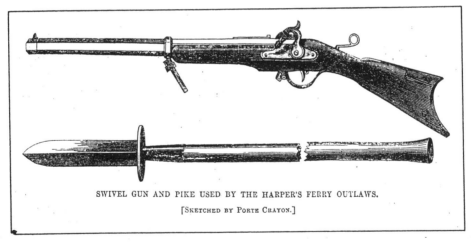

SWIVEL GUN AND PIKE USED BY THE HARPER'S FERRY OUTLAWS.

[SKETCHED BY PORTE CRAYON.]

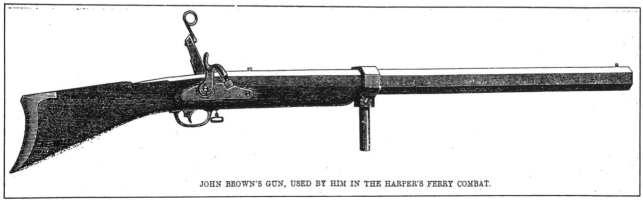

JOHN BROWN'S GUN, USED BY HIM IN THE HARPER'S FERRY COMBAT.

From the Baltimore Sun.

Important Documents

CONCERNING THE REBELLION AT HARPER'S FERRY.

The Washington *Constitution* publishes a number of additional letters found at the house of "Old Brown," the leader of the rebellion at Harper's Ferry." All those signed "John Smith" are said to be in the handwriting of one of the sons of Ossawattomie (old) Brown, and are endorsed in the handwriting of the latter. These documents clearly establish a most extensive conspiracy, extending throughout portions of Ohio, New York, and New England, and some towns in Pennsylvania. The batch opens with a letter signed "J. Smith," dated West Andover, Ohio July 30, 1859, enclosing a draft for $100 from "a mutual friend Isaac." It is addressed to J. Henrie, Chambersburg, Pa., and also states that fifteen boxes of freight had previously been sent off by the writer to Henrie, and that six boxes and one chest, containing "household stuff," would be despatched in a couple days. The contents of the six boxes are believed to have been as follows:

[A] Comfortables, blankets, rose blankets and boots. (Box A not delivered.)
[B] Tents, blankets and woolen sheets.
[C] 2 or 3 blankets, pants, coats, vests, caps, drawers, undershirts and boots.
[D] Comfortables, blankets, rose blankets and Luke's S. G., hand mills and axes.
[E] Tents, wagon-covers, tackle-blocks, ropes.
[F] Blankets, comfortables, frying pan.
[G] (or red chest)—Cloth, some clothing, carpet bag of "J. H. K.," 3 S. R.'s; a lot of school books, knives and forks; articles belonging to J. E. C.; a can, and sundry other little things.

The second letter, dated Harper's Ferry, July 17, 1859, is signed Isaac Smith, who says he has hired from James Magraw a mule for thirty days, when he is to return her or pay him $160.

Letter No. 3, dated "Pa., Aug., 1859," acknowledges the receipts of shipments of freight, and begs for a little more money for J. Smith & Sons, say $200 or $300, as "the harvest opens before me with increasing encouragement." The writer (evidently Old Brown, for there is no signature) adds:

"I am highly gratified with all our arrangements up to the present time, and feel certain that no time has yet been lost. Our freight is principally here, but will have to go a little further. Our hands, so far, are coming forward promptly, and better than I expected, as we have called on them. We have to move with all caution."

Letter No. 4 is from J. Henric, dated Chambersburg, September 8, 1859, in which he says he has received a letter from J. Smith, of West Andover, and adds:

"He has engaged two mechanics at Cleveland, who, he says, will go to work in a few days. He will at once endeavor to get subscriptions of stock in the manner talked between you. He is, however, now out of means, and wishes you to send him $25 or $30. To enable you to do this, if you wish, without making a trip to H. or here, I send you enclosed a check for $50, which I received from F., of Concord."

Letter No. 5, also from Henric, dated September 14, informs I. Smith & Sons that a quantity of freight for them arrived that day, in care of Oaks & Caufum, consisting of 32 bundles and 4 boxes. On the 16th, Henric, in a line or two, writes that Mr. Anderson had just arrived in the cars.

Letter No. 6 is dated at West Andover, Ashtabula county, Ohio, September 21, 1859, and addressed to "Dear Father." The writer says:

"I am now at work to raise the $50 or more for the purpose you mentioned, and have no doubt I shall succeed. Am busy forming associations of the kind I have previously written you. Already stock in them is beginning to be taken quite freely, and I am of the opinion that for the present, at least, I can aid the cause more in this way than in any other I can imagine. However, I hope you will be able to remit me some little means, as I am entirely out, and unless I have something to subsist upon I could not devote my whole time to this work, as it is my wish to do."

Enclosed in No. 6 are several other letters received by the writer, one of which, from J. M. Bell, dated September 14, says:

"One hand (Anderson) left here last night, and he will be found an efficient hand. Richardson is anxious to be at work as a missionary to bring sinners to repentance. He will start in a few days. Another will follow immediately after, if not with him. More laborers may be looked for shortly. 'Slow, but sure.'"

"Alexander received yours; so you see all communications have come to hand so far. Alex. is not coming up to the work as he should; I fear he will be found unreliable in the end. Dull times affect missionary matters more than anything else; however, a few active laborers may be looked for as certain. I would like to hear of your congregation numbering more than '15 and 2' to commence a good revival; still our few will be adding strength to the good work."

Another from Akron, Ohio, Sept. 13, signed "your affectionate son John," says:

"Perhaps I shall not visit you immediately, but at any rate you can depend upon my working in our cause to the utmost of my ability all the time, and wherever there is good reason to believe I can render the most efficient service. As I believe an All-wise Providence is directing this matter, no other prayer is demanded of me than the prayer of work."

Letter No. 7, is signed John Smith, and dated West Andover, Ohio, September 21st, addressed to "Friend Henric," in which he says:

"Glad to learn that the 'wire' has arrived in good condition, and that our 'R.' friend was pleased with a view of those 'pre-eventful shadows.' Shall write Leary at once; also all our other friends at the North and East. Am highly pleased with the prospect I have of doing something to the purpose now right away here and in contiguous sections, in the way of getting stock taken. I am devoting my whole time to our work."

Letter No. 8 is also from John Smith, addressed to "Friend Henric," under date of Sept. 27, 1859. He says:

"Since I became aware that you intended opening the mines before spring, I have spared no pains, and have strained every nerve to get hands forward in season. I do not, therefore, feel to blame for any error in respect to time. I had before never heard anything else than that the spring was the favorable time, unless uncontrollable circumstances should otherwise compel! At this distance I am not prepared to judge, but take it for granted that wisdom, or perhaps necessity dictates the change of programme. Immediately on receipt of your urgent communications I have dispatched copies where they would be most likely to avail anything, and have devoted, and am still devoting my whole time to forming associations for the purpose of aiding. There will be a meeting of stockholders at my house this eve; a distinguished gentleman from New Hampshire, who is anxious to invest, will also be present.

"Whether it is best for me to come to you now or not I cannot say; but suppose it will be impossible for me to remain here when you are actually realizing your brightest prospects. When in C., and in all other places, I have at all times urged all hands to go on at once, since necessity might render their presence an imperative want at any time."

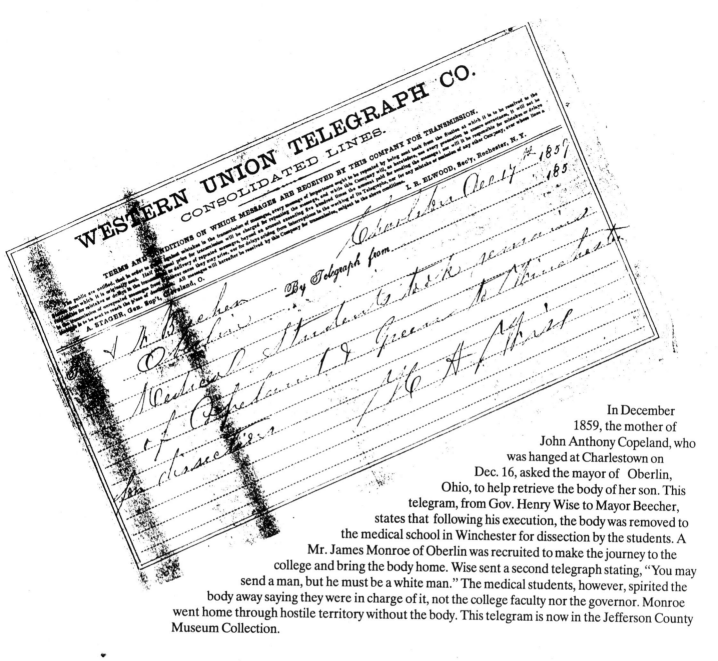

In December 1859, the mother of John Anthony Copeland, who was hanged at Charlestown on Dec. 16, asked the mayor of Oberlin, Ohio, to help retrieve the body of her son. This telegram, from Gov. Henry Wise to Mayor Beecher, states that following his execution, the body was removed to the medical school in Winchester for dissection by the students. A Mr. James Monroe of Oberlin was recruited to make the journey to the college and bring the body home. Wise sent a second telegram stating, "You may send a man, but he must be a white man." The medical students, however, spirited the body away saying they were in charge of it, not the college faculty nor the governor. Monroe went home through hostile territory without the body. This telegram is now in the Jefferson County Museum Collection.

The Winchester Medical College

Virginia's first medical college, The Medical College of the Valley of Virginia, founded in 1826, figured in the saga of John Brown's legacy.

The college became dormant three years later and was reopened in 1847 as the Winchester Medical College. All the students left at the outbreak of the Civil War.

In October 1859 students heard of the Harpers Ferry attack and hurried to the scene. Apparently they went for the excitement, but when they found a cadaver lying on the river bank, they packed it up and sent it back to the college. Cadavers were in short supply for study at the college.

There is some controversy as to whose body was sent south. Some said it was Owen Brown, but he had escaped following the raid. The body was probably that of Watson Brown, also killed during the raid.

In May 1862, Union Gen. Nathaniel Banks' army occupied Winchester. The troops searched the college and apparently found a negro boy on a dissection table. They also found what they thought were bones of one of the Brown boys. Because of the body and bones found in the hospital, Banks ordered the college burned to the ground. Watson's bones were apparently retrieved either before or after the burning as his remains were eventually reburied at North Elba, N.Y. The hospital site is now 302 West Boscawen Street in Winchester.

Heyward Shepherd and His Monument*

A free black man named Heyward Shepherd was the first man killed in Brown's raid on Harpers Ferry. Although Shepherd was from Winchester, Virginia, he worked as a porter in the Harpers Ferry train station. In addition, he attended the railroad office when the station agent was absent. He was well-liked in both communities where he lived and worked, quite an accomplishment considering Virginia was a slave state.

There are different accounts as to how Shepherd died. But it is known that about 1:30 a.m. on Oct. 17, shortly after the Baltimore & Ohio express train arrived from Wheeling, Virginia, Shepherd walked to the Potomac River railroad bridge where he was confronted by two of Brown's men. He apparently ignored their order to halt, turned and ran back toward the station. He was shot in the back, just below the heart. He was seriously injured but made it back to the station where he died later in the day.

Through the years there have been many stories about what really happened that morning. One reported that Shepherd actually started to help the raiders but then changed his mind. Another was that he was asked to join the raiders but refused. Shepherd himself stated on his deathbed that he merely went to the bridge in search of a missing watchman and knew nothing of the impending raid. Other reports indicate that Shepherd was simply in the line of fire, or in the wrong place at the wrong time.

Regardless of the correct scenario, Shepherd became a symbol for Southerners who suggested that he resisted Brown's war on slavery and stuck by the position he was hired for.

Several Virginia militia groups and white citizens accompanied his body through Winchester to his burial place in the colored cemetery. This was unusual for this time and place in American history.

For years afterward, a movement was fostered to erect a monument to this black man, the first casualty of Brown's attempt to free the blacks of the South. After many years of bitter controversy within the United Daughters of the Confederacy as to the appropriateness of a monument to a black man, they voted, in 1920, to contribute $500 toward the monument. The Sons of Confederate Veterans, in turn, voted to donate $500.

The monument would be called the Faithful Slave Memorial and would be worded to represent the devotion of the slaves to their masters before and during the Civil War. It would be placed in Harpers Ferry at the approximate site of Shepherd's encounter. Historian Matthew Page Andrews, who had proposed the monument's erection years before, was asked to write the inscription.

Andrews, a devout Southerner, also wanted to honor James, a hired slave of Col. Lewis Washington. James was taken hostage along with Washington and was thought to have drowned while attempting to escape from the raiders. He was eventually deleted from the inscription because of too many inaccuracies in the story.

The placement and inscription on the proposed monument stirred a huge controversy, not only in Harpers Ferry but within the UDC and the academic community at nearby black Storer College. In 1918, the college's alumni had placed a tablet on John Brown's Fort, located on the college campus, honoring the actions of Brown in 1859.

Finally in 1930, political conditions changed in Harpers Ferry and the town council finally approved the monument. However, the B&O Railroad had not given approval for placement on its property so a local druggist gave the UDC permission to place the monument on his property located across Potomac Street from the John Brown Fort obelisk.

On Oct. 10, 1931, the monument was finally dedicated with many local dignitaries and descendants of Col. Lewis Washington and Shepherd. This dedication was also embroiled in controversy with speakers giving varying views of slavery and their role in the Civil War. The next year the NAACP wanted to place a counter tablet to the Shepherd memorial on John Brown's Fort, but this was rejected due to a disagreement as to its wording.

As Mary Johnson states in her *West Virginia History* article, in recent years, it (the memorial) has been a renewed subject of controversy between those who claim the memorial is an appropriate tribute to Shepherd and local blacks and those who claim it is a misrepresentation of history and black attitudes toward slavery. The monument site is now owned by the National Park Service.

In the 1970s, the monument was moved so restoration work could proceed on the nearby

* Shepherd's first name has been spelled both as Heyward and Hayward. His monument spells it Heyward, but his records spell it Hayward.

buildings. There was talk that the monument was being held hostage by those who didn't like its message. It was put back in place in 1981 but covered with plywood due to possible vandalism. Finally in 1995 it was again unveiled by the National Park Service with an interpretive plaque placed next to it. The NAACP continues to oppose its display. The UDC and SCV support the memorial.

HEYWARD SHEPHERD

The Evening Star,
Winchester, Va. 8-29-01

The only known picture of Heyward Shepherd was sketched by David English Henderson in 1859. Fontaine Beckham, stationmaster and mayor of Harpers Ferry is thought to be the man sitting next to Shepherd on the baggage cart. NPS HF-521

Dedication of the Heyward Shepherd Monument
in Harpers Ferry on Oct. 10, 1909. Storer College president Henry T. McDonald is shown on the speaker's platform. Also in attendence were relatives of Col. Lewis Washington and Shepherd; UDC president-general Elizabeth Bashinsky; memorial committee chairwoman Mary Dowling Bond; SCV representatives Col. Braxton Gibson and Matthew Page Andrews; the Storer College Singers; local residents James Ranson and his father B.B. Ranson, who was a member of a militia company present at Brown's execution and James Moten, a black man holding the same job Shepherd had at the railroad station. NPS HF-1233

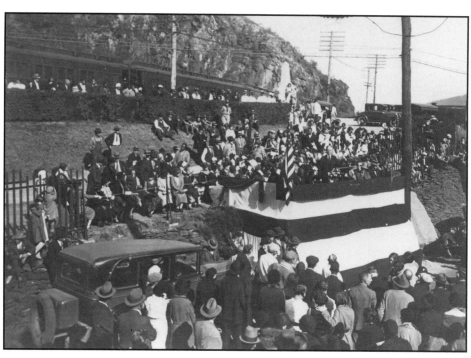

Vol. VI. No. 49.

FIRST VICTIM OF
JOHN BROWN RAID

Hayward Shepherd's Neglected Grave
at Colored Cemetery.

Practically neglected and gradually merging into the characterless undulations of the Old Colored Cemetery in this city, is a grave that the colored people should especially honor. Over its apparently neglected surface they should raise some sort of testimonial as beneath the disappearing mound sleeps Hayward Shepherd, the first victim of the John Brown raid and hence one of the minor characters in the great chain of events leading up to one of the deadliest conflicts in the world's history, when this fair land was bathed in the blood of thousands of her noblest sons, while the world looked on aghast as the terrible struggle waged from Bull Run to the final scene at Appomattox.

Hayward Shepherd was a colored resident of Winchester and was in the employ of the old Winchester and Potomac Railroad at Harpers Ferry. On Sunday night, Oct. 10, 1859, he was aroused by a commotion at the bridge at Harpers Ferry. The Brown raid was in its incipiency and two of his men had made a prisoner of Patrick Higgins, who had gone to relieve the watchman at the bridge. Pat had awaited his opportunity and succeeded in breaking away from his captors, after knocking one of them down. Shepherd hearing the scuffle went to investigate and the two raiders, furious at the escape of their first prisoner, called on him to halt, but Shepherd fled, only to receive a bullet that laid him low. Thus the first victim of these ruffians who claimed to have the sacred obligation of liberating the negroes was one of the very race they professed to have a desire to save.

Shepherd's corpse was brought to this city and buried in the colored cemetery. The ceremony made a profound impression and his remains were highly honored. His death was not long being avenged for on Dec. 2, the same year, Brown was hanged and subsequently his companions in crime also died upon the gallows.

Shepherd, the unconscious martyr, sleeps silently. Four long and terrible years of war swept over his head and close by his grave marched the tens of thousands of armed men. Nearly forty years have passed and his people are now enjoying the privileges of the free born, but his grave remains solitary and impoverished and unnoted.

COOK'S CONFESSION.—The confession of John E. Cook, one of Brown's accomplices, has been published. It does not implicate any persons whose names have not already been mentioned publicly as having been in correspondence with Brown. Cook first became acquainted with Brown at his camp, just after the battle of Black Jack, Kansas, early in 1856. Met him again at Topeka, July 4th the same year. About the 1st of November, near Lawrence, the nucleus of a company was formed for the purpose of putting a stop to the aggressions of the pro-slavery men. A few days aftewards John Brown, Owen Brown, A. D. Stephens, Richard Robertson, Colonel Richard Realf, L. F. Parsons, William Leeman and Cook, started eastward. When Brown disclosed his plan for going to Virginia, several of the party objected, but finally agreed to go. They did not go to Harper's Ferry all at once. The arms and munitions were carted from Chambersburg to Brown's rendezvous, about five miles from Harper's Ferry. Among the arms there were a breech-loading gun and a pair of muzzle-loading pistols, given to Brown by Dr. Howe. The attack was precipitated by letters from the east, complaining of delay and the consequent expense. Seven of the party were not sworn to the constitution until the Sunday evening previous to the attack. Brown's orders to his men were not to take life, except it should become necessary to do so to save their own lives.

The Case of John E. Cook.—A Virginia correspondent states that the State authorities propose to hand John E. Cook, old Brown's chief "captain," over to the United States Court for trial. This course has been determined upon with a view to compel the attendance of Mr. Seward, Mr. Greeley, Mr. Wilson, Dr. Howe and the other outsiders, who are suspected of complicity in the Harper's Ferry insurrection. If in the progress of the trial, their guilt as aiders or abbettors shall be established, the probability is that they will be assigned positions in the dock beside Cook, and subjected to the same ordeal that led to the majority of them being brought forward as witnesses. The list to be summoned will embrace every individual, wheresoever he may reside, whose name has been identified with this movement in any connection, however remote. As to their appearance in obedience to the summons, that must be presumed as certain, inasmuch as it is a question involving the ability of the federal government to enforce obedience to its summons. This is the only means to insure a full development of the origin and progress of this movement, and of the relations to it of the prominent men of other States, whose moral complicity, at least, has been already fixed. It will prove the most interesting and important trial in the criminal annals of this country.

The bodies of nine of Brown's raiders were gathered up after the raid and a local resident, James Mansfield, was paid $5 to get rid of them. He put the bodies in two wooden boxes and buried them in an unmarked grave at the edge of the Shenandoah River. In 1899, the grave was unearthed, and the remains dug up and sent up to North Elba and reburied at the John Brown farm. NPS HF-261

The Burial of the Dead Revolutionaries in a Common Grave at Midnight

This letter was written by John Brown Jr. to A.H. Harsban of New Wilmington, Ohio, from his home in Put-in-Bay Island, Lake Erie, on March 1, 1874. Notice that Cook's name is mispelled.

Put-in-Bay Island Lake Erie
Ottawa Co Ohio
March 1st 1874

A.H. Harsban Esqr
New Wilmington Pa.

Dear Sir:

Your kind favor of the 21st ___ to my brother Owen, he received last evening; and as he is somewhat troubled with lameness of his right arm, requests me to reply for him and to express his thanks for the very kind sentiments contained in your letter. He is greatly obliged to you for the item of information in regard to the capture of John E. Cooke. It has always seemed to my brother a very strange thing that the accounts of Cooke's capture no statement has appeared that he at the time made any resistance. He was known by his friends to have been so expert with a pistol, and he being so fully aware that capture was equivalent to a loss of his life; it has indeed been one of the mysteries that he should have been taken and no mention made of a desperate struggle. The account you have sent throws much light on that matter. At the moment he probably thought that to refuse them his pistol would bring suspicion upon him ___ that having begun to play the part of a "lost hunter" in which he had succeeded only two days before, it would be unwise to show any distrust of them then. We know now how fatal was his mistake. My Brother thinks that had he refused his pistol and thus incurred suspicion while it would have greatly increased their hazzard, he believes they all might have got through. But we can well imagine Cooke's estimate of the risk at the moment he allowed them to take his pistol. It was hard for Cooke to endure hunger. We know how extreme it must have been and how much he lost for want of a resolute will to control himself.

As you say of Mr. Keeler's article that "it purports to be my brothers' account of his own escape" ___ it affords me pleasure to say that the article in the Atlantic is correct in all its statement of facts, and is published in nearly the very words as given to Mr. Keeler last summer by my brother Owen.

Thanking you on my own behalf not less than on his, for your expressions of kind interest in our family. I am, Very Truly Yours
John Brown Jr.

FRANK LESLIE'S ILLUSTRATED NEWSPAPER

Entered according to Act of Congress in the year 1859, by FRANK LESLIE, in the Clerk's Office of the District Court for the Southern District of New York.

No. 206.—Vol. VIII.]   NEW YORK, SATURDAY, NOVEMBER 12, 1859.   [PRICE 6 CENTS.

OUR ILLUSTRATIONS.

We continue this week the Illustrations of the

HARPER'S FERRY INSURRECTION.

Our large cut representing the important and interesting trial of the

CHIEF CONSPIRATOR, JOHN BROWN,

can be relied on for its accuracy,

BEING TAKEN ON THE SPOT BY OUR OWN SPECIAL ARTIST. The portraits of Judge Parker and the counsel are likewise reliable, being taken at personal interviews by our artist. The Jury were sketched as they sat, by the same hand, and were pronounced admirable likenesses by their friends. The picture of Brown returning to prison after receiving sentence of death is also strictly exact, and cannot fail to be deeply interesting.

We may as well state that, on the first news of the outbreak, we immediately

DESPATCHED TWO ARTISTS
and a
SPECIAL REPORTER

to the scene, and that

THEY STILL REMAIN THERE

to furnish us with every incident of interest.

BOGUS ILLUSTRATIONS.

A paper facetiously called a *Journal of Civilization* has been foisting upon the public a series of fancy pictures of scenes at Harper's

CANNON PLANTED OUTSIDE THE COURT-HOUSE DURING THE TRIAL.

Ferry. It coolly states that the fancy sketch of "Governor Wise examining Brown" is from a sketch on the spot by Porte Crayon This is a sheer fabrication, for with the exception of the officials, no outsiders were present but the *Herald* reporter and our special artist.

This statement, however, agrees with the whole course of that picture paper, which places at its head another deliberate romance in regard to its circulation, which it over-rates preposterously, a fact known well to news agents, advertisers and ourselves.

It is conceded by every competent authority, that FRANK LESLIE'S is the

ONLY ILLUSTRATED PAPER

WHICH FAITHFULLY AND PROMPTLY DEPICTS THE INCIDENTS OF THE TIMES; and the faith in our immense, bona-fide circulation is evidenced by an influx of advertisements so great, that we are frequently compelled to leave out TWO PAGES OF THIS MATTER.

This "Journal of Demoralization," for its want of truth renders the change of name imperative, is very humorous without intending it. One picture represents—so says the caption—"Brown, his son and another of the outlaws awaiting examination." Now, Brown's son was dead, and therefore likely to wait a long time for his examination. Brown is certainly there in an unimaginable attitude, but of the third outlaw nothing is to be seen but his boots, which are supposed to be anxiously awaiting cross-questioning! Of such character are the general cuts in this picture paper. No reliance can be placed upon any of them, if we except the countless transfers from the English papers, which are used without credit.

Our Illustrations of the Harper's Ferry Insurrection this week are

---

THE ST. LOUIS DEMOCRAT
(Free Soil)

Reprinted in *The Liberator* (Boston), Fri., Nov. 4, 1859.--We should be better pleased if Brown and his followers, instead of being shot down like soldiers in battle, were made to die the ignominious death of traitors and murderers. They should have been saved for the gallows--every one of them. Were the Slaves themselves to rise in revolt, their guilt, however great, would be light in comparison with the guilt of those white rebels, or rather rapparees. They not only spilled innocent blood, but they did their utmost to draw down destruc-

tion on the slave population of Virginia and Maryland, whose good they pretended to have in view, but who would be undoubtedly exterminated in the event of their uprising. Therefore, we say, they were the enemies of black and white.... And here we would protest against the weakness of making any plea of abatement, on the ground that 'old Brown' is not in his right mind. The madness engendered as the spirit of unholy vengeance is not a mood on which the Spirit of Mercy can look with a benignant eye. Like the drunkenness which culminates in crime, it is but a preliminary stage of that instigation by the devil, which the law itself makes emphatic mention of.

The newspaper articles on the following page show the sentiment in the South over John Brown's raid at Harpers Ferry. The article from Charleston, South Carolina, appears to be promoting secession from the Union two years before it actually happened. It even mentions the possibility of civil war.

THE RICHMOND ENQUIRER

Fri., Oct. 21, 1859.--The "irrepressible conflict" was initiated at Harper's Ferry, and though there, for the time suppressed, yet no man is able to say when or where it will begin again or where it will end. The extent of this iniquitous plot cannot be estimated by the number of men detected and killed or captured...; the localities from whence these men came-- . . .New England...Iowa...Ohio,...Kansas--show an extent of country embracing the whole Northern section of the Union, as involved in the attempt at instigating servile insurrection in Virginia. Alarming as is the fact that so extended a conspiracy has been detected, a yet more serious circumstance is presented in the amount of pecuniary means at the disposal of these leaders.

..."*tents, blankets, spades, and about fifteen hundred Sharps Rifles with ammunition.*" *From whence came the money to buy these things?* When the known economy of our *Northern brethren* is considered, the fact that so large a sum has been furnished for the pillage of our property and the murder of our persons, will give some idea of what the South may expect ere the "irrepressible conflict" just begun is finally ended, either by our triumph or subjugation....

The Harper's Ferry *émeute* failed by a mistaken idea of the temper of Virginia slaves.--The late effort was made after passing into a slave State; but how long before the Abolition fanatics of Cincinnati may seize Newport, in Kentucky, away from the Marines at Washington, and within hailing distance of the depot of Western Abolitionism? Virginia has been assailed. All the memories of her sacrifices for the Union availed nothing to protect the soil that gave permanency to the Union.--The name and family of Washington offered no protection from the assaults of these fanatics. Since these things are patent, what safety had Kentucky from the hordes that swarm upon her border on the Ohio side? The aid of the Federal government was near the

"higher law" of an "irrepressible conflict" urge on and strengthen the hands that murder our families and pillage our property. Is there no remedy? Shall the South, divided by useless conflicts about Federal politics, fall as single victims to marauding bands of Northern fanatics? Can there by no union of council, actions and *arms* among States so vitally interested in the integrity of each?....

THE RICHMOND ENQUIRER

Tues., Oct. 25, 1859.--...It is but just that a disclaimer should be made by the Northern press; but...the voice of the *people* at the North, through the polls, is necessary to restore confidence and to dispel the belief that the Northern people have aided and abetted this treasonable invasion of a Southern State.

If the success of a party is of more importance than the restoration of good feeling and attachment to the Union, let that fact go forth from the polls of New York at her approaching election. Upon her soil, the treason, if not planned, was perfected; the money of her citizens gave vitality to the plot; the voice of her people should speak words of encouragement to the outraged sovereignty of a sister State. The vile clamor of party, the struggle of Republicanism for power, has given an impetus to the abolition zeal of old Brown and his comrades, that impelled them forward in their mad career of treason and bloodshed. The leader of the Republican forces gave utterance to the treasonable declaration of "an irrepressible conflict," and if the people of New York really repudiate [that] dogma let them send from the polls greetings of overthrow that shall, if possible, restore confidence, and cement the broken fragments of attachment for the Union....

The Harper's Ferry invasion has advanced the cause of Disunion more than any other event...since the formation of the Government; it has rallied

THE RICHMOND ENQUIRER

Tues Nov. 15, from Charleston, S.C., Nov. 7, 1859.--With all due reverence to the memory of our forefathers, I think the time has arrived in our history for a separation from the North...The Constitution..has been violated..., if the Union stands we have no security either for life or property..., emissaries are in our midst, sent here by a party which claims to have the good of the country at heart, but in fact are assassins...,there are papers in the South, supported by Abolition money.... We must separate, unless we are willing to see our daughters and wives become the victims of a barbarous passion and worse insult.

With five millions of negroes turned loose in the South, what would be the state of society? It would be worse that the "Reign of Terror".... The day of compromise is passed.... We should not listen to the words of Northern men who are continually telling us we are safe, while they attempt to ridicule this "Harper's Ferry business." Watch those fellows.... Gentlemen may cry peace, but there is no peace. Every gale that sweeps from the North brings new instruments of death in our midst. We publish to the world the causes that impel us to a separation, and throw ourselves upon the justice of God.... The hour has now come. The curtain falls, and the Republic framed by the hands of Washington and Jefferson fades from the view. Better civil war than injustice and oppression.

(cont.)
to that standard men who formerly looked upon it with horror; it has revived, with ten-fold strength, the desire of a Southern Confederacy. The heretofore most determined friends of the Union may now be heard saying, "if under the form of a Confederacy our peace is disturbed, our State invaded, its peaceful citizens cruelly murdered...by those who should be our warmest friends...*and the people of the North sustain the outrage,* then let disunion come."....

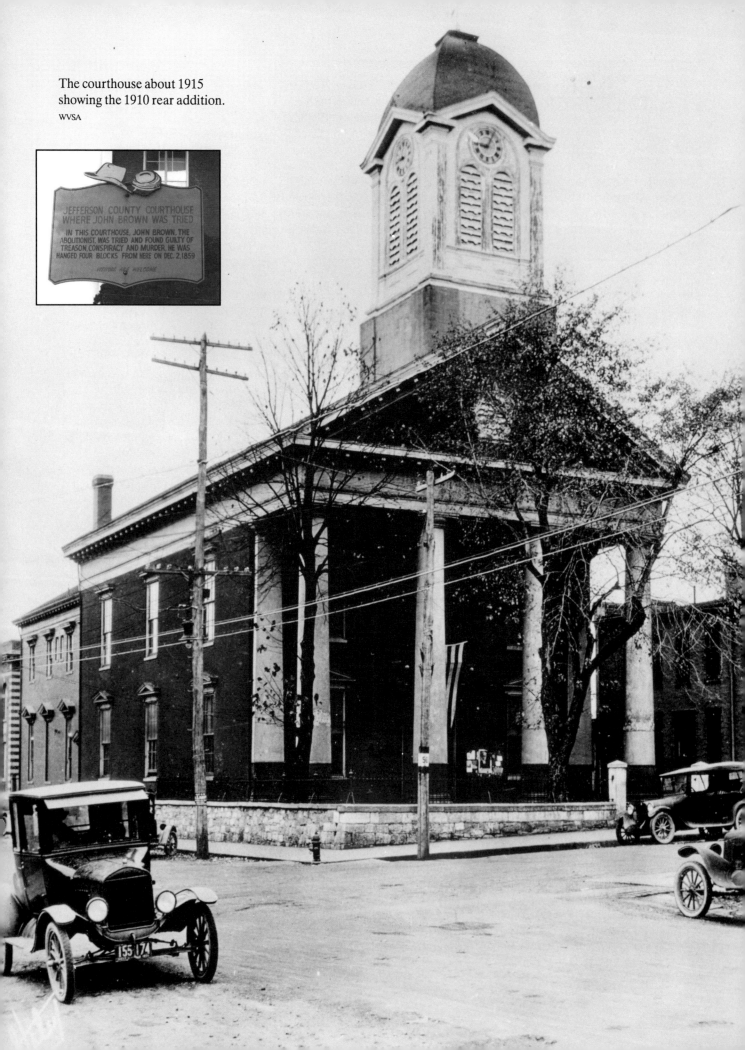

The courthouse about 1915
showing the 1910 rear addition.
WVSA

JEFFERSON COUNTY COURTHOUSE
WHERE JOHN BROWN WAS TRIED

IN THIS COURTHOUSE, JOHN BROWN, THE
ABOLITIONIST, WAS TRIED AND FOUND GUILTY OF
TREASON, CONSPIRACY AND MURDER. HE WAS
HANGED FOUR BLOCKS FROM HERE ON DEC. 2, 1859

VISITORS ARE WELCOME

Charlestown - the Trials and Executions

The Jefferson County Courthouse

One of the most historic and oldest courthouses in West Virginia still stands at the northeast corner of Washington and George streets in Charles Town. The present building dates to 1836-37, built on the site of the 1803 courthouse. By the 1830s the county had grown large enough to construct a new building as a Doric Temple in the Greek Revival style.

The ground floor was one big courtroom with windows in all four walls and heated by large iron stoves. An elevated platform behind a railing with turned balusters held the judge and court officials. In this room was held one of the most famous trials in American history—that of John Brown and five of his raiders in 1859. Part of this courtroom still serves as a hearing room for the County Commission.

During the Civil War the county records were removed to Lexington, Virginia. On Oct. 18, 1863, Confederate troops surrounded the building then occupied by Union troops. After a brief battle, which caused some damage, the courthouse was used as a stable and by war's end the county seat was moved to Shepherdstown.

Charles Town again became the county seat in 1872 and the courthouse was rebuilt with the walls and columns made higher, and a broad cornice or entablature added below the roof line. Above the portico, the bell tower was enlarged to include a clock. Walls were added to the first floor interior, creating offices and supporting the floor above. On the second floor a new courtroom, with a 25-foot ceiling was added. In 1910 an annex was built on the backside to house the judge's chambers, jury and witness rooms and a clerk's officer. This is the courthouse seen today.

A second treason trial was held in the courthouse in 1922 involving leaders in a southern West Virginia coal fields insurrection. Up until World War II, two of the three treason trails held in the United States were held in the Jefferson County Courthouse.

An on-the-scene sketch by Alfred Berghaus for *Leslie's Weekly*, Nov. 19, 1859. The three-story building across from the courthouse is the Charlestown City Hall, an 1810-built Federal-style building. wvsa

This jail building at the southwest corner of Washington and George streets housed John Brown until his execution on Dec. 2, 1859. In 1919, a new jail was built behind the courthouse and the site was sold to the United States government for the town's post office building. WVSA

The residence of Col. John Gibson at 515 South Samuel Street in Charles Town, was built in 1892 on the site of the scaffold upon which John Brown was hanged on Dec. 2, 1859. At the time, this was a field on the Rebecca Hunter Farm. On the morning of Dec. 2, the wagon carrying Brown and its accompanying procession moved out on George Street to this site. Nearly 800 troops under the command of Col. Gibson were posted to keep order. The gallows stood at a spot just to the north of where the house now stands.

Gibson Residence, built on the spot where John Brown was hanged, December 2, 1859. Charles Town, W. Va.

A modern view of the Jefferson County Courthouse, still in use.
GERALD RATLIFF PHOTO

JOHN BROWN SCAFFOLD
WITHIN THESE GROUNDS A
SHORT DISTANCE EAST OF
THIS MARKER IS THE SITE OF
THE SCAFFOLD ON WHICH
JOHN BROWN, LEADER OF
THE HARPERS FERRY RA'D,
WAS EXECUTED DECEMBER
THE SECOND, 1859.
ERECTED BY THE JEFFERSON COUNTY
HISTORICAL SOCIETY OF WEST VIRGINIA 1932

HISTORIC
HOUSE·GARDEN
TOUR
APRIL 25th 26th
INFORMATION CENTER

From the Baltimore Sun of Wednesday.

The Rebellion at Harper's Ferry.

PRELIMINARY TRIAL OF THE PRISONERS—EXCITED CROWD—APPEARANCE OF THE PRISONERS—SPEECH OF BROWN, ETC.

The preliminary or examination trial of the Harper's Ferry insurgents commenced at Charlestown, Va., yesterday. We have received the following report from our special reporter:

CHARLESTOWN, Va., October 24.—The County Court of Jefferson county, sitting as an examining court, with five justices (reported yesterday) Chas. D. Hording, State's attorney, Andrew Hunter, Esq., assisting in the prosecution. At 10½ o'clock the prisoners were brought into the court-room, old John Brown and Edwin Coppee coupled together, Stevens by himself, the negros Green and Copeland manacled together. The doors were thrown open to the crowd, and the court room was instantly filled. A military guard was also in attendance. The court requested that the evidence given on the examination trial should not be reported, but the testimony of the witnesses examined is substantially the same as the statements heretofore made by them and published. Brown's eyelids were very much swollen, and he looked haggard. Stevens looked much improved, but sallow.

The warrant of Justice Chew, summoning the Justices of the Court, was then read by the clerk, Thomas A. Moore, and also the warrant of commitment to jail—both heretofore reported in the *Sun*.

Mr. Hunter, assistant counsel for the State, suggested that the court should assign counsel to the prisoners, as, upon inquiry, they were unprovided. The presiding justice, Col. Braxton Davenport, appointed Hon. C. J. Faulkner and Lawson Botts, Esq., as their counsel. At this moment, Brown arose and said in a clear and distinct voice:

"Virginians, I did not ask for any quarter or to have my life spared. I have the Governor's assurance that I should have a fair trial. I do not know the object of this examination. I have applied for counsel from abroad, but I have not heard from them. There are mitigating circumstances which might be presented. If you seek my blood you can have it at any moment without the mockery of a trial. If I am to be hurried to execution, you can spare yourselves the expense and trouble of an examination and trial. I have made a free admission of my acts and objects, and I hope not to be insulted as cowardly, guilty barbarians insult those who are in their power."

After the counsel for the defence had a conference with Brown and his associates—

Mr. Faulkner stated to the court that he was always ready to discharge any duty which the court assigned him. He doubted if they possessed the power to appoint counsel on an examination trial. The prisoners say that they consider this examination a mockery of justice, and he would, therefore, prefer to be excused from acting, from that as well as for other reasons.

Mr. Botts then stated to the court that his position was not one of his seeking, nor one that he felt authorized to retire from. He would discharge his duty in the case.

Brown then stated that he believed Mr. Botts was one who had previously declined to act as his counsel. He cared nothing about having counsel for his defence if he was to be hurried to execution.

Mr. Botts said he sent the prisoner word by the Sheriff that he would defend him if appointed by the court.

Mr. Hunter then suggested that each of the prisoners should be interrogated if he desired Messrs. Faulkner and Botts to act as their counsel.

Brown responded that he left it to them to exercise their own pleasure. The other prisoners accepted their services.

The following witnesses were then sworn and examined, viz: Lewis W. Washington, A. M. Kiltzmiller, A. M. Bull, John H. Allstedt.

Alexander Kelly testified to the shooting of Turner.

At this stage Stevens became prostrated from weakness; the court sent him a glass of water, and his physicians, Drs. G. F. Mason and John A. Straith, had a mattress brought into court upon which Stevens was laid.

Wm. Johnson testified as to the taking of Copeland.

Andrew E. Kennedy testified to the confessions of Copeland.

Joseph A. Brua was also examined generally.

The evidence being closed, and the counsel having submitted the case, the presiding Justice said:

"It is the opinion of the court that the prisoner should be sent on for further trial."

The prisoners were taken to jail.

The grand jury sits this evening, and the result of their investigations can hardly be a subject of doubt.

Mr. Alex. R. Boteler, member elect to Congress from this district, has collected from fifty to one hundred letters from citizens in the neighborhood of Brown's house, who searched it before the arrival of the marines.

The letters are in the possession of Andrew Hunter, Esq., who has also a large number of letters obtained from Brown's house by the marines and other parties. It is requested that their contents shall not be published until after the trial of the prisoners. Among them is a roll of the conspirators, containing forty-seven signatures; also a receipt from Horace Greeley for letters, &c., received from Brown, and an accurately traced map from Chambersburg to Brown's house; copies of letters from Brown stating that the arrival of too many men at once would excite suspicion; they should arrive singly; a letter from Merriam stating that of the 20,000 wanted, G. S. was good for one-fifth. Brown told them to let the women write the letters and not the men. There is also a pathetic letter from Elizabeth Leeman to her brother. Also a letter from J. E. Cook, stating that "the Maryland election is about to come off; the people will become excited, and we will get some of the candidates that will join our side." Then follows four pages in cypher. There is also a letter from Col. Craig, of the ordnance department, Washington, answering inquiries as to the disposition of the United States troops &c.

There is also a collection of autographs and important papers in the possession of the State and general government.

The case of Lynch, arrested yesterday, will not probably be acted upon this term. The trial of Brown separately will commence to-morrow.

Nothing has been heard of counsel from abroad, but the best talent of the bar will defend him, if none arrive.   W.

I, John Avis, a Justice of the Peace of the County of Jefferson, State of West Virginia, under oath do solemnly declare that I was Deputy Sheriff and Jailor of Jefferson County, Virginia, in 1859 during the whole time that Captain John Brown was in prison & on trial for his conduct in what is familiarly known as the Harper's Ferry Raid; that I was with him daily during the whole period; that the personal relations between him and me were of the most pleasant character; that Sheriff James W. Campbell & I escorted him from his cell the morning of his execution one on either side of him; that Sheriff Campbell & I rode with Captain Brown in a wagon from the jail to the scaffold one on either side; that I heard every word that Captain Brown spoke from the time he left the jail till his death; that Sheriff Campbell (now deceased) and I were the only persons with him on the scaffold.

I have this day read, in the early part of Chapter 8 of The Manliness of Christ *by Thomas Hughes, the following paragraph....*

Respecting the statements contained [therein] I solemnly declare:--

First, that Captain John Brown...was furnished with a change of clothing as promptly as prisoners in such condition usually are; that he was allowed all the clothing he desired; and that his washing was done at his will without any cost to himself....I saw that he was at all times...treated kindly.... In further proof of the kindness he received at my hands I will state that Captain Brown in his last written will & testament bequeathed to me his Sharps Rifle and a pistol. Furthermore, on the night be-

fore the execution Captain Brown and his wife, upon my invitation, took supper with me and my family at our table in our residence which was a part of the jail building.

2....The only remarks made by Captain Brown between his cell and the scaffold were commonplace remarks about the beauty of the country and the weather.

3. The statement that "he kissed a negro child in his mother's arms" is wholly incorrect. Nothing of the sort occurred...for his hands, as usual in such cases, were confined behind him before he left the jail; he was between Sheriff Campbell and me, and a guard of soldiers surrounded him, and allowed no person to come between them and the prisoner, from the jail to the scaffold, except his escorts.

4. Respecting the statement that he "walked cheerfully to the scaffold," I will say that I did not think his bearing on the scaffold was conspicuous for its heroism, yet not cowardly.

5. Whether he was "thankful that he was allowed to die for a cause and not merely to pay the debt of nature as all must," or not, I cannot say what was in his heart; but if this clause means, as the quotation marks would indicate, that Captain Brown used any such language or said anything on the subject, it is entirely incorrect. Captain Brown said nothing like it. The only thing he did say at or on the scaffold was to take leave of us & then just about the time the noose was adjusted he said to me: "Be quick."
CHARLESTOWN, W.VA.   (Signed) JOHN AVIS
April 25, 1882.

Deputy Sheriff John Avis was the jailer at Charlestown. He was responsible for John Brown and the other captured raiders up until the time of their executions. On the scaffold Avis asked Brown to step forward onto the trap. "You must lead me," Brown replied, "for I cannot see." As Avis made the last adjustment of Brown's noose, the condemned man spoke his last words, "Be Quick." A few days after Brown's execution his wife, Mary received a letter from Avis. He expressed his heartfelt sorrow for her bereavement and enclosed a note that Brown had drawn up early in the morning on the last day of his life. He left instructions for inscriptions to be engraved on the old family stone that had recently been hauled to North Elba from Canton, Conn. He wrote:*

Oliver Brown born March 9, 1839, was killed at Harper's ferry Nov. 17th 1859
Watson Brown born October 7, 1835, was wounded at Harper's ferry November 17, and died November 19, 1859.
John Brown born May 9, 1800, was executed at Charles Town, Va., December 2, 1859.

*Brown got his dates mixed up. This should be October 17.

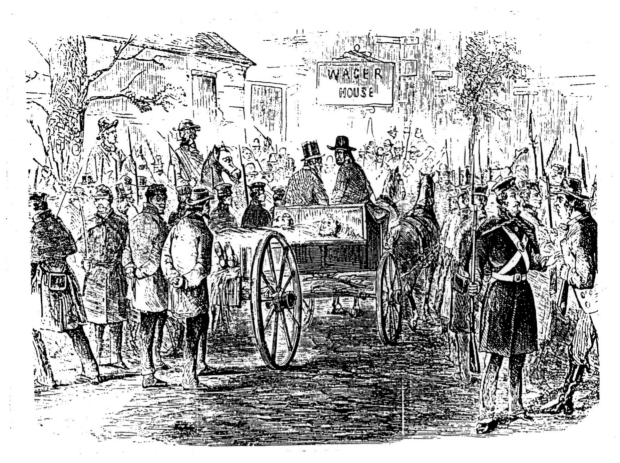

The Alfred Berghaus sketch of the prisoners being moved from the railroad station at Harpers Ferry to Charlestown for trial. *Leslie's Weekly*, Nov. 12, 1859. WVSA

John Brown's First Speech in Court

October 25th, 1859

"Virginians: I did not ask for my quarters at the time I was taken. I did not ask to have my life spared. The Governor of the State of Virginia tendered me his assurance that I should have a fair trial; but under no circumstances whatever, will I be able to attend to my trial. If you seek my blood, you can have it at any moment without this mockery of a trial.

"I have had no counsel. I have not been able to advise with any one. I know nothing about the feelings of my fellow prisoners, and am utterly unable to attend in any way to my own defense. My memory don't serve me. My health is insufficient, although improving.

"If a fair trial is to be allowed us, there are mitigating circumstances, that I would urge in our favor. But, if we are to be forces with a mere form—a trial for execution—you might spare yourselves that trouble. I am ready for my fate. I do not ask a trial. I beg for no mockery of a trial—no insult—nothing but that which conscience gives or cowardice would drive you to practise.

"I ask again to be excused from the mockery of a trial. I do not know what the special design of this examination is. I do not know what is to be the benefit of it to the Commonwealth. I have now little further to ask, other than that I may be not foolishly insulted, only as cowardly barbarians insult those who fall into their power."

FROM JAMES REDPATH'S, *The Public Life of Capt. John Brown*

The Trial

On Oct. 18, Brown and his surviving raiders—Copeland, Stevens, Green and Edwin Coppoc—were taken, under heavy guard, to the Charlestown jail. Since the Jefferson County grand jury was in session and Judge Richard Parker was presiding over the semi-annual term of the circuit court, it was decided to try the conspirators right away.

On Oct. 25 they were arraigned at the Jefferson County courthouse. The attack was against a federal facility at Harpers Ferry. But since it happened in the state of Virginia, the trial would be conducted under the laws of the state.

The court appointed Lawson Botts, who helped with the capture and Thomas Green, mayor of Charlestown, to defend Brown, who would be tried first. Prosecutors for the state were Charles Harding and Andrew Hunter.

All of the conspirators pleaded "Not Guilty."

The trial, which lasted three and one-half days, began on Oct. 27. Brown, still suffering from his wounds, had to be carried to and from the jail and had to lie on a cot in the courtroom. Botts astounded the court, and Brown too, by reading a telegram from A.H. Lewis of Akron, Ohio:

"A.H. Lewis of Akron, Ohio, dated October 26:
"John Brown, leader of the insurrection at Harper's Ferry, and several of his family, have resided in this county for many years. Insanity is hereditary in that family. His mother's sister died with it, and a daughter of that sister has been two years in a Lunatic Asylum. A son and daughter of his mother's brother have also been confined in the lunatic asylum, and another son of that brother is now insane and under close restraint. These facts can be conclusively proven by witnesses residing here, who will doubtless attend the trial if desired."

Botts entered the telegram as evidence of Brown's insanity to save his life. But Brown refused to agree to this and countered this in a speech before the court. A young Boston lawyer, George Hoyt, was sent to Charlestown to help with the defense, but his main job was to gather information for a possible rescue of Brown.

Brown became increasingly upset with Botts and

Green and they resigned. Samuel Chilton and Hiram Griswold were sent to the trial by Brown's friends to take over his defense and try to save his life.

The outcome of the trial was inevitable no matter how Brown's case was presented to the jury. The prosecutor's case was convincing: The death of several innocent people at Harpers Ferry and the attempt to arm the slaves, which was against federal and state laws of the time.

Brown's lawyers countered that as commander-in-chief of a provisional army he should be tried according to the laws of war and not as a common criminal. Their argument was rejected. The case went to the jury on Oct. 31 and after a 45-minute deliberation the verdict was read: guilty on all three counts—treason against the Commonwealth of Virginia, for conspiring with slaves to rebel, and for murder.

On Nov. 2, Brown was sentenced to hang on Friday, Dec. 2, 1859. Coppoc, Copeland, Green and Stevens were tried, found guilty and sentenced to die by hanging on Dec. 16. John Cook and Albert Hazlett, who had escaped to Pennsylvania, were brought back to Charlestown and put on trial in February 1860. They, too, were found guilty, sentenced to die and were hanged on March 16, 1860.

The liberation of Brown and his conspirators was also a constant threat to authorities in Jefferson County. After the death sentence was issued, Gov. Henry Wise of Virginia and President Buchanan sent additional troops to the area to thwart any rescue attempt. Martial law was declared in Charlestown and armed patrols kept the peace. No serious rescue attempt was ever made.

Between the day of sentencing and his execution, Brown spent his time receiving visitors and writing letter to friends and family. He was not afraid of death and thought perhaps his death would do more good to free the slaves than his abortive try by force.

He was right—he became a martyr for the entire abolitionist cause.

Mary Brown came to Charlestown on Dec. 1 to visit her husband. They had his last supper with his jailer, Captain Avis and his wife. Two days later, Mary accompanied John Brown's body to his final burial site in New York.

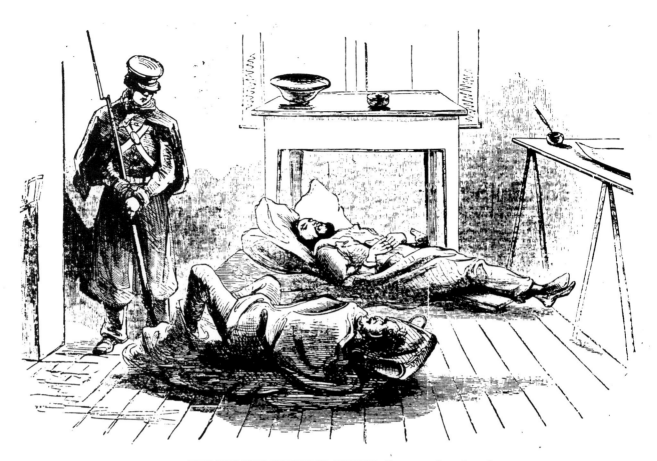

THE GUARD-ROOM, WITH THE WOUNDED PRISONERS.—[SKETCHED BY PORTE CRAYON.]

John Brown and his raiders were in jail in Charlestown, and there were hundreds of militiamen on picket duty scattered all over town to thwart any escape attempt. Many militant abolitionists in Massachusetts and Kansas formulated several schemes to rescue Brown and his men. All came to naught either because of a lack of money or the impracticality of their plans. There was even a plan to abduct the governor of Virginia and hold him for an exchange for brown.

After Brown was executed, John Cook and Edwin Cooper did break out of their cell the day before they were to hang but did not make it out of the jail yard. A last attempt was planned for Stevens and Hazlett, but by this time the area was too secure, and word was received that the two condemned men did not wish any further bloodshed to be on their hands.

If an attempt by a group of northern abolitionists had actually been made, the Civil War could have conceivably started right in Charlestown in late 1859 or early 1860.

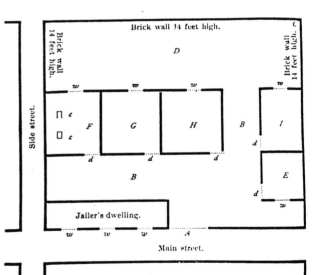

A Main entrance; *B* Space between walls, Avis's house, and the jail building; *C* Point of wall which Cook and Coppoc reached on the night of Dec. 15th in their attempt to escape; *D* Jail yard *d d d d d*, cell doors; *E* Reception-room; *F* Cell occupied by Brown and Stevens, afterwards by the latter and Hazlett; *G* Cell of Green and Copeland; *H* Cell of Coppoc and Cook; *I* Cell first occupied by Albert Hazlett, *w w w, w w*, windows, those of cells look into the jail yard; *c c* cots of Brown and Stevens.

Plan of Brown's Prison Printed in the New York TRIBUNE *to Encourage a Rescue*

FROM REDPATH'S *LIFE OF CAPTAIN JOHN BROWN*

- 80 -

Brown's warning as he lay wounded outside of the enginehouse:

"I wish to say furthermore, that you had better—all you people of the South—prepare yourselves for a settlement of that question that must come up for settlement sooner than you are prepared for it. The sooner you are prepared the better. You may dispose of me very easily; I am nearly disposed of now; but this question is still to be settled—this Negro question I mean—the end of that is not yet."

Congressman Andrew Hunter was a prominent Jefferson County attorney and the prosecuting attorney for the State of Virginia at John Brown's trial. He vowed to see Brown "arraigned, tried, found guilty, sentenced and hung, all within 10 days."

Representative Charles Faulkner of Berkeley County, Virginia, was asked by Judge Parker to help defend Brown. But Faulkner had to refuse since, as a member of the Jefferson Guards, he had taken part in the fighting. NPS HF-165

Hiram Griswold from Cleveland, Ohio, was sent by Brown's friends to take over the defense from Lawson Botts and Thomas Green. NPS HF-164

Thirty-six-year-old Lawson Botts was one of Brown's first defense attorneys but was replaced by Hiram Griswold as Brown did not believe that Botts could provided an adequate defense. Botts was from Spotsylvania County, Virginia, and a 1844 graduate of the Virginia Military Institute. He was a colonel in the 2nd Virginia Infantry and was mortally wounded at the 2nd Battle of Manassas and died on Sept. 16, 1862. NPS HF-271

Samuel Chilton, a native Virginian and an attorney in Washington, D.C., was sent by Brown's friends to help George Hoyt in his defense. NPS HF-268

T. Clairborne Green, the 39-year-old mayor of Charlestown, was one of Brown's court-appointed counsels but was soon replaced due to Brown's distrust of him. During the Civil War he joined the Confederate Army and in 1863 was appointed Chief Collector of Confederate taxes in Virgina. In 1876 he was appointed to the West Virginia Court of Appeals and continued to his death in 1899. NPS HF-272

George Hoyt was a 21-year-old Boston lawyer sent to Charlestown by Brown's New England supporters to help in his defense. His real mission, however, was to gather information for people plotting to free Brown from the Charlestown jail. WVSA

THE TRIAL OF JOHN BROWN, AT CHARLESTOWN, VIRGINIA, FOR TREASON AND MURDER.—[Sketched by Porte Crayon.]

This drawing from *Frank Leslie's Illustrated Newspaper* shows the courtroom during the trial with portraits of the presiding judge, the twelve jurors, the counsel for the prisoner and prosecution and Brown reclined on his couch. WVSA

John Brown is arraigned before the federal Court at Charlestown, from a drawing made at the trial by James E. Taylor

- 83 -

THE ARRAIGNMENT.—Drawn by Porte Crayon.—[See Page 729.]

The arraignment of Brown and his raiders by Porte Crayon. Left to right: Copeland, Green, John Brown, Edwin Coppoc (chained to Brown) and Stevens (assisted by two guards.)

Brown had no spiritual advisor while in jail, especially from the local clergy. Norval Wilson, a Methodist preacher, and others of the cloth called on him. Brown asked Wilson, "Do you believe in slavery?" Wilson replied, "I do under the present circumstances." "Then," said Brown, "I do not want your prayers. I don't want the prayers of any man who believes in slavery." Brown wrote to a friend: "You may wonder, are there no ministers of the gospel here? I answer no. There are no ministers of <u>Christ</u> here. These ministers who profess to be <u>Christian</u>, and hold slaves or advocate slavery, I cannot abide them. My knees will not bend in prayer with them while their hands are stained with the blood of souls."

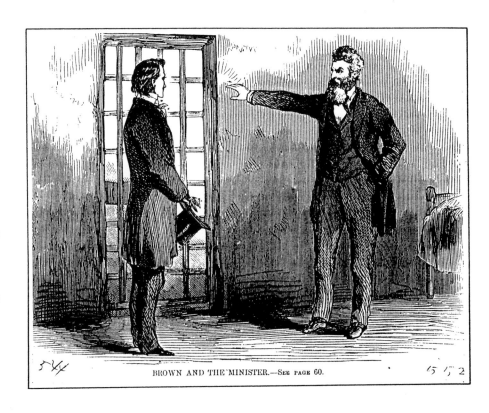

BROWN AND THE MINISTER.—See page 60.

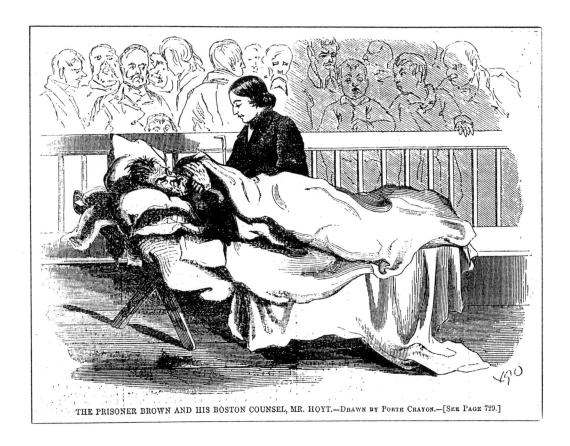
THE PRISONER BROWN AND HIS BOSTON COUNSEL, MR. HOYT.—Drawn by Porte Crayon.—[See Page 729.]

RETURN OF MR. HOYT, ONE OF BROWN'S COUNSEL.—Mr. George H. Hoyt, who acted as counsel of John Brown, arrived in this city on Saturday. He has just returned from Ohio, where he has been seeking evidence of the insanity of Brown. We learn from him that he obtained eighteen affidavits from persons of good character and standing, the reliability of whose statements are vouched for by public officials, which establish the fact that John Brown's grandmother, his only sister, two aunts, two uncles, five cousins, one niece, and two of his sons, John Brown, Jr., and Frederick Brown, have all been subjects of insanity. The affidavits also affirm that since the death of Brown's first wife, a number of years ago, he, at times, has exhibited signs of insanity, and instances are given of his monomania in regard to slavery. Mr. Hoyt states that to the energetic coöperation of Judge Daniel R. Tilden, of Cleveland, he is mainly indebted for these affidavits. On Wednesday last Mr. Hoyt had an interview with Gov. Wise in Washington, the latter being on his return from Charlestown to Richmond, and he there presented to him a petition, praying that the execution might be stayed until the issue of Brown's insanity could be framed and tried according to the laws of Virginia. He also gave the affidavits to Gov. Wise, who stated that he would examine them with pleasure. Mr. Hoyt met a large number of Brown's friends in Ohio, and is convinced that there is no truth in the stories of an organization to attempt the rescue of Brown.

CHARLESTOWN, JEFFERSON COUNTY, VA.,
Oct. 21, '59

HON. RUFUS CHAPMAN, Springfield, Mass.

DEAR SIR: I am here imprisoned with several saber cuts in my head and bayonet stabs in my body. My object in writing to you is to obtain able and faithful counsel for myself and fellow prisoners, five in all, as we have the faith of Virginia pledged through her Governor and numerous other prominent citizens to give us a fair trial. Without we can obtain such counsel from without the slave state, neither the facts in our case can come before the world, nor can we have the benefit of such facts as might be considered mitigating in the view of others upon our trial. I have money in hand here to the amount of $250, and personal property sufficient to pay a most liberal fee to yourself or to any suitable man who will undertake our defense. If I can have the benefit of said property, can you or some other good man come immediately on for the sake of the young men prisoners at least? My wounds are doing well. Do not send an Ultra Abolitionist.

Very respectfully yours,
JOHN BROWN.

Judge Richard Parker

Parker was the presiding judge at the trial of John Brown. He was born in Richmond, Va., in 1810 and came from a long line of distinguished jurists. Judge Parker graduated in law from the University of Virginia and practiced in Winchester, Va.

In 1849 he was elected to the U.S. House of Representatives, and while serving there, was appointed a General Court Judge and later on the Circuit Court which embraced Winchester, Frederick and Jefferson counties.

As the Circuit Court Judge in 1859, he was to controlled the fate of John Brown. His charge to the jury was as follows:

"In all your presentments you shall present the truth, the whole truth, and nothing but the truth. Do but this, gentlemen, and you will have fulfilled your duty. Go beyond this, and in place of that diligent inquiry and calm investigation which you have sworn to make, act upon prejudice or from excitement or passion, and you will have done a wrong to that law in whose services you are engaged. As I said before, those men are now in the hands of justice. They are to have a fair and impartial trial. We owe it to the cause of justice, as well as to our own characters, that such a trial shall be afforded them."

After his conviction, Brown stated, "Let me say one word further. I feel entirely satisfied with the treatment I have received on my trial. Considering all the circumstances, it has been more generous than I expected."

No mention was noted as to Parker's service during the Civil War but he spent the rest of his life in Winchester. He died in 1893 and is buried in Winchester's Mt. Hebron Cemetery.

Judge Richard Parker. WVSA

Sheriff James W. Campbell was responsible for hanging John Brown and six of his men. NPS HF-166

"Had I interfered in the manner which I admit in behalf of the rich, the powerful, the intelligent, the so-called great, or in behalf of any of their friends, it would have been all right, and every man in this court would have deemed it an act worthy of reward rather than punishment."

John Brown

WM. A MARTIN

GEORGE W. TAPP

WM. RIGHTODALE

JOHN C McCLURE

ISAAC DUST

JACOB J. MILLER

JOSEPH MYERS

THOMAS OSBORNE

RICHARD TIMBERLAKE

GEORGE W BOYER

THOMAS WATSON JR.

JOHN C. WILTSHIRE

Members of the jury for John Brown's trial.
Sketches are by William Morris Stutler.
WVSA

A number of envelopes have survived from people writing to John Brown when he was imprisoned in Charlestown. Some were addressed to John Brown, some to "Osawatomie Brown" and some in care of Colonel Washington. WVSA

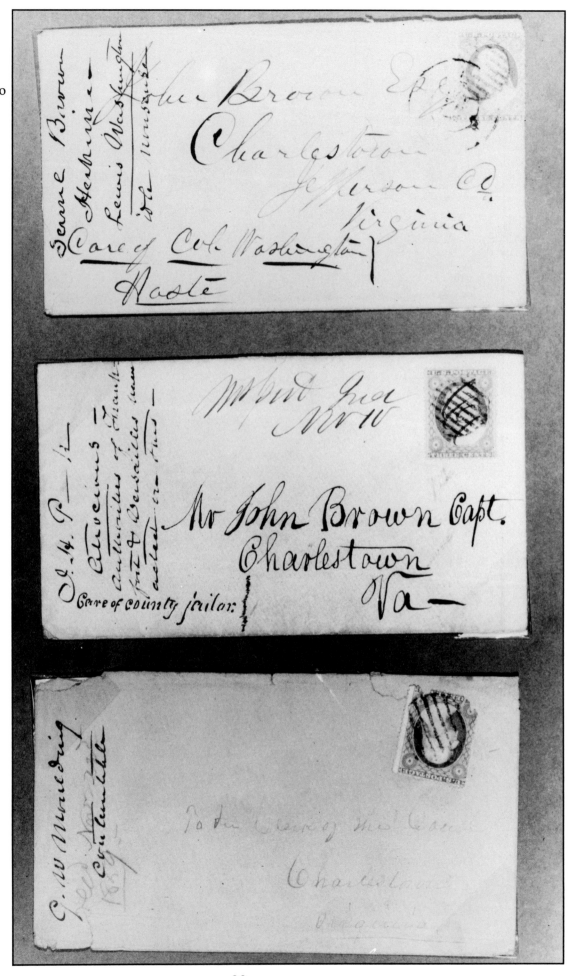

Capt'n John Brown

Charlestown

Jefferson County

Va—

Fred. Douglass Sympathy

Capt John Brown

Charlestown

Verginia

care of his Custodian

Ingol: Brown

Mr. Ossawatomie "Brown

(care of U.S. Marshal) Charlestown

Mr. Martin Esq.) Va

Sketch by David C. Hitchcock for the *New York Illustrated News*, Dec. 10, 1859.

BROWN AND STEVENS IN THEIR CELL, THREE DAYS BEFORE THE EXECUTION.

Jailor   Cook.   Coppic.   Correspondent.   Artist.

OUR ARTIST AND SPECIAL CORRESPONDENT VISITING COOK AND COPPIC IN THEIR CELL, PREVIOUS TO THEIR EXECUTION.

Artist and correspondent from the *Baltimore Clipper*, along with officials, visit Cook and Coppoc in their cell before their execution.

Artist and correspondent from the *Baltimore Clipper*, along with officials making their last visit to Brown in his cell before his execution.

Charlestown Prison, Jefferson County, Virginia—December 1, 1859*

My dearly beloved wife, sons, daughters, everyone:

As I now begin what is probably the last letter I shall ever write to any of you, I conclude to write to you all at the same time... I am waiting the hour of my public murder with great composure of mind and cheerfulness, feeling the strongest assurance that in no other possibly way could I be used to so much advance the case of God and of humanity, and that nothing that either I or all my family have sacrificed or suffered will be lost...

I have now no doubt but that our seeming distaste will be ultimately result in the most glorious success. So my dear shattered and broken family be of good cheer & believe & trust in God "With all your heart & with all your soul" for "he doeth All things well." Do not feel ashamed on my account, nor for one moment despair of the cause, or grow weary of well doing. I bless God; I never felt stronger confidence in the certain and near approach of a bright morning & a glorious day than I have felt, and do now feel, since my confinement here...

I beseech you every one to make the Bible your daily and nightly study, with a childlike honest, candid, teachable spirit out of love and respect for your husband and father, and I beseech the God of my fathers to open all your eyes to a discovery of the truth. You cannot imagine how much you may soon need the consolations of the Christian religion. Circumstances like my own, for more than a month past, convince me beyond all doubt of our great need of something more to rest our hopes on than merely your own vague theories framed up, while our prejudices are excited or our vanity worked up to its highest pitch.

Do not be vain and thoughtless, but sober minded. And let me entreat you all to love the whole remnant of our once great family "with a pure heart fervently." Try to build again your broken walls, and to make the utmost of every stone that is left. Nothing can so tend to make life a blessing as the consciousness that you love and are beloved and "love ye the stranger" still. It is ground of the utmost comfort to my mind to know that so many of you as have had the opportunity have given full proof of your fidelity to the great family of man...

I beseech you all to live in habitual contentment with very moderate circumstances and gains of worldly store and most earnestly to teach this to your children & children's children after you, by example as well as by precept... And John Brown writes to his children to abhor with undying hatred...that "sum of all villanies," slavery.

Remember that "he that is slow to anger is better than the mighty, and he that ruleth his spirit than he that taketh a city." Remember also that "they that be wise shall shine, and they that turn many to righteousness as the stars forever and ever." And now, dearly beloved, farewell, to God and the word of his grace I commend you all.

Your affectionate husband and father,

John Brown

*From *Life and Letters of John Brown: Liberator of Kansas and Martyr of Virginia,* edited by F.B. Sanborn, Roberts Brothers, Boston, 1891.

*Brown wrote this letter the day before his execution.

Edmund Ruffin was a 66-year-old South Carolina Veteran of the War of 1812 and a well-known agricultural expert. He stood with the cadets from Virginia Military Institute to witness Brown's execution. Two years later, as a private in the Palmetto Guards of Charleston, South Carolina, he would yank the lanyard that fired the shot at Fort Sumter--the shot that started the Civil War.

Arrival of Brown's wife, women's rights advocate Lucretia Mott and a Captain Moore in Charlestown on Dec. 1, 1859. Sketched by Alfred Berghaus for *Leslie's Weekly*, Dec. 17, 1859.

The Last Supper. John Brown and his wife in the parlor of John Avis, Brown's jailer, the night before his execution.

NEW EXCITEMENT AT HARPER'S FERRY.

The excitement caused by the Harper's Ferry foray has broken out afresh. According to the dispatches it is evident that at Charlestown, Harper's Ferry, Richmond, and other towns in Virginia, the people are feverishly apprehensive of an attempt to rescue Old Brown and his fellow-culprits. The burning of several barns and outhouses in the vicinity of Charlestown, which were, it is believed, fired by sympathizing friends of the conspirators, has served to confirm the fears of the citizens. In this state of affairs Governor Wise has ordered troops to proceed to Charlestown forthwith to guard the prisoners and preserve the peace. Great excitement exists in Virginia, though at the latest dates no plot had been discovered.

JOHN BROWN IN PRISON.

A lady, who visited Charlestown to assist Mrs. Lydia Maria Child, obtained two interviews with John Brown, the first of an hour, and the other for a shorter period.

Mrs. ——, on entering, found Captain Brown lying on a cot, and Stephens on a large bed. Captain Brown arose from his bed to receive his guests, and stood a few moments leaning against the bedstead, immediately lying down again from weakness. His visitors were struck with the cheerfulness of his expression, and the calmness of his manner. He seemed not only passively resigned to his fate, but cheerful under it, and more than willing to meet it.

She said to him,

"I expected Mrs. Child would be here to introduce me; I am sorry not to find her, for her presence would make this room brighter for you."

He smiled, and replied,

"I have written to her the reasons why she should not come; but she was very kind—very kind!"

Some questions were then asked as to the treatment and care he had received; to which he said,

"I wish it to be understood by every body that I have been very kindly attended; for if I had been under the care of father or brother I could not have been better treated than by Captain Avis and his family."

Captain Avis is the jailer, of whom all the reports speak in high terms for his humane and courteous conduct, not only to these, but to all prisoners.

When another allusion was made to Mrs. Child, Captain Brown remarked,

"The reason why I did not wish her to come, and why I did not wish my wife to come, was for fear lest they would be harassed and annoyed, and that on this account I would be troubled myself."

HIS STATE OF MIND.

Mrs. —— had carried with her into the jail a large bunch of autumn leaves, gathered in the morning from the woods. There was no nail on the wall to hang them by, and she arranged them between the grated bars of the window. She gave to the sufferer a full-blown rose, which he laid beside his cheek on his pillow. The old man seemed to be greatly touched with these tokens of thoughtfulness. He is said to have always been a great lover of nature, particularly of the grandeur of forest scenes.

Mrs. —— drew a chair near his bedside, and taking out her knitting, sat by him for an hour. She has preserved his complete conversation, of which I can give only a small portion. She says:

"I never saw a person who seemed less troubled or excited, or whose mind was less disturbed and more clear. His remarks are pointed, pithy, and sensible. He is not in the least sentimental, and seems to have singularly excellent common sense about every thing."

HIS PRINCIPLES ON SLAVERY.

She asked him the direct question—"Were you actuated, in any degree, in undertaking your late enterprise, by a feeling of revenge?" adding that a common impression to that effect had gone abroad.

He manifested much surprise at this statement, and after pausing a moment, replied:

"I am not conscious of ever having had a feeling of revenge; no, not in all the wrong done to me and my family in Kansas. But I can see that a thing is wrong and wicked, and can help to right it, and can even hope that those who do the wrong may be punished, and still have no feeling of revenge. No, I have not been actuated by any spirit of revenge."

He talked a good deal about his family, manifesting solicitude for their comfort after he was gone, but expressing his great confidence and trust in God's kind providence in their behalf.

When some allusion was made to the sentence which he had received, he said, very deliberately and firmly, and, as my friend says, "almost sublimely:"

"I do not think I can better serve the cause I love so much than to die for it!"

She says that she can never forget the impressive manner in which he uttered these solemn words. She replied:

"It is not the hardest thing that can happen to a brave man to die: but it must be a great hardship for an active man to lie on his back in prison, disabled by wounds. Do you not dread your confinement, and are you not afraid that it may wear you down, or cause you to relax your convictions, or regret your attempt, or make your courage fail?"

"I can not tell," he replied, "what weakness may come over me; but I do not think that I shall deny my Lord and Master Jesus Christ, as I certainly should if I denied my principles against slavery."

When the conversation had proceeded thus far, as it was known outside the jail that a Northern lady was inside, a crowd began to collect, and although no demonstration of violence was made, yet there were manifest indications of impatience; so that the Sheriff called to the jailer, and the jailer was obliged to put an end to the interview.

HARPER'S WEEKLY.

SATURDAY, OCTOBER 29, 1859.

INSURRECTION AT HARPER'S FERRY.

A WEEK ago people were astounded by news that a servile insurrection had broken out at Harper's Ferry, in Virginia. It is now well understood that, though negroes were implicated in the affair as well as white men, and one of the designs of the movement was to liberate slaves, the insurrection was merely the work of a half-crazed white, whose views and aims were, to say the least, extremely vague and indefinite. Ossawottomie Brown, as he loved to be called, was an old soldier of fortune, who had fallen upon evil days in Kansas where he lost two of seven sons; misfortune had imbittered his temper and turned his brain; he fancied he was charged with the mission of liberating slaves by force; and the sad recurrence of Harper's Ferry, with the loss of life which it occasioned, is the miserable result.

It is hardly necessary to add that the event will possess marked political significance at the present time. The admitted affiliations between Gerrit Smith and old Brown, and the peculiar sympathy expressed for him and his friends by certain organs of the Republican party, are likely to increase the vote against the Republican candidates this fall.

For, whatever opinions a man may hold in reference to the slavery controversies which are agitated in this country, all are unanimous against any thing like compulsory emancipation and servile revolts. The horrors of servile war, with its necessary accompaniments in the shape of murder, rape, outrage, rapine, and incendiarism, are vividly realized by men of all parties; even the warmest friends of the slave—with a few crazy exceptions, perhaps—would, like Mr. Everett, shoulder a musket at any time to prevent such atrocities. And though the leading Republican politicians and papers may and do repudiate the acts of Brown and his associates, it is likely that a large section of the people of this country will hold them responsible for what has happened. It will be said that men of Brown's stamp would never have ventured upon the outrages they have committed but for the open sympathy expressed by persons of high standing with the cause they espoused; and though this inference may be unjust, it presents sufficient superficial plausibility to be very generally accepted. Mr. Brown, we think, will have cost the Republicans many thousand votes.

Is the Republican Party responsible for Brown's Insurrection.

We are accused by the republican paper of this county with exhibiting "paltry partisan villainy," in connecting the Harper's Ferry insurrection in any manner with the republican party. The terms used in reference to us are the mildest which can give utterance to the bitterness which abolitionism nurses towards all who oppose its schemes, whether in the South or the North. Had our neighbor the faculty of seeing himself as others see him, he would, at least, clothe his spite in more becoming language; for where can there be found a more diligent scavenger for "political capital" than his paper has ever been? Descending from public acts, and the principles of public men and political parties, which are legitimate subjects of newspaper comment, the *Union* has never failed to charge upon the democratic party any and every act that could inflame opposition and hatred to it, whether such act were properly attributable to the party or not; and for "political capital" how often has it dragged private acts and private character before the public—neither sparing the family, the school district, or the town, if by any distortion of events it could gather a little "political capital." It is little consequence, that such political *rag-pickers* rail at us or the democratic party.

How long ago was it that the republican papers (and they have not yet wholly ceased) uniformly designated democrats as "border ruffians," because there were disorders in Kansas? Now we see, in the case of Brown, what sort of innocents they were who brought these charges against the democracy. Brown was then in Kansas—a leader under the auspices of New England republicans—furnished with arms and money by them—and all the outrages he, and the like of him, committed were charged to the democracy; and he is only thought to be *crazy* when he *gets caught* in his treasonable and murderous "Kansas work."

How long ago was it that republican papers designated all democrats as "rummies," and charged them with all the intemperance that cursed the community, because they did not believe in the efficacy of a remedy which the republican party itself (being in power) now disclaims obligation to enforce?

How long ago was it that the republicans held the whole democratic party responsible for a blow struck in anger by a single individual, and made that act a principal item in their "*political capital?*" How many weeks ago that they charged Mr. Buchanan and his administration with guilt for the death of a Senator who fell in a duel of his own acceptance?

These are instances of the practices of the republican party, to raise "political capital." We will not refer in detail to the political *rag-picking* of the *Union* in particular, for its feats in this line are familiar to men of all parties in this vicinity.

We have affirmed, and we repeat, that the republican party is in a great measure responsible for the insurrectionary attempt of Brown and his associates. The very foundation of that party was laid in spite, hatred, and revenge to the Southern States of the Union.— The acts of Congress of 1854 were represented as an *aggression* upon the North, for which vengeance should be visited upon the South. The republican party, through its press, its orators, associations of men and women, churches, and preachers, has constantly labored to stir up hatred to the South and its institutions. This has been the very life as well as the chief political capital of the party, and a prominent article in its religious creed. It has taught that the time for moral suasion had passed, and that the South must be subjugated to the North. In this spirit it organized its "Kansas aid societies," and sent arms and munitions of war to that territory; and when collisions happened, (as happen they must when men thus inflamed by passion meet with arms in hand) they charged them wholly to the South and the democracy. In the same spirit of hatred, the party has deliberately set about annulling or circumventing the laws of the Union relative to any institution of the South; and has, by its prominent men, justified bloodshed and armed resistance to law. Such fanaticism as Brown and his associates have exhibited is the natural product of republican teachings; and armed resistance to law, and attempts to overturn Southern institutions by force, are but the *ripened grain* from republican sowing. Let such sowing continue, and be encouraged as it has been, and before another generation passes our Union must be broken up, and wide spread civil war desolate this happy land.

It is time that Northern people look this matter seriously in the face, if they would avert the evil. What we sow that shall we reap. If people put away all sober thought and consideration, because those who fan the flames of passion and hatred cry out "political capital," that will not prevent the evil consequences.

"It was not Carolina, but Virginia, not Fort Sumter, but Harpers Ferry, not Major Anderson but John Brown who began the war that ended slavery and made this a free republic...when John Brown stretched forth his arm the sky was cleared—the armed hosts stood face to face over a chasm of a broken union and the clash of arms was at hand."

FREDERICK DOUGLASS

Brown would "....make gallows as glorious as the Cross."

RALPH WALDO EMERSON

"The death of no man in America has ever produced so profound a sensation. A feeling of deep and sorrowful indignation seems to possess the masses."

LAWRENCE, *KANSAS REPUBLICAN*

Brown was "....a crucified hero."

HENRY DAVID THOREAU

"In firing his gun, John Brown has merely told what time of day it is. It is high noon, Thank God."

WILLIAM LLOYD GARRISON

The Republican Party and John Brown. The Republican party denies any knowledge of Brown's conspiracy, or having aided it in any way. A trumpeter, says Æsop, being taken prisoner in a battle, begged hard for quarter. "Spare me, good sirs, I beseech you," said he, "and put me not to death without cause, for I have killed no one, nor have I arms save only this poor trumpet." "For that very reason," said his captors, "shall you the sooner die; for without the spirit to fight, yourself, you stir up others to bloodshed."—*Boston Courier.*

FREE PRESS
Extra.

Friday Morning, Nov. 11.

Yesterday morning Cooke, Coppee, Green and Copeland, were brought into Court to receive sentence. When asked by the Clerk if they had any thing to say why sentence should not be passed upon them, Coppee arose and addressed the Court for a few minutes—declaring that he had been seduced into the project—that the sole object was to liberate the slaves, not murder, &c.

Shields Green said he had nothing to say, whilst Copeland remained *mum.*

John E. Cooke then stated that he had not been acting as a spy—that he had not taken the relics of Washington as plunder but that as they had been used by the Father of his Country to disenthrall the people of America from bondage, so they were to be used to liberate the slaves of the South, &c., &c.

After Cooke had finished his remarks, Judge PARKER in a solemn, affecting and impressive manner passed sentence.

It will be seen that *Friday, the 16th of December next*, has been fixed for their execution. Green and Copeland between the hours of eight in the morning and twelve noon—and Cooke and Coppee between the hours of twelve and five o'clock. Brown's execution the 2nd of December.

SENTENCE.

JOHN E. COOKE, EDWIN COP-PEE, SHIELDS GREEN, AND JOHN COPELAND:

Your trials, on which we have been so long employed, have at length ended; and all that remains to be done to complete these judicial proceedings, is to pronounce and record the judgments which by law must follow upon the crimes for which you have been tried, and of which you have been found guilty.

These crimes have all grown out of a mad inroad upon this State, made with the predetermined purpose to raise in our midst the standard of a servile insurrection. In the execution of this purpose, in the darkness of a Sabbath night, you seized upon a portion of our territory, captured several of our best citizens—holding them as hostages of war until your party was itself overcome by force—armed such of our slaves as you could seize upon with deadly weapons which they were to use against their owners, whom you denounced to them as their oppressors—and in your efforts to push your bold and unholy scheme through to a successful issue, you have taken human life in no fewer than five instances. The evidence most abundantly proved that all these things had been done—and by the force of that evidence jury after jury has felt itself compelled to bring in its verdict of *GUILTY* against each one of you.

Happily for the peace of our whole land, you obtained no support from that quarter whence you so confidently expected it. Not a slave united himself to your party, but so soon as he could get without the range of your rifles, or as night gave him opportunity, made his escape from men who came to give him freedom, and hurried to place himself once more beneath the care and protection of his owner.

When we reflect upon all the mischief and ruin, the dark and fearful crimes which must have attended even your partial success—men, everywhere, should be thankful that you were so soon and so easily overpowered.

For these offences the Law denounces the penalty of Death, and imposes upon me the duty of pronouncing that sentence. It is the most painful duty I have ever been called upon to perform. In spite of your offences against our laws, I cannot but feel deeply for you; and sincerely, most sincerely, do I sympathise with those friends and relations, whose lives are bound up in yours, and whose hearts will be so wrung with grief when they shall hear of the sad fate which has overtaken you, the objects of their warmest and holiest affections. For them we all do sorrow. Whilst a due regard for our safety may not permit us to forgive the offences of which you have been guilty, I hope that they will turn for consolation, and you for pardon, to that good Being, who in His wrath remembereth mercy. Make, then, your peace with Him—for, you must soon be ushered into His presence, there to be dealt with as His Justice, and His Mercy may ordain.

To conclude this sad duty, I now announce that the sentence of the law is that you and each of you, JOHN E. COOKE, EDWIN COPPEE, SHIELDS GREEN and JOHN COPELAND, be hanged by the neck until you be dead; and that execution of this judgment be made and done by the Sheriff of this county, on Friday, the Sixteenth day of December next, upon you Shields Green and John Copeland, between the hours of eight in the forenoon and twelve noon, of that day—and upon you John E. Cooke, and Edwin Coppee, between the hours of twelve (noon), and five in the afternoon of the same day. And the Court being of opinion that the execution of this sentence should be in public, it is further ordered that this judgment be enforced and executed, not in the jail yard but at such public place convenient thereto, as the said Sheriff may appoint—and may God have mercy upon the soul of each one of you!

The prisoners are remanded to jail, there to await execution of this judgment.

THE MILITARY PARADE

At eight o'clock the troops began to arrive; and at nine the first company took position. Horsemen clothed in scarlet jackets were posted around the field at fifty feet apart, and a double line of sentries was stationed farther in. As each company arrived, it took its allotted position. The following diagram will explain the position of the military forces:

The first companies of infantry and cavalry having taken their position, the artillery then arrived, with a huge brass cannon, which was so placed and pointed that, in the event of an attempted rescue, the prisoner might be blown into shreds by the heavy charge of grape shot that lay hidden in it. Other cannon were stationed, with equal care, to sweep the jail and every approach to it. From eight o'clock till ten, the military were in constant motion. The extent of these precautions may be inferred from the fact that lines of pickets and patrols encircled the field of death for fifteen miles, and that over five hundred troops were posted about the scaffold. Nearly three thousand militia soldiers were on the ground. There were not more than four hundred citizens present; for the fears of a servile insurrection, or an anti-slavery invasion, had kept them at home to watch the movements of their slaves. REDPATH'S *LIFE OF CAPTAIN JOHN BROWN*

Description of the Field of Death

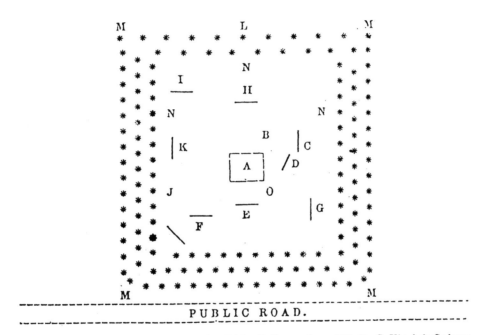

DESCRIPTION OF THE FIELD. — A, Scaffold; B, Generals and Staff; C, Virginia Cadets; D, Cadet Howitzers, with cannon pointed at scaffold; E, Richmond Company; F, Winchester Continentals; G, Fauquier Cavalry; H, Company A of Richmond; I, Alexandria Riflemen; K, Riflemen, and part of Capt. Ashby's Cavalry, to keep order in the small crowd. J, Hunter's Guard, at entrance gate, supported by a piece of Artillery under command of Lieut. Green of the United States Marines; L, Woods scoured by the Woodis Rifles, to have the first brush at the enemy, if approaching from Harper's Ferry; M M M M, Pickets of the Fauquier Cavalry; N N N, Two lines of Sentries; O, Petersburg Grays, as Body Guard to prisoner in wagon.

This telegram was sent from Charlestown to Vergennes, Vermont, on Dec. 2, 1859. Brown's body traveled by railroad to Vergennes, then crossed Lake Champlain and traveled by horse and wagon to his North Elba farm.

Vergennes, Dec. 2d 1859 4 o'clock 45 minutes
from Charlestown to CJ and CO Stevens

John Brown was taken to the scaffold in a furniture wagon about 11:00. He spoke freely to the soldiers around him. The body hung ___ minutes. He died apparently easy. The body will be sent to Harpers Ferry at 4:00. He was hanged at a quarter past 11:00.

John Brown's Will

CHARLESTOWN, JEFFERSON CO., VA., Dec., 1859

I give to my son John Brown, Jr., my surveyor's compass and other surveyor's articles if found; also, my old granite monument, now at North Elba, N.Y., to receive upon its two sides a further inscription, as I will hereafter direct; said stone monument, however, to remain at North Elba so long as *any of my children and my wife* may remain there as resident.

I give to my son Jason Brown my silver watch with my name engraved on the inner case.

I give to my son Owen Brown my double-spring opera-glass, and my rifle gun, (if found,) presented to me at Worchester, Mass. It is globe-sighted and new. I give also to the same son fifty dollars in cash, to be paid him from the proceeds of my father's estate, in consideration of his terrible suffering in Kansas, and his crippled condition from his childhood.

I give to my son Solomon Brown fifty dollars in cash, to be paid him from my father's estate, as an offset to the first two cases above named.

I give to my daughter Ruth Thompson my large old Bible, containing the family record.

I give to each of my sons, and to each of my *other* daughters, my son-in-law Henry Thompson, and to each of my daughters-in-law, as good a copy of the Bible as can be purchased at some bookstore in New York or Boston, at a cost of five dollars each in cash, to be paid out of the proceeds of my father's estate.

I give to each of my grandchildren that may be living when my father's estate is settled, as good a copy of the Bible as can be purchased (as above) at a cost of three dollars each.

All the Bibles to be purchased at one and the same time, for cash, on the best terms.

I desire to have ($50) fifty dollars *each* paid out of the final proceeds of my father's estate to the following named persons, to wit: To Allen Hammond, Esq., of Rockville, Tolland County, Conn., *or* to George Kellogg, Esq., former agent of the New England Company at that place, *for the use and benefit of that company.* Also, fifty dollars to Silas Havens, formerly of Lewisburg, Summitt County, O., at Canton, who sued my father in his lifetime, through Judge Humphrey and Mr. Upson of Akron, to be paid by J.R. Brown to the man in person, if he can be found. His name I cannot remember. My father made a compromise with the man by taking our house and lot at Manneville. I desire that any remaining balance that may become my due from my father's estate my be paid in equal amounts to my wife, and to each of my children, and to the widows of Watson and Owen Brown, by my brother.

JOHN AVIS, *Witness.*   JOHN BROWN

D.H. Cockrill erected this scaffold on the morning of Dec. 2, 1859. After Brown's execution it was dismantled and taken to the jail and stowed away. On the morning of Dec. 16, 1859, it was again erected at the same site for the execution of four additional raiders, then removed again and taken to the jail. On the morning of March 16, 1860, it was erected for the execution of Stevens and Hazlett, then removed to the jail once more. Soon afterwards Cockrill used some of the lumber to build a front porch on the residence of Daniel Sheets at the corner of Lawrence and Liberty streets in Charlestown. The porch was torn down in 1883 when Col. John M. Coyle purchased the property. The scaffold – or pieces – were exhibited at the 1893 Chicago World's Fair. Remains are on display in Charlestwon and Harpers Ferry.
WVSA

Opposite page – This contemporary proclamation was found in the Stutler collection. It is a farce, published just prior to Brown's execution and apparently posted around the town of Charlestown.

PROCLAMATION!

WHEREAS, Charlestown is now held by a Military force, and its citizens kept prisoners in their own domicils, and whereas, there are numerous Reports, Proclamations, Fizzles, and other divers fuzzy guzzys, issued by the Governor, Commanding and Chief officers, as well as other Small "toot horns" of the same kind by the Assistant Prosecuting Attorney, and the Mayor, Sheriff, &c. Now, be it known by the citizens of Charlestown and its vicinity, that I, Gen. Fugo Tumblebug, by virtue of the authority vested in me by Lieut. Common Sense, do hereby issue the following orders.

The Soldiers, for fear of an attack by Brown's men, will remain in their Barracks, as in case they expose themselves on the streets, they may run the risk of being hurt.

The General commanding, the Mayors, Attorneys, Colonels, Majors, Captains, Lieutenants and Corporals being *more numerous* than the rank and file, and therefore, of more consequence, are hereby *particularly* warned to remain in their Quarters, as in case of attack, *especially during the night*, the citizens who are able and willing to defend the town from all attacks, either by Brown's men or anybody else, may be incommoded in the performance of their duties. All of the above mentioned Honorables, will be arrested and Court Martialed, if found disregarding this order.

Citizens of the State of Virginia and of the Southern States, and the well disposed citizens of the Northern States, are requested to visit our town as heretofore, and they will be protected by the citizens from the insults of the mushroom, corn-stalk military, now quartered among us.

Citizens of the town will hereafter be allowed to pass to their homes and places of business, without being arrested as insurgents or nigger stealers.

By order

GEN. TUMBLEBUG,

Commander-in-Chief.

BOB DUNGHILL,

Military Secretary.

Charlestown, November 30th, 1859.

N. B. Citizens from other portions of the State, desirous of witnessing Ossawattama's *persecution* will be protected from the "woepons" of the valliant Cornstalkers, as the design of hanging him in public was to allow everybody a sight at him, as a warning to all future nigger-stealers.

P. S. Come, one! come all! The military shan't monopolize the show!

JOHN BROWN LEAVING JAIL, ON HIS WAY TO THE SCAFFOLD·

A contemporary drawing showing the procession to the scaffold along George Street in Charlestown. The large building on the left shows the back of the county jail and its exercise yard where Brown was kept. Brown is sitting on his coffin in a wagon in the center of the drawing. NPS HF-516

DEATH FOR TREASON !

CHARLESTOWN CRIMINAL EXECUTIONS.

UNCLE SAM'S NATIONAL EXPRESS!

Urged for the solemn and friendly consideration of the American People, by JAMES STERRET, *the sightless American Traveller and Unionist.*

SPEED ye this Express through our States,
Welcome your friend, unbar your gates;
Admit the blind man, freely choose
Him to assist—let none refuse.

Ye Friends of Peace, attend his call,
Our Nation's threatened with a fall;
Rebels would break the chain of Union,
And thus destroy our State communion.

When savage passions rule mankind,
Mischief will always be designed;
Like angry dogs, fools will delight
In ranc'rous hate, to growl and fight.

When wolfish men, with Judas' faces,
Through frauds engross official places,
Ruffians and thieves, like beasts of prey,
May growl for booty, night and day.

When fiends would murderous deeds commit,
And for perdition thus grow fit.
Loud cries and shrieks we soon may hear
Among the friends we hold most dear.

When brethren's blood cries from the ground,
Ere Vengeance scatters death around,—
Ere war, or pestilence, or dearth,
Shall scourge our quarter of the earth.

Let hostile parties yield to reason,
And justice crush all deeds of treason,
Let patriots gain the world's applause,
By prompt enforcement of our laws.

NOTES.

JOHN BROWN, the savage traitor, who was guilty of the most atrocious theft, robbery and murder, in KANSAS, several years ago, and who made an inglorious attack on HARPER'S FERRY, on the 17th of OCTOBER, 1859, on which occasion he and his fellow-conspirators were defeated, was hung in CHARLESTOWN, on the 2nd of DECEMBER following—and on the 16th of the same month, COOK and COPPOC, *white men*, and GREEN and COPELAND, *negroes*, were hung for having been associated with him in similar crimes and misdemeanors.— Again, to-day, (FRIDAY, the 16th of MARCH,) between the hours of 12 and 2, AARON D. STEVENS and ABSALOM HAZELETT, were executed for the most nefarious transgressions against the Constitution and Laws of the United States.
—— Let Demagogues, Black Republicans, *alias* Amalgamators, Official Traitors, and especially all who have sworn the oath of allegiance for the maintenance of our sacred Constitution and Laws, remember not to perjure themselves—let all such especially remember the awful fate of Brown, Cook, Coppoc, Stevens, Hazelett, Green and Copeland, and from their example take warning, not to rebel against the Government instituted by the Fathers of our Country at a vast expense of blood and treasure. Let disunionists, whether of a public or private character, be regarded as political incendiaries who would burn and destroy the glorious fabric of of our liberty. ——
CHARLESTOWN, MARCH 16th, 1860.
N. B. The above lines (with appropriate additions and revisions,) have been copied from a sheet of verses and notes which were printed and circulated in Charlestown, on the day of the execution of Stevens and Hazelett, and are now made fit to set up in frames, or on boards, as an awful warning to Black Republican maniacs; and also, as an indelible record of the ignominious death of Brown, the notorious ringleader, and of the other six of his white and black confederates, who were executed on the gallows as principal conspirators against the sacred laws and peace of our nation.

Charles C. Conklyn at age 87 was the last survivor of the Special Military Detail of six men to guard John Brown, from the time of his capture at Harpers Ferry to his execution at Charlestown. WVSA

The well-known actor John Wilkes Booth joined the Richmond Grays just before Brown's execution. He got sick after viewing the event. In 1865 Booth's name would join Brown's in the pages of American history. USAMHI

Nimrod Milton Green had this photo taken of himself while on guard duty in Harpers Ferry in 1859. Green was one of the original members of the "Black Horse Troop" from the Warrenton, Virginia area. They all rode black horses and wore black plumes in their hats. As part of the Virginia Militia, they were called up to guard Brown while he was in jail in Harpers Ferry. Brown is said to have admired the gentlemanly conduct of these young men from Fauquier County. The troop became the 4th Virginia Cavalry, which Green enlisted in, on April 25, 1861. He was captured twice during the war and after the war moved to Augusta County, Virginia, where he died in 1882. ROBERT D. WALKER, CUMBERLAND, R.I.

Brown mounts the scaffold, from *Frank Leslie's Illustrated Newspaper,* Dec. 17, 1859.

Sketch of Brown's execution by David C. Hitchcock for the *New York Illustrated News.*

THE EXECUTION OF JOHN BROWN.

The Cadets at Harpers Ferry
The Hanging of John Brown
The cadets' first military expedition

The commander of the State Arsenal at Lexington had offered the services of the Virginia Military Institute Cadets in preserving law and order after the John Brown Raid at Harpers Ferry. The Governor had declined the offer but requested that the corps be ready in case of a call.

On Nov. 19, 1859, the corps of cadets listened to an order from Superintendent F.H. Smith stating that in anticipation of orders from the Governor for the services of a portion of the Corps of Cadets on special duty at or near Charlestown, Virginia, those cadets who had been detailed for such service would hold themselves in readiness to take up the line of March at a moment's notice. The infantry would be under the command of Major Gilham and the artillery detachment under the command of Maj. T.J. Jackson, who had been especially prepared for the use of Howitzers.

The Governor's long-expected order of movement was sent from Harpers Ferry on Nov. 22 at 3:56 p.m.—it read:

General W.H. Harmon or
J.H. Skinner   Staunton

"Despatch message to Col. F.H. Smith, Superintendent of Virginia Military Institute, that his corps of Howitzers is required at Charlestown by the first of December next. He will come ahead and let his corps follow."

The message was received at the Institute early in the afternoon of the following day and Colonel Smith set out for Charlestown at once. Before leaving, he informed the Governor of arrangements that had been made. He stated that a detachment of 80 cadets with a battery of Howitzers had been kept ready and that the command was provided with all the appliances for taking care of themselves upon the field of duty, that the commissary had his cooks and cooking implements in order. He stated that Messrs. Harman and Co. had placed their stages and entire stock at Lexington and Staunton at the Superintendent's command and would transport the detachment at a moment's call, free of charge.

Other orders reached Lexington at 8:00 p.m. on Nov. 25 and two hours later the detachment of 85 cadets, 64 infantry and 21 artillery with two Howit-

zers were en route. The cadets traveled by stagecoach to Staunton, then proceeded by train to Washington, D.C.

Colonel Smith, accompanied by Maj. J.T.L. Preston, arrived ahead of the cadets. The cadet schedule called for reveille at 6:00 a.m.—breakfast at 7:30 a.m.—guard mounting at 8:30 a.m.—dinner at 2:00 p.m.—dress parade at 3:30 p.m., and retreat at 6:00 p.m. No cadet was permitted to be absent from quarters after retreat at 6:00 p.m. Major Jackson in a letter to his wife wrote that about a thousand troops assembled but everything was quiet, and that about six others slept in the room with him.

The next few days were occupied in picket duty, special drills and instruction pertaining to handling mobs. Four companies of United States Army troops under Lt. Col. Robert E. Lee arrived on Nov. 30 to help keep order.

The day before the execution the following order was given to the cadets:

"Every cadet will have his musket in perfect firing order for inspection this evening at 3-1/2 o'clock and 12 rounds of ball cartridges in good order in his cartridge box. The cadets will lie down in their clothes and accoutrements, with their arms loaded by their sides, to be ready at a moments warning for any emergency tonight."

The muskets, sabres and ammunition used by the cadets on this expedition had been specially issued from the Arsenal and were not those customarily used by the corps of cadets.

Sixty-six-year-old Edmund Ruffin had begged permission to join the cadets for a single day in order to see the execution and stood among them in his cadet overcoat. He later wrote "when I made my appearance, I could see what was very natural and excusable that my position was very amusing, and perhaps ludicrous, to the young men and it required, all the restraint of their good manners to hide their merriment." he later referred to the "trim cadets from Virginia Military Institute, in their scarlet flannel shirts crossed by two white belts and given dignity and maturity by their long gray overcoats." (In 1887 the lining of the gray overcoats was made of red flannel. In 1859 the corps appeared to have worn red flannel shirts and were referred to by Major Preston in his account of the execution of Brown.)

Jackson in writing to his wife of the execution stated that the gibbet was erected in a field southeast of town, and the Brown's face upon the scaffold was turned a little east of south and in front of him were the cadets, under the command of Major Gilham. "My command," he wrote, "was still in front of the cadets all facing south. One howitzer I assigned to Mr. Trueheart on the left of the cadets, with the other. I remained on the right."

An account written by Maj. J.T.L. Preston, who was on the staff of Colonel Smith and dated Dec. 2, 1859, stated "that Col. Smith had been assigned the superintendency of the execution and he (Smith) and his staff were the only mounted officers on the ground until the Maj. General (Taliaferro) and his own staff appeared. The cadets were immediately in rear of the gallows, a howitzer on the right and left, a little behind, so as to sweep the field. They were uniformed in red flannel shirts, which gave them a gay, dashing zouave look, and were exceedingly becoming especially at the Battery. They were flanked obliquely by two corps, the Richmond Grays and Company F which, inferior in appearance to the cadets were superior to any other company I ever saw outside of the regular army."

The corps of cadets and other troops remained at Charlestown several days after the execution and at first it was the intention to hold them until after five of his conspirators were hung on Dec. 16, but things quieted down to such an extent that the plans were changed. The cadets left by train at 10:30 a.m. on the sixth for Richmond where they had been ordered. The cadet detachment proceeded to Washington and spent the night there before going on to Richmond. The cadets under the command of Major Gilham arrived in Richmond on Dec. 7 and were quartered at the St. Charles Hotel. Colonel Smith, with the Howitzer Corps did not arrive due to the difficulty of getting his guns on the train. At one o'clock (Dec. 7) the cadets paraded and marched to the Richmond, Fredericksburg and Potomac Railroad depot to receive their Colonel, but to their great disappointment, he had stopped at Fredericksburg to await the arrival of an extra train to bring down his howitzers. Colonel Smith in a letter to Lawson Botts, dated Dec. 14, 1859, thanking him for his comfortable meals and other courtesies, stated that the return trip had been a very unpleasant one, more so to himself and the artillery detachment for they missed connection with the Fredericksburg boat and thus were detained at Fredericksburg for six hours. They reached Richmond at midnight.

The cadets were dressed in gray bunting, with gray pants and wearing their white cross belts just as they did at Charlestown.

The cadets on Dec. 8 drilled on the Capitol Square under Major Jackson and the next morning left for Lexington. The worst part of the trip before them and letters tell of the dreadful ride from Staunton to Lexington.

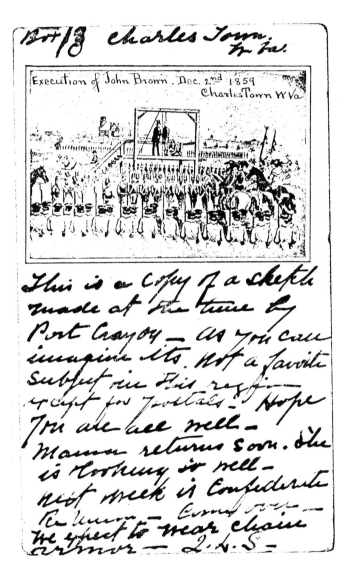

This is a copy of a sketch made at the time by Port Crayon—as you can imagine its not a favorite subject in this region except for postals. Hope you are all well. Mama returns soon. She is looking so well—Next week is Confederate Reunion—come over—We expect to wear chain armor. J.L.S.

This Porte Crayon sketch was apparently made on the spot but was rejected by *Harpers Weekly*. It shows the VMI cadets in the foreground along with Edmond Ruffin. Strother (Crayon) even drew himself at the bottom of the stairs. WVSA

Posted proclamation warning all strangers found loitering in the county were subject to arrest. There was concern that Brown's followers would try and rescue him before his scheduled execution on Dec. 2, so a large contingent of troops was requested to prevent this and to keep order. NPS, HF-664

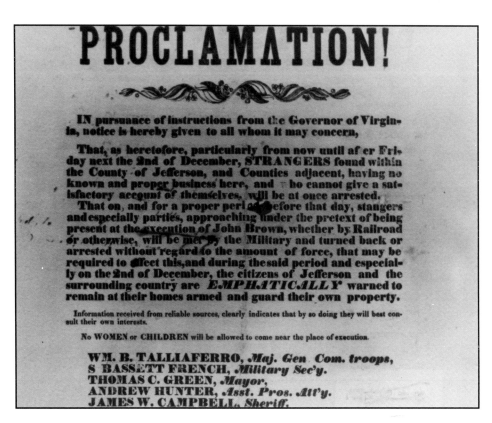

The trial of JOHN BROWN.

Mrs. JOHN BROWN.

The EXECUTION of JOHN BROWN in a stubble field, Near CHARLESTOWN, VA.

JOHN BROWN in his cell at Charlestown receiving the last visit from Newspaper Correspondents & Jail Officials, just before his Execution.

COOK & COPPIC, in their cell, just previous to their Execution, receiving a visit from Newspaper Artist and Correspondent.

Trial and Execution of John Brown. A montage made from illustrations in *Leslie's Weekly* in 1859. Lithograph by Robert F. Bennett, 1897. LC

The Hanging of John Brown*

This unpublished story of the execution by an eyewitness was lost for over 90 years until surfacing in the 1950s. The author was David Hunter Strother, who is better known under his *nom de plume* of Porte Crayon, and who was one of the literary lights of the middle period of the last century. Strother was present at the execution as the artist-writer representative of *Harper's Weekly*, but because his publishers found the John Brown theme too hot to handle, his sketches and news story of the hanging were rejected. Some little background notes are needed to make this Strother (Porte Crayon) manuscript clear to modern readers.

Not only was the day notable for the execution of John Brown, but in retrospect it can be seen as a milestone in the development of American journalism. Modern field reporting for American newspapers may well be said to have come of age in the "John Brown war." Never before had such an aggregation of professional writers and artists been sent from a distance by metropolitan newspapers to report an event.

Through fortuitous circumstance (he was calling on a young lady at Charlestown who later became his second wife) Strother was on the scene of the "John Brown war" from first to last. At Harpers Ferry on Monday morning, Oct. 17, he saw the militia skirmishing with the John Brown army of liberation, and on Tuesday morning he witnessed the final assault on the enginehouse where Brown, his surviving men and his citizen hostages had taken refuse. He attended the trial a few days later, held in the old pillared courthouse at Charlestown and was present when the sentence of death by hanging was pronounced.

Fresh from the scene, Strother's sketches and reports of the raid and trial were grabbed by *Harper's Weekly* and were given top position. *Leslie's Illustrated Newspaper*, then the only rival in the weekly pictorial field, had hurriedly dispatched Alfred Berghaus, one of its chief artists, to Harpers Ferry and was making a field day of the affair in full-page pictures and graphic stories. Strother's reporting did well for a few weeks, and *Harper's* was holding its own with *Leslie's*. Then came the explosion.

Strother came of an old Virginia family and was closely related by blood or marriage to most of the ruling families in the Potomac-Shenandoah area, nearly all of whom were slaveholders. Though himself an intense Unionist, he was by no means friendly to the abolition cause or to the immediate emancipation of slaves. He wanted to preserve the *status quo*. His treatment of the raid and raiders violently displeased the anti-slavery element in the North, and did not go far enough to please the pro-slavery advocated in the South. The *Weekly* soon came in for sharp criticism.

Thus caught between two fires, the *Weekly* dropped the John Brown story like a hot potato: it contented itself thereafter by publishing a news symposium, culled from the newspapers, inconspicuously placed in the "Domestic Intelligence" column.

Strother apparently was not advised of the change of policy. At least he was not recalled from duty. He continued to write and sketch down to the last act in the tragedy, but all this work went for naught.

The press was not tenderly treated at Charlestown. Gen. William B. Taliaferro, commander of the Virginia troops, looked with suspicion on all strangers and had publicly announced that he wanted no "abolitionists or Republicans" in Charlestown on the day of the execution. Many newspapermen were turned back at Baltimore. Henry S. Olcott, New York *Tribune*'s man, went to Petersburg, Virginia, and through Masonic connections made his way to Charlestown with the Petersburg Grays. Edward H. House, another *Tribune* man, spent weeks in Charlestown very much incognito. He needled and castigated the exasperated Virginia officers almost daily in the *Tribune*.

Strother had no difficulty in wangling an advantageous place. He was admitted to the staff of Andrew Hunter, his kinsman, special prosecutor at Brown's trial and the personal representative of Governor Wise. Strother took his position at the foot of the 13 steps that led to the scaffold platform.

Crosby S. Noyes, Washington *Star*'s man, said in his telegraphic dispatch: "Porte Crayon Strother, the artist, a thin, sickly-looking young man, with others visited the platform for a moment." But Andrew Hunter was more explicit in an article in the New Orleans *Times-Democrat*, Sept. 5, 1887: "While the body was hanging, Strother slipped up, raised the cap from his face and took a sketch of him hanging. He said that the celebrated Lydia Maria Child [a prominent abolitionist leader] had published that she wanted to have a portrait or likeness of Brown in every condition of life to hang in her room, and that he had taken this sketch to send her."

Strother wrote his story and made careful drawings of the execution scene, but when submitted to the Messrs. Harper both the story and sketches were rejected and returned to the artist-writer.

Less than 18 months later the Civil War started and Strother hastened to offer his services to the Union. He served well, through many campaigns and some 30 battles, and emerged a Brevet Brigadier General. When the war was over he resumed his connection with *Harper's*.

When he died at his home at Charlestown on Mar. 8, 1888, his papers and sketches were widely scattered. His manuscript story of the execution of John Brown, signed D.H.S., was found in the papers of a Shenandoah Valley family. It is published here with Strother's spelling and punctuation intact.

John Brown's Death and Last Words
by David Hunter Strother (Porte Crayon)

On Friday, December 2nd the notorious John Brown was executed at Charlestown, Virginia, according to the sentence of the law. It may be a matter of curiosity to the public, to know how a man, whose late acts have created so much disturbance, deported himself in his last hours. Although very guarded in his conversation on the subject, it was quite evident that up to a certain date, he indulged in the hope of a rescue or possibly a pardon. When, however, he ascertained that the Court of appeals had confirmed the sentence, and saw the formidable military preparations made to insure its execution, there was a marked change in his manner. The great gulf between the simple probability and the gorgon head of certainty was not passed without a visible struggle. He became more thoughtful & serious, less dogmatic in the expression of his opinions, and somewhat softened toward those who had treated him with civility & consideration (and this included all whose official duties had brought them in contact with him during his confinement).

He expressed a disinclination to receive visitors and sent for his wife whom he had heretofore refused to see. Their meeting, which took place in the afternoon of the 1st of December is represented to have been a most businesslike affair without visible emotion on either side.

On the morning of the 2nd, Brown sent for an eminent legal gentleman of Charlestown to write his will, or rather a codicil to a former will disposing of some property which had been overlooked. His manner then was cold & stony, his discourse altogether of business. After the completion of the writing, he enquired sharply and particularly about a dollar which had been mentioned in one of his letters but which had not come to hand. He was assured that all the money enclosed in letters had been delivered to him. This he insisted was an error, he had the letter mentioning the enclosure but the money was not there.

Unwilling to dispute, the gentleman said that the note might have been dropped accidentally and if found, the amount would be transmitted to his wife.

But Brown was by no means satisfied, and at length informed his visitor that in consideration of the service just rendered in writing his will, he might keep the dollar.

This the Lawyer politely but peremptorily declined, as he intended to accept no remuneration for what he had done, and again expressed a doubt as to whether the money had been sent.

The letter was produced. In the body of the writing the enclosure of the dollar was named, but on the margin, it was noted in pencil that it had been withdrawn & sent to his wife.

Thus was the mystery cleared up, to the very great apparent satisfaction of the old man and thus was concluded the last business transaction of his life. An hour after he was called on by the officers who were to convey him to the place of execution. His farewell scene with his late followers and fellow prisoners was peculiar and characteristic. To Coppock and the two negroes he gave a scolding and a quarter each, remarking that he had now no further use for money. To Stephens who had occupied the same room with him he also gave a quarter, and charged them all to die like men and not to betray their friends. To Cook he gave nothing but sharp & scathing words charging him with falsehood & cowardice. Cook denied the charges and attempted to dispute the points with his former commander but was authoritatively silenced. As to the question of veracity between them, circumstances seem decidedly to favour the truth of Cook's statement, and he may be readily excused for not caring to prolong a dispute with a man on his road to the gallows. Governor Wise and others, who were imposed upon by Brown's apparent frankness during his first examination at Harpers Ferry, have long since had occasion to change their opinions in regard to his honesty & veracity.

However, of all these matters I was not an eye nor ear witness, but had them from those who were.

As early as nine o'clock on Friday morning, the field (adjoining the town of Charlestown), which had been selected for the place of execution, was occupied by a considerable body of soldiers, horse, foot & artillery. A line of sentinels encircled the enclosure preventing access by the fences and a guard of infantry and artillery was posted at the gate by which spectators were required to enter.

I repaired to the field some time before the appointed hour that I might choose a convenient position to witness the final ceremony. The gibbet was erected on a gentle swell that commanded a view of the country for many miles around. From the scaffold which I ascended the view was of surpassing beauty. On every side stretching away into the blue distance were broad & fertile fields dotted with corn shocks and white farm houses glimmering through the leafless trees—emblems of prosperity and peace. Hard by was the pleasant village with its elegant suburban residences and bordering the picture east & west were the blue mountains thirty miles apart. In the Blue Ridge which lay to the eastward appeared the deep gap through which the Potomac and Shenandoah pour their united streams at Harpers Ferry, eight miles distant.

Near at Hand stood long lines of soldiers resting on their arms while all the neighboring hills in sight were crowded with squadrons of cavalry. The balmy south wind was blowing which covered the landscape with a warm & dreamy haze reminding one rather of May than December. From hence thought I, the old man may see the spot where his enormous crime first took the form of action—he may see the beautiful land his dark plots had devoted to bloody ruin, he may see in the gleaming of a thousand swords and these serried lines of bayonets—what might be well calculated to make wiser men than he, thoughtful.

At eleven o'clock escorted by a strong column of soldiers the Prisoner entered the field. He was seated in a furniture waggon on his coffin with his arms tied down above the elbows, leaving the forearms free. The driver with two others occupied the front seat while the jailer sat in the after part of the wagon. I stood with a group of half a dozen gentlemen near the steps of the scaffold when the Prisoner was driven up. He wore the same seedy and dilapidated dress that he had at Harpers Ferry and during his trial, but his rough boots had given place to a pair of particoloured slippers and he wore a low crowned broad brimmed hat (the first time I had ever seen him with a hat). He had entirely recovered from his wounds and looked decidedly better & stronger than when I last saw him. As he neared the gibbet his face wore a grim & greisly smirk which, but for the solemnity of the occasion might have suggested ideas of the ludicrous. He stepped from the waggon with surprising agility and walked hastily toward the scaffold pausing a moment as he passed our group to wave his pinioned arm & bid us good morning. I thought I could observe in this a trace of bravado—but perhaps I was mistaken, as his natural manner was short, ungainly and hurried. He mounted the steps of the scaffold with the same alicrity and there as if by previous arrangement, he immediately took off his hat and offered his neck for the halter which was as promptly adjusted by Mr. Avis the jailor. A white muslin cap or hood was then drawn over his face and the Sheriff not remembering that his eyes were covered requested him to advance to the platform. The Prisoner replied in his usual tone, "you will have to guide me there."

The breeze disturbing the arrangement of the hood the Sheriff asked his assistant for a pin. Brown raised his hand and directed him to the collar of his coat where several old pins were quilted in. The Sheriff took the pin & completed his work.

He was accordingly led forward to the drop the halter hooked to the beam and the officers supposing that the execution was to follow immediately took leave of him. In doing so, the Sheriff enquired if he did not want a handkercheif to throw as a signal to cut the drop. Brown replied, "no I dont care: I dont want you to keep me waiting unnecessarily."

These were his last words, spoken with that sharp nasal twang peculiar to him, but spoken quietly & civilly, without impatience or the slightest apparent emotion. In this position he stood for five minutes or more, while the troops that composed the escort were wheeling into the positions assigned them. I stood within a few paces of him and watched narrowly during these trying moments to see if there was any indication of his giving way. I detected nothing of the sort. He had stiffened himself for the drop and waited motionless 'till it came.

During all these movements no sound was heard by the quick stern words of military command, & when these ceased a dead silence reigned. Colonel Smith said to the Sheriff in a low voice—"we are ready." The civil officers descended from the scaffold. One who stood near me whispered earnestly—"He trembles, his knees are shaking." "You are mistaken," I replied, "It is the scaffold that shakes under the footsteps of the officers." The Sheriff struck the rope a sharp blow with a hatchet, the platform fell with a crash—a few convulsive struggles & a human soul had gone to judgement.

Thus died John Brown, the strange, stern old man; hard and uncouth in character as he was in personal appearance, undemonstrative and emotionless as an indian. In the manner of his death there was nothing dramatic or sympathetic. There was displayed neither the martial dignity of a chieftain nor the reckless bravado of a highwayman—neither the exalted enthusiasm of a martyr nor the sublime resignation of a christian. His voice and manner were precisely the same as if he had been bargaining for a sixpence worth of powder slightly anxious to get through the job but not uncivilly impatient. A stony stoicism, an easy indifference, so perfectly simulated that one could hardly perceive it was acting.

As with John Brown, so it seemed with the spectators around him. Of Sympathy there was none—of triumph no word nor sign. The fifteen hundred soldiers stood mute and motionless at their posts—The thousand civic spectators looked on in silence. At the end of half an hour the body was taken down & placed in the coffin—the people went home, the troops wheeled into columns & marched to their quarters, and the day concluded with the calm & quiet of a New England sabbath.

No man capable of reflection could have witnessed that scene without being deeply impressed with the truth that then & there was exhibited, not the vengeance of an outraged people, but the awful majesty of the law.

DAVID H. STROTHER

*This article was written by Boyd B. Stutler in 1954 and is reproduced here with some minor editing. All spelling was left as originally written.

Charlestown, Va, 2ᵈ December, 1859.
I John Brown am now quite certain that the crimes of this guilty, land: will never be purged away; but with Blood: I had as I now think: vainly flattered myself that without very much bloodshed; it might be done.

Brown wrote this, his last prophecy, on Dec. 2, 1859, the day of his execution. It reads:

Charlestown, Va., 2ⁿᵈ December 1859

I John Brown am now quite certain that the crimes of this <u>guilty, land</u>: <u>will</u> never be purged <u>away</u>; but with Blood. I had <u>as I now think</u>: vaily flattered myself that without <u>very much</u> bloodshed; it might be done.

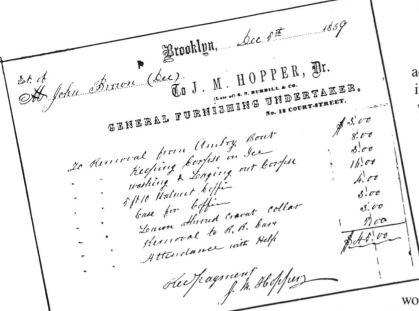

Brown's Journey Back to New York

After Brown's execution on Dec. 2 his wife accompanied his body to New York City where it was kept on ice. For $45 a new walnut coffin was made along with arrangements for the body to be taken to the farm in North Elba. An honor guard stood vigil over the casket in the county seat courthouse at Elizabethtown. Six days after his execution, Brown was buried on his farm with friends and family at the site. From Vermont, Unitarian minister Joshua Young came to lead the prayers. When he returned home, he was relieved of his church duties because of this service. In 1899, Young would again travel to North Elba to preside over the reburial of Brown's son, Oliver and ten others.

JOHN BROWN IN HIS COFFIN—"His mouth was partly open and his eyes somewhat protruded from their sockets."

John Brown was described as "striking figure—not really tall but so weasel-lean that his five-foot-ten inches seemed so; a slow, springy walk; foxy-brown, bristly hair shot with gray, grass-thick down over his narrow forehead; and glaring blue eyes."*

*Furnas, *The Road to Harpers Ferry*, page 19.

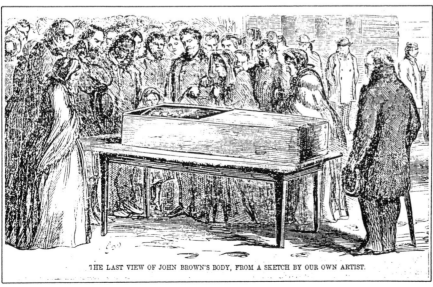

THE LAST VIEW OF JOHN BROWN'S BODY, FROM A SKETCH BY OUR OWN ARTIST.

These two drawings by L. Thomas Nash appeared in the *New York Illustrated News* in December, 1859.

Abolitionist James Redpath, who had been with Brown in Kansas, wrote of his execution:

"There was but one spasmodic effort of the hands to clutch at the neck, but for nearly five minutes the limbs jerked and quivered. He seemed to retain an extraordinary hold on life.... After the body had dangled in mid-air for twenty minutes, it was examined by the surgeons for signs of life. First the Charlestown physicians went up and made their examination, and after them, the military surgeons...."

Richmond, Va., January 30th, 1860.

To the Ladies of Charlestown:

The approving testimonial presented, Dear Ladies, in your name, by Governor Wise, would alone, and independently of the beautiful accompanying token, have been out of all proportion to the unimportant services so kindly alluded to by you.

I thank you, especially, for thus setting the seal of your approbation on the acts of our late Commander in Chief, that great and patriotic Governor, who at the first alarm, threw around you an impregnable wall of chivalry, and himself stood ready to shed his blood in your defence. His energetic measures and prompt display of forces will have a lasting effect, and render improbable any future fanatical raid upon our border. But should Providence otherwise direct, and allot to our hands the infliction of further punishment on our enemies, I ask no higher privilege than a place in the ranks of your own citizen soldiers, as brave and true as any on earth.

Believe me, Dear Ladies, every volunteer who rallied to the scene of danger, at the call of our Great Chief, will join me in admiration and gratitude, in view of the self-sacrificing spirit of the citizens of Charlestown, and especially of your own unwearied attention to the health and comfort of the volunteer soldiery.

The remembrance of your kindness to my comrades will be no less cherished than the inestimable gift and unmerited honor you have thought proper to confer on

Your most obedient,

Humble servant,

J. Lucius Davis.

Col. J. Lucius Davis was in charge of the troops in Charlestown during the trial of John Brown. On Jan. 30, 1860, Davis sent this letter to the Ladies of Charlestown thanking them for housing officers in their homes. WVSA

Order 3

I. The following order of arrangements will govern the troops of this Command on tomorrow, in connection with the Execution of the prisoners Stephens & Hazlett

1. Captain Rowan's company will occupy the designated in line in front of the Gallows at 10. A. M.

2. Captain Botts' company will take position on the right flank of Capt Rowan's

3. Capt Boteler's Company will constitute the escort of the prisoners from the jail, and on reaching the ~~leaving~~ the scaffold will take position as a flanking Company on the left of Capt. Rowan's company.

4. Capt. Reinhart's Company of Cavalry will occupy the ground immediately ~~in~~ within the fenced enclosure of the field of execution, to prevent all persons from entering the field Except at the main gate, & to assist in preserving order in the enclosure.

5. Capt. Campbell's Company will be detailed on duty as special sentinels to maintain order within the enclosure, & to keep all persons from entering within the line of sentinels.

II Lt. Col. Grantham is assigned to the duty of placing the Companies in their designated positions.

III Major Lewis is assigned to the Command of the escort from the jail.

On the night previous to the execution, the [...] will be doubled, around the [jail], and precautions taken to prevent the escape [of] prisoners. Major Hooff is detailed on as special officer of the day on the [...]. + he will see that the sentinels [are properly] instructed in their duty + are [...]

By order of Col. J. T. Gibson

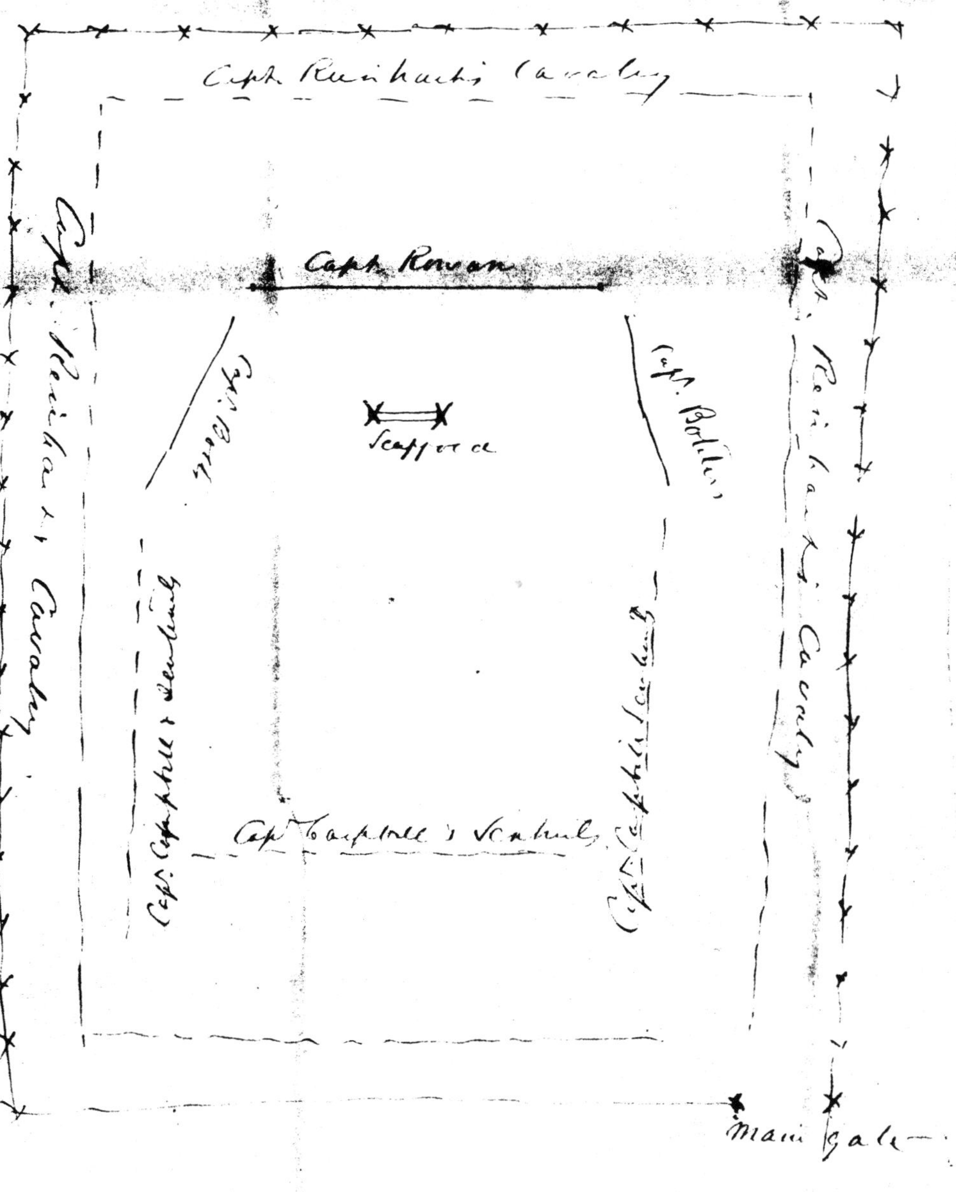

General order by Col. John T. Gibson from the Headquarters of the 55th Regiment of the Virginia Militia, dated March 15, 1860, to designate company duties at the execution of Albert Hazlett (1837-1860) and Aaron Dwight Stevens (1831-1860) on March 16, 1860. The diagram below, in Gibson's handwriting, details the companies' assigned positions on the field of execution. JCM

H5

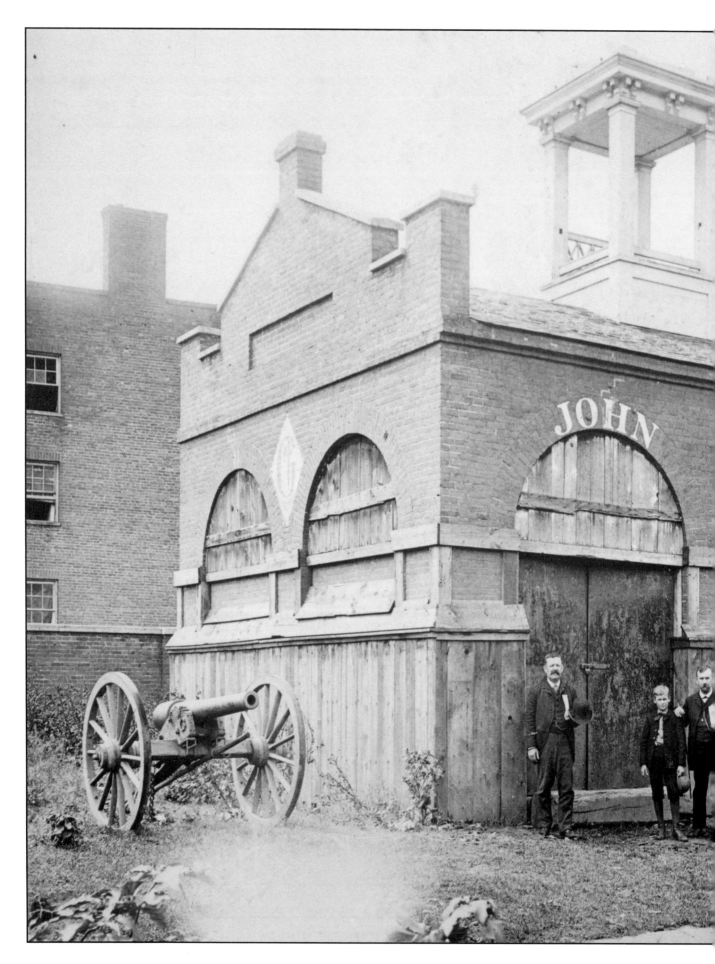

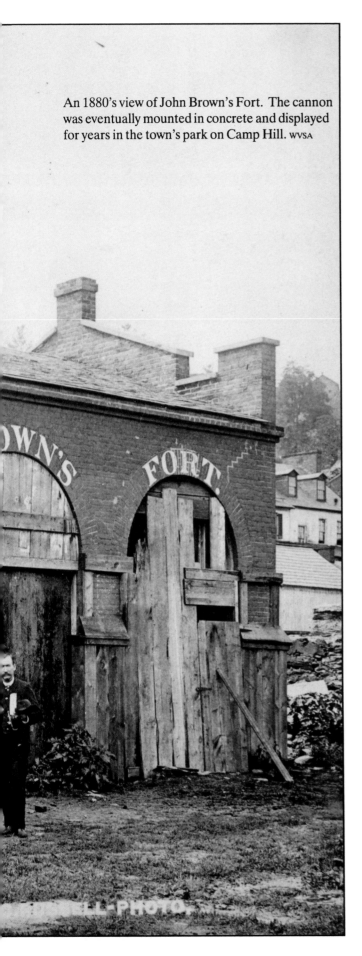

An 1880's view of John Brown's Fort. The cannon was eventually mounted in concrete and displayed for years in the town's park on Camp Hill. wvsa

John Brown's Fort
The Arsenal Enginehouse

The building was built in 1848 as a fire enginehouse for the United States Arsenal at Harpers Ferry. In it were located two hand fire engines with hose carts and the usual fire appliances used before the days of steam fire engines.

The two engines in the building at the time of the raid were the *Rough and Ready,* an old-style bucket machine, and the *Liberty*, a modern double-deck suction engine. They were used by Brown to barricade the enginehouse doors. When the Civil War started the Confederates took the two engines south where they were later demolished.

The building was 35 and one-half feet by 24 feet, one story, built of brick, covered with slate and had copper gutters and downspouts. It was the only armory building to escape burning during the Civil War. During and after the war the building was a victim of vandalism by troops and curiosity-seekers. The bell in the cupola was removed in 1861.

In 1892 the building was dismantled brick by brick and transported to Chicago to be exhibited at the 1893 World's Columbian Exposition. It was only opened for 10 days with very few people interested in viewing it. Before it was to be converted to a stable, Kate Field, a newswoman from Washington, D.C., raised money to return it to the Harpers Ferry area. She rebuilt it on a lot three miles from Harpers Ferry in 1895 in hopes of starting a national park in the area. Fields died in 1896, and A. Murphy, who already owned the property, resumed control.

There the building stood until the 50th anniversary of the raid in 1909 when the local all-black Storer College raised $2,000 to buy it and move it to their campus on Camp Hill next to Brackett Hall. The college closed in 1954 and the building and grounds were purchased by the National Park Service.

The Park Service moved the building in 1968 to a location less than 200 feet from its original site, which is now covered by a railroad embankment.

In the 1880s a committee was formed by Frederick Douglass to raise $10,000 $12,000 to place a granite shaft at the site of the enginehouse. It was dedicated in 1895 along with five cast iron markers placed by the War Department describing the capture of Harpers Ferry.

In 1864 the enginehouse was used as a magazine for gunpowder as the burned-out armory was the site of a Union Army quartermaster depot. NPS

Photo circa 1882-86 showing advertising aimed at rail travelers painted on surrounding walls and buildings. Many Harpers Ferry structures can be seen; St. John's Church, Marmion Row, Harper House, former armory grounds, armory gate and wall. NPS HF-379

This view was probably taken just prior to its dismantling in 1892 for shipment to Chicago. The building is in a state of deterioration with a make-shift plank entry door. NPS HF-1159

An 1898 scene of the fort site after the railroad embankment was built. The monument was placed at the approximate site of the fort. The five cast-iron markers were placed there by the War Department describing the capture of Harpers Ferry by Confederate forces in 1862. They were removed years ago. NPS

The fort in July 1890. Loudoun Heights can be seen in the background. NPS HF-570

On Oct. 1, 1862, President Abraham Lincoln visited Harpers Ferry and John Brown's Fort. He was there to see Gen. Edwin V. Sumner at his Camp Hill headquarters. USAMHI

The great flood of 1889 inundated Harpers Ferry and swept away the Shenandoah River Bridge. The fort can be seen in the middle of the photo. NPS

The fort standing in a field on the Murphy Farm, three miles from Harpers Ferry on Bolivar Heights. It stood here from 1895 to 1909 when it was reconstructed on the campus of Storer College as a symbol of the college's mission and as a preservation effort. NPS HF-77

Interior view of the fort in 1936 when it was situated on the Storer College Campus. NPS HF-564

Top:Members of the Colored Women's League pose before the fort when it was sitting on the Murphy Farm property. The women were attending their annual meeting in Washington, D.C. in July 1896. NPS HF-599

Middle: The fort on Storer College campus held a small museum. Brackett Hall (now demolished) is in the background, circa 1923. NPS HF-581

Bottom: The fort, circa 1950's on the campus of Storer College.

Moving John Brown's fort to its final resting place in 1968. NPS

In 1906, the second annual meeting of the Niagara Movement, an early civil rights organization led by W.E.B. DuBois, was held on the Storer College campus. The last day of the meeting, Aug. 17, was John Brown's Day.

John Brown's Day started early. At six in the morning his admirers left the site of the convention, Storer College, a Baptist-controlled school founded in 1867 for blacks, to make a pilgrimage to the brick-walled fire-engine house, a mile away. As they neared their destination they formed a procession, single file, led by Owen M. Waller, a physician from Brooklyn. Defying stone and stubble, Waller took off his shoes and socks and walked barefoot as if treading on holy ground.

Halting outside the engine house, the pilgrims listened to prayer, followed by remarks from Richard T. Greener, Harvard's first black graduate and former dean of the Howard University Law School....

Following Greener's reminiscences, the group marched around the fort single file. Almost as if to keep in step singing "The Battle Hymn of the Republic," supplementing it with additional verses from the John Brown song.

— Benjamin Quarles, from *Allies for Freedom*, 1974

The 1895 granite shaft at the approximate site of the enginehouse. The base of the shaft is about the height of the fort's cupola.

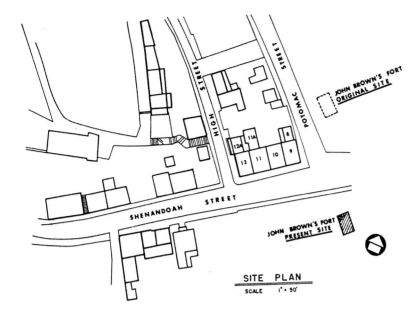

HISTORIC STRUCTURES
REPORT DRAWINGS
JOHN BROWN'S FORT
HARPERS FERRY NATIONAL
HISTORICAL PARK
NATIONAL PARK SERVICE

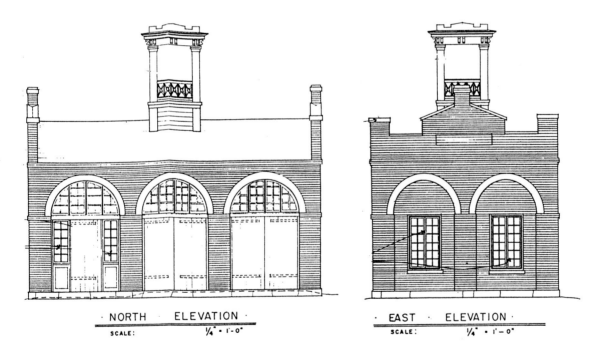

The Fort at the 1893 Chicago World's Fair

Ex-Congressman A.J. Holmes of Iowa formed a company in 1892 to buy the fort from the Baltimore & Ohio Railroad and move it, brick by brick, to Chicago. It was enclosed in a frame structure, stocked with Brown artifacts and opened for exhibit to people attending the 1893 World's Columbian Exhibition. Since it was not on the actual fairgrounds attendance was poor and the company soon closed the exhibit. The historic enginehouse languished at the site for several years, eventually becoming a stable for a local department store. When it was to be razed, Kate Field and others purchased it and brought it back to the Harpers Ferry area in September 1895. The building could not be placed on its original site as the Baltimore & Ohio Railroad had relocated its tracks over the site in 1892 with a new embankment. So the historic building was placed on the farm of Alexander Murphy on Bolivar Heights, about three miles from its original location.

The Brown family house as it looked in the 1890s. The porches were not part of the original home and were removed in the 1950s restoration. The house now looks as it did in 1859. WVSA

The John Brown Farm

John Brown's Farm and Grave

In 1846 Brown heard of the abolitionist Gerrit Smith of Petersboro, New York. Smith had opened up thousands of acres of land in the upper region of New York State for the express purpose of small farm cultivation. Much of this land was in the untamed Adirondack Wilderness.

These parcels, averaging 40 acres each, were given away to free blacks from New York. These people came from all walks of life but few knew the fundamentals of farming. Most of the land Smith gave away was unfit for cultivation, it was either low and swampy or on mountain slopes, rocky and inaccessible.

The community was called "Timbucto" and despite of lack of money, food and supplies, men came to the colony and struggled for years.

In 1849, Brown moved his family there to help teach the colonists how to farm. He rented a farm nearby and soon bought a 244-acre tract for one dollar per acre. This is the present John Brown Farm State Historic Site.

He surveyed his neighbors land, showed them how to clear land, build cabins, and become self-sufficient; but as an experienced farmer, he soon realized few of the farms could ever be productive and only the hardiest of the colonists could survive. Business reasons forced Brown to move back to Ohio in 1851. In 1855 the family moved back to the farm and the present house was built.

Only a few of Brown's surviving children ever lived at the farm but his widow lived there until 1863 when she moved her family to Red Bluff, California. The farm was sold to a neighbor in 1866 for $700. In 1870, Kate Field, a journalist and lecturer, and 19 others who were interested in John Brown's cause bought the farm for $2,000. In 1895, this group donated the farm to New York State. In the 1950s, the house was restored to its 1855 appearance with some of the original furnishings.

Although Brown was very active in helping slaves escape to freedom, his farm was never used for the "Underground Railroad."

Brown is buried in front of the glass-enclosed headstone by the large boulder. Watson Brown's remains were moved here in 1882 and in 1899, Oliver Brown and 10 of the raiders killed at Harpers Ferry were reburied here.

Arrival of Brown's body at North Elba. Sketch by Thomas Nash for the *New York Illustrated News*, Dec. 24, 1859.

Thomas Nash was present at Brown's burial on Dec. 8 and sketched the event for the *New York Illustrated News*. The sketch was used to help in the 1950s restoration of the farm.

Hauling the granite monument to be erected in the rear of the great stone at Brown's burial site in 1896. The monument memorializes Kate Field and her associates who purchased the John Brown Farm and presented it to the state. wvsa

This large granite stone, with John Brown's inscription on it, is located on his farm site. His grandfather's gravestone, which was originally located in the Canton, Conn., cemetery was moved to the site by John Brown in 1857. wvsa

An early view of John Brown's grandfather's headstone. The inscription on the front reads: "In memory of Capt. John Brown who died in New York, Sept Ye, 1776, in the 48 year of his Age. Below this inscription reads: "John Brown, born May 9, 1800, was executed at Charleston, (sic) Va., Dec. 2, 1859." "Oliver Brown, born Mar. 9, 1839, was killed at Harper's Ferry, Oct. 17, 1859." On the back it reads: "In Memory of Frederick, son of John and Dianthe Brown, born Dec. 21, 1830, and murdered at Osawatomie, Kansas, Aug. 30, 1856, for his adherence to the cause of Freedom." (Frederick's inscription was cut on the stone in his memory. He is buried in Kansas.) Below reads: "Watson Brown, born Oct. 7, 1835, was wounded at Harper's Ferry, Oct. 17 and died Oct. 19, 1859." USAMHI

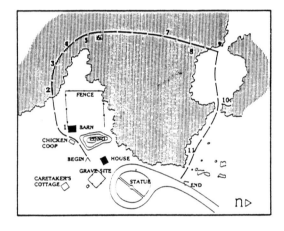

Ceremony for the transfer of John Brown's farm to the State of New York in 1895. Brown moved his family to this site in the Adirondack Mountains in 1849 and the original 244 acres encompass the historic site today. WVSA

A life-sized bronze statue of John Brown with a Negro boy stands in the entrance circle of the John Brown Farm State Historic Site. It was created by sculptor Joseph P. Pollia and unveiled on May 9, 1935. It was a gift of the John Brown Memorial Association, an organization that made annual pilgrimages to the farm for many years. WVSA

JOHN BROWN
1800 – 1859

John Brown in Movies, Plays and Literature

The saga of John Brown has spawned numerous plays, books and several movies since his death in 1859. Brown became a martyr for the abolitionist cause immediately upon his execution and also became one of the most controversial figures in American history. A compatriot of Brown's, James Redpath wrote the first biography of him the year after his death—*The Public Life of Captain John Brown*. After Redpath learned the details of the Kansas Pottawatomie Massacre however, he repudiated his work. Many other biographies have been written through the years, some treating him as a saint, some as a villain. The most recent work on Brown (1998) is Russell Banks' novel, *Cloudsplitter*. Theatrical works commenced immediately after the execution. The first was probably *Pottawatomie Brown/A Drama in Three Acts* performed in New York in late 1859. In 1950, Seyril Schochen's play on the struggle and differences of the characters within the Brown family, *The Moon Beseiged*, was produced. The title comes from an astrological forecast in which Stewart Taylor, one of Brown's raiders, predicted his death and the destruction of the group. In 1953, Paul Gregory produced Benét's *John Brown's Body* for the stage. It starred Tyrone Power, Judith Anderson, and Raymond Massey, and was directed by Charles Laughton. *The Anvil*, a play based on the trial of John Brown, was written by Julia Davis in 1962. Numerous poems have been written about Brown from the obscure to Benét epic drama. The few movies made about Brown have treated him both historically inaccurate,--*Santa Fe Trail*--and accurate,--*Seven Angry Men*. Many television mini-series have dealt with the Civil War era. In 1982, in *The Blue and the Gray*, Sterling Hayden played John Brown, and in 1985's *North and South*, Brown was portrayed by Johnny Cash.

Leftist writers wrote of Brown as one of their own. These included Michael Gold's 1924 *Life of John Brown*, David Karsner's 1934 *John Brown: Terrible Saint*, and Muriel Rukeyser's 1940 poem *The Soul and Body of John Brown*. Brown is also included in Dos Passos' 1921 antiwar novel *Three Soldiers* and Sinclair Lewis' 1935 anti-Fascist novel *It Can't Happen Here*.

A scene from *Santa Fe Trail.*

George Pauncefort was the first actor to appear as John Brown in *Pottawattomie Brown* at Worcester, Mass. in 1859. wvsa

Lucille Western appeared in *Pottawattomie Brown* in 1859. wvsa

Howard Bosworth portrayed John Brown in Ronald Gow's *Gallows Glorious* at the Pasadena Community Playhouse in 1935. wvsa

Tim O'Conner completes his make-up as John Brown in the Goodman Memorial Theatre production of the prize-winning play, "The Moon Beseiged," by Seyril Schocken. Date unknown. wvsa

It's Here!
The thundering story that challenges all filmdom to match its excitement!
*"Iron Rails to Kansas . . .
Iron Nerves from there on!"*

WARNER BROS. PRESENT

ERROL FLYNN
OLIVIA DeHAVILLAND
in
Santa Fe Trail

A thousand miles of danger with a thousand thrills a mile!

Original Screen Play
by Robert Buckner
Music by Max Steiner

with RAYMOND MASSEY
RONALD REAGAN · ALAN HALE
Wm. Lundigan · Van Heflin · Gene Reynolds
Henry O'Neill · Guinn 'Big Boy' Williams
DIRECTED BY MICHAEL CURTIZ

WATCH!
The big hit right after 'Santa Fe Trail' will be 'FOUR MOTHERS'! It's the wonderful new Warner Bros. picture starring the 'Four Daughters'!

-133-

Santa Fe Trail

Santa Fe Trail was released by Warner Brothers in 1940. Robert Buckner wrote the screen play, Michael Curitz directed, Jack L. Warner was in charge of production and Hal. B. Wallis was executive producer. It starred Raymond Massey as John Brown, Errol Flynn as Jeb Stuart, Ronald Reagan as George Custer, Gene Reynolds as Jason Brown, Moroni Olsen as Robert E. Lee, Olivia De Havilland as Kit and Van Heflin as Carl Rader.

The following description was released in the January 1941 issue of *Movie Story Magazine*:

It was Commencement at the United States Military Academy at West Point, New York, in the year 1854, and the warm June sunlight shone down brightly on the eager faces of the young soldiers as they sat, flanked by their families and friends, at the graduating exercises. There were only forty-one in the class, for at that time the army was as young as the country it was preparing to protect. But under the leadership of the new Commandant, Robert E. Lee, that gentleman from Virginia who had won the respect and love of West Point, the army was beginning to develop real soldiers.

Now the young men were listening to their leader as he spoke to them of their new commissions, and none listened more eagerly than three young men in the front row. They were Jeb Stuart from Virginia, George Custer from Ohio, and Bob Holliday from the Kansas territory, and these three had been friends for four years. They had been through a lot together, and no escapade had compared with that of last night. The events of the past evening had almost cost them their diplomas. Jeb Stuart and another classmate named Carl Rader had had a duel, culminating an enmity which had existed for four years. Now Carl Rader had been dishonorably discharged, and Jeb and George and Bob were to be sent, as punishment, to Fort Leavenworth, the Suicide Station—the last outpost of civilization, where the railroad stopped and the Santa Fe Trail began!

The quarrel between the two boys had been a deep one and had involved many things. Carl Rader had hated the South, and Jeb Stuart had loved it. Carl Rader was a hard-looking cadet, and Jeb with his warm blue eyes, his clean-cut face, had always felt there was something furtive and dishonest and cowardly in the other boy. But what had brought it all to a head was the pamphlet Carl had read to the younger boys—and Abolitionist pamphlet written by a man named John Brown. It had declared that in the name of the Cause—that of ridding the United States of Slavery—one could lie, murder, terrorize communities, speak treason, for these were not sins compared to this greater sin.

Jeb Stuart had recognized the underlying truth about slavery—that it must be wiped out—but his faith in the South he knew and loved so well was boundless. They would abolish slavery themselves. They need not be terrorized by the fanatical, Bible-reading bandit. He knew, too, that the pamphlet spoke treason—and that it was an offense to read such matter in the Military Academy.

So the boys had quarrelled, and now Carl Rader had gone. The three friends received their diplomas from Commandant Lee, shook his hand, and went back to their rooms to pack for Fort Leavenworth. None of them suspected that all of them would meet again in the not too distant future.

Bob Holliday was secretly thrilled that he and his two friends were to be stationed at Fort Leavenworth, for this was his home, and his father, Cyrus Holliday, with his *Holliday Freight Yard*, was the very soul of the raw, colorful frontier town. It was his father who dreamed of a railroad which would go from Fort Leavenworth to Santa Fe, using the old trail. If only the trail wasn't, as he put it, blood-soaked! But blood-soaked it was—for John Brown and his band had descended upon them, bearing with him groups of terrified Negroes; and anyone who objected to his releasing these Negroes was shot down in cold blood. So there would be no railroad until this wholesale murdering was curbed—and it was up to the army, it was up to Jeb Stuart and George Custer and Bob Holliday, to curb it!

Jeb Stuart was thrilled to be in Fort Leavenworth for many reasons. First of all it was exciting and dangerous. And then he had met Bob Holliday's sister—a brown-haired, browned-eyed girl named Kit Carson Holliday. They knew each other very slightly and she seemed to treat him in the same gay, casual manner she treated George Custer and the rest of the soldiers, but sometimes Jeb thought he saw a glimmer of sympathy in her eyes as she looked up at him.

But there was little time for romance in Fort Leavenworth, for there was work to be done. The next afternoon when Kit came down to say good-bye to the soldiers, only a brief smile passed between the two. With its military escort, the caravan set out down the Santa Fe Trail.

Jeb, in his heart, had longed to meet the now legendary figure of John Brown, and his wish was granted. The next afternoon, at sundown, they met him.

The skirmish which ensued was like many which had occurred that year. In the caravan was a crate of guns that had been sent to Brown from his Boston friends; the crate was addressed to a Reverend Newton in Wichita, and was marked on the outside in bold black letters—Holy Bibles. John Brown descended upon the little troupe and demanded the Bibles, and the fight was on. Almost immediately Jeb recognized the tall spare man with the long gray beard and the flaming eyes of a fanatic. But he was unprepared to see in the group of raiders, the figure of his erstwhile enemy, Carl Rader.

Jeb Stuart and his men fought valiantly, but John Brown and his Abolitionist band escaped. Only John's son—Jason Brown, was left behind—a terrified boy of seventeen, wounded badly and lying the dust.

Jeb lifted the boy gently to his saddle and ordered his men to return with him to Leavenworth. All the next day they tried to question the boy. Where was his father? Where were his headquarters? But Jason was stubborn—or speechless with pain.

In the end it was the gentleness of Kit that broke the boy, for she stayed with him all that night, and just before dawn, an hour before he died, he told her where his father was.

With tears streaming down her face, Kit ran to Jeb. John Brown was at Palmyra, at the home of one Shubel Morgan.

Palmyra! It was a dangerous town. Jeb would have to go alone. Kit stared at the young soldier as he unfolded his plan to her—and then silently put her arms around him and kissed him. Kit knew now that Jeb was different. He was braver than the rest—that was certain, but what was more important, she loved him.

The fight that night in Palmyra was memorable. Although Jeb disguised himself as a civilian, no one had realized that his army horse would be recognized. Immediately he was covered by a gun and taken to the house of Shubel Morgan. There sat John Brown conferring with his disciples, among whom was Carl Rader. With not a semblance of a trial, Jeb was taken to the barn behind the house. There by the eerie light of torches a scaffolding was constructed. Carl Rader had asked for the privilege of hanging his classmate, and as he advanced toward Jeb, the soldier realized that this was the end.

But he had forgotten his faithful regiment headed by his friend, George Custer, and even as he felt the rope about his neck, he heard a shout outside—a shot and then another and another, and the full power of the regiment burst upon the executioners.

John Brown's power was broken that night, but he, himself, and Rader escaped—only to lay plans for the destruction of Harper's Ferry, the entrance to the South.

No one knows what might have happened if John Brown had not been stopped at Harper's Ferry, but his own confidant—Carl Rader—betrayed him and sent word to Jeb Stuart of his leader's plans. Jeb and George and the Hollidays were in Washington that night, for Jeb and George had been called there to receive promotions. It was the same night, in fact, that Jeb and Kit officially announced their engagement. But when word came that John Brown was in Harper's Ferry, all the fighting instincts in Jeb came to the fore.

Harper's Ferry was John Brown's Waterloo—and the next week he was hanged. But his spirit—as the yet unwritten song was to say—kept marching on. He was a fanatic, but there was truth behind him—a truth with no one in the United States could deny. It was as Jeb Stuart told Kit that night. This was a fight that was just beginning. Soon the whole nation would have to settle this problem. John Brown was a shadow of coming events.

The movie's description in Leonard Maltin's *1996 Movie & Video Guide* makes the following comment: Lopsided picture, can't make up its mind about anything: what side it's taking, what it wants to focus on, etc. Worthless as history, but amid the rubble are some good action as Jeb Stuart and cohorts go after John Brown.

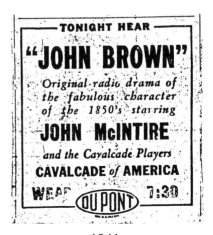

1941

History Distorted

John Brown Slandered in Hollywood Version of Fight for Free Men

"Santa Fe Trail," a Warner Brothers picture directed by Michael Curtz, starring Raymond Massey, Errol Flynn, Olivia de Havilland, Ronald Reagan, Alan Hale, at the Fox Theater in San Francisco.

By AL RICHMOND

It was Abraham Lincoln's fervent wish that the men who died at Gettysburg "shall not have died in vain." But they did, at least so far as Hollywood's latest abortion on American history, "The Santa Fe Trail," is concerned. The men who went to battle singing, "John Brown's body lies a-moldering in the grave but his soul keeps marching on!" were dupes or rogues, marching in the name of a crazed murderer and enemy of humanity. This is the message of Warner Brothers' malicious distortion of one of the most significant periods in American history.

Customarily, one is inclined to shrug one's shoulders at Hollywoodian distortion of history, as it is generally movivated either by a vulgar sensationalism or sheer ignorance. But when the malice of design is as apparent as it is in Warner Bros'. epic, one is more inclined to shake one's fist than shrug one's shoulder.

"The Santa Fe Trail" purports to cover the period of John Brown's activities from the middle 1850s in "Bloody Kansas," to the sortie against Harper's Ferry in Virginia and the subsequent hanging of the great Abolitionist on Dec. 2, 1859. The story centers around the career of Lieutenant "Jeb" Stuart (Errol Flynn), West Point graduate, who together with some five of his fellow classmates is commissioned to the Army post at Fort Leavenworth, Kansas. Here he encounters John Brown and their paths cross until Brown meets his doom and Stuart-Flynn marries the girl, Kit Carson Holliday (Olivia de Havilland).

In addition to Stuart, the aristocratic officer and gentleman from Virginia, the two other chief heroes of the film are Robert E. Lee, who was to lead the rebel armies of the Confederacy against the Union, and Jefferson Davis, president-to-be of the slaveowners' junta.

Lee and Davis are pictured as the noble defenders of the Union and democracy (the latter even makes a speech for freedom in the film), while Brown is portrayed as the nefarious villain who brought the Civil War to the United States.

The "little civil war" in Kansas, which preceded the big Civil War later, is presented as the excessive doing of John Brown's fanaticism. Forgotten completely is the role of the "Border Ruffians," the notorious gangs sent into Kansas by the slaveowners in order to terrorize the populace into accepting entrance into the Union as a slave state. Brown's band of men are portrayed by actors who have so long played the roles of villains and gangsters in films that they have been so "typed" in the public eye.

Slavery is interpreted as an exclusive problem of the South, to be settled by the South in its own way. In one scene where Brown sets free a group of slaves, smuggled up from the South through the Underground Railway, the picture's message definitely is that freedom for the slaves was a stupid notion and they would have been much better off back on their owners' plantations.

The opening sequence of the film tells of an incident in West Point where an Abolitionist is singled out as the "traitor" to the United States and is expelled from the military academy by none other than Colonel (later, General) Lee. It is an ironic note, for Lee was later to turn traitor to the army and his oath and take up arms against the Government. Not only Lee, but a large number of the West Pointers whom he trained were to turn traitor. At the outbreak of the Civil War, of the 1,106 commissioned officers in the United States Army, more than a third (387) were to desert to the rebels.

But these would-be traitors, these defenders of slavery, are Hollywood's heroes! And John Brown, he who was honored by some of the finest contemporary Americans like Ralph Waldo Emerson and Henry Wadsworth Longfellow, is the villain of the piece.

From the *Peoples World*, January 4, 1941

Movies and History

Sir: — Your magazine recently published a very timely letter by Oswald Garrison Villard criticising the picture "Santa Fe Trail," which greatly misrepresented the life of John Brown. It is to be hoped that Mr. Villard and many others will continue to raise their voices in a mighty protest against the distortion of historical figures and facts in the pictures. So many great people and events in history have been so grossly misrepresented. This, in a measure, is most dangerous to the young, who often get an impression which will be as lasting as it is false. To the grown ups it is nothing less than an insult to their intelligence and education to see a historical picture which is a very poorly presented history lesson to say the least. Educational groups should put this protest into real action and demand that history and people should be presented with truth. Is it possible that the picture producers do not know the truth is not only stranger than fiction but far more dramatic?

(Mrs.) FLORENCE MUNSAN.
Jersey City, N.J.

From the *Saturday Review of Literature*, May 3, 1941

Scenes from the movie,
Santa Fe Trail. COURTESY
ACADEMY OF MOTION PICTURE
ARTS & SCIENCES

THEIR RENDEZVOUS MADE
A NATION TREMBLE!

ALLIED
ARTISTS
presents

SEVEN
ANGRY
MEN

Starring

RAYMOND MASSEY
DEBRA PAGET
JEFFREY HUNTER

with

LARRY PENNELL • LEO GORDON • JOHN SMITH

Produced by VINCENT M. FENNELLY

Directed by   Story and Screenplay by
CHARLES MARQUIS WARREN • DANIEL B. ULLMAN

Seven Angry Men

The second movie produced about John Brown was released in 1955 by Allied Artists. *Seven Angry Men* was directed by Charles Marquis Warren and starred Debra Paget, Jeffrey Hunter, James Best, Dennis Weaver, Dabbs Greer, Ann Tyrrell, and again, Raymond Massey as John Brown. Larry Pennell, Leo Gordon and John Smith were also cast members. Produced by Vincent M. Fennelly. Directed by Charles M. Warren with story and screenplay by Daniel B. Ullman. It was a good historical drama of Brown and his family fighting to free the slaves.

Raymond Massey played John Brown in two movies — *Santa Fe Trail* and *Seven Angry Men*. He was born in Ontario in 1897 and was Oxford educated. He made his stage debut in 1922 and his film debut in 1931. He was wounded in both world wars serving with the Canadian Army but became a U.S. citizen in 1944. He became closely identified not only with John Brown but with the role of Abraham Lincoln, which he played in both the stage and screen versions of *Abe Lincoln in Illinois*. He appeared in 49 movies from 1929 to 1969. In the early 1960s, he portrayed Dr. Gillespie in the "Dr. Kildare" TV series. Massey died in 1983.

Sterling Hayden portrayed John Brown in the 1982 CBS television mini-series *The Blue and the Gray*.
COURTESY DAVID WOLPER PRODUCTIONS

Scenes from *Seven Angry Men*.

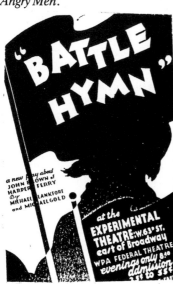

Promotional poster for *"Battle Hymn,"* a play in three acts by Michael Blankfort and Michael Gold. It was presented by the Federal Theatre Project of the Works Progress Administration. (WPA).

John Chenoweth played John Brown in RKO's 1940 movie *Abe Lincoln in Illinois*. Other major parts were played by Gene Lockhart and Ruth Gordon. It is an adaptation of Robert E. Sherwood's Pulizer Prize-winning play of the same name. John Brown is only a very small part of the movie which concentrates on the life of Lincoln from 1833 to his presidency in 1861.

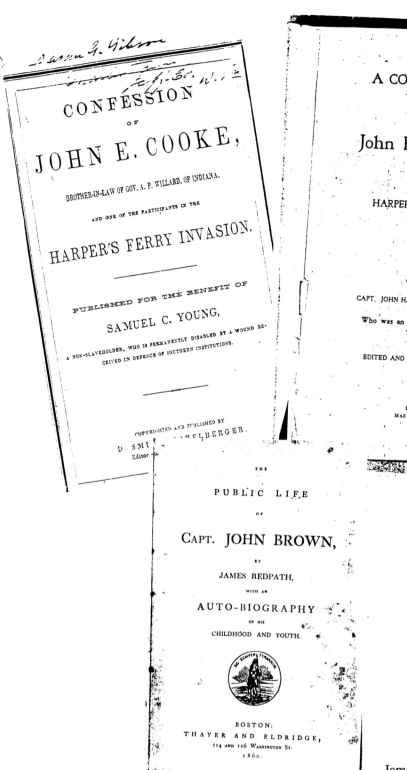

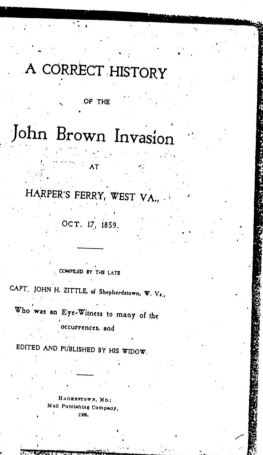

CONFESSION
OF
JOHN E. COOKE,

BROTHER-IN-LAW OF GOV. A. P. WILLARD, OF INDIANA.

AND ONE OF THE PARTICIPANTS IN THE

HARPER'S FERRY INVASION.

PUBLISHED FOR THE BENEFIT OF

SAMUEL C. YOUNG,

A NON-SLAVEHOLDER, WHO IS PERMANENTLY DISABLED BY A WOUND RE-
CEIVED IN DEFENCE OF SOUTHERN INSTITUTIONS.

COPYRIGHTED AND PUBLISHED BY
D. SMI   ELBERGER.
Editor

A CORRECT HISTORY

OF THE

John Brown Invasion

AT

HARPER'S FERRY, WEST VA.,

OCT. 17, 1859.

COMPILED BY THE LATE

CAPT. JOHN H. ZITTLE, of Shepherdstown, W. Va.,

Who was an Eye-Witness to many of the
occurrences, and

EDITED AND PUBLISHED BY HIS WIDOW.

HAGERSTOWN, MD.:
Mail Publishing Company,
1905.

THE

PUBLIC LIFE

OF

CAPT. JOHN BROWN,

BY

JAMES REDPATH,

WITH AN

AUTO-BIOGRAPHY

OF HIS

CHILDHOOD AND YOUTH.

BOSTON:
THAYER AND ELDRIDGE,
114 AND 116 WASHINGTON ST.
1860.

James Redpath, abolitionist newspaper editor from
Scotland, first met John Brown in Kansas where he
was the local correspondent for the *New York
Herald*. Redpath wrote about the fictitious incident
of Brown kissing the baby just before his execution
and also the first biography of him shortly after his
execution. After Redpath learned the truth about the
Pottawatomie Massacre and Brown's part, he
disavowed his biography of him. He also helped
Jefferson Davis write his *Short History of the
Confederate States* in 1885.

Oswald Garrison Villard, who wrote *John Brown:
1800-1895 — A Biography Fifty Years After* in 1909,
was the son of journalist and financier, Henry
Villard. Oswald was the owner of the New York
Evening Post and was the owner and editor of the
Nation from 1908 to 1933. He was a founder along
with Joel Springson and W.E.B. Du Bois of the
NAACP.

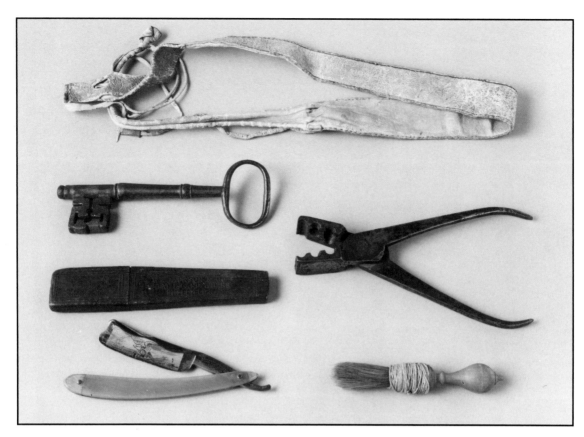

Artifacts of John Brown on display at the Ohio Historical Society Museum in Columbus.

John Brown artifacts which are in the West Virginia State Museum collections, Charleston. The lock and key are from his cell door, the rope is from the scaffold and the hand cuffs and collar are fom his imprisonment. PHOTO BY MICHAEL KELLER.

John Brown Artifacts

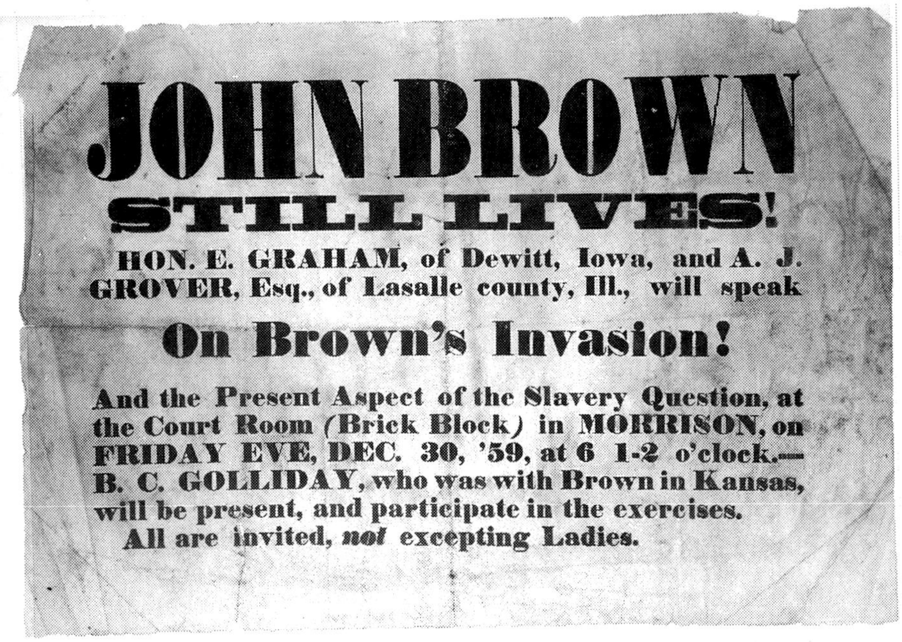

JOHN BROWN
STILL LIVES!

HON. E. GRAHAM, of Dewitt, Iowa, and A. J. GROVER, Esq., of Lasalle county, Ill., will speak

On Brown's Invasion!

And the Present Aspect of the Slavery Question, at the Court Room (Brick Block) in MORRISON, on FRIDAY EVE, DEC. 30, '59, at 6 1-2 o'clock.— B. C. GOLLIDAY, who was with Brown in Kansas, will be present, and participate in the exercises. All are invited, *not* excepting Ladies.

This rare broadside sold at a 1998 auction for over $5,300.

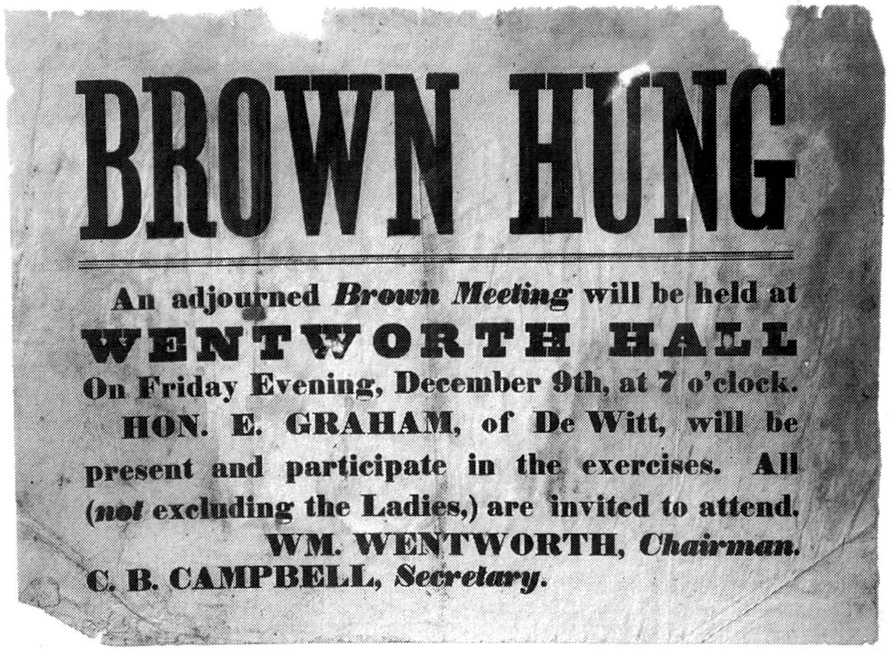

BROWN HUNG

An adjourned *Brown Meeting* will be held at

WENTWORTH HALL

On Friday Evening, December 9th, at 7 o'clock. HON. E. GRAHAM, of De Witt, will be present and participate in the exercises. All (*not* excluding the Ladies,) are invited to attend.

WM. WENTWORTH, *Chairman.*

C. B. CAMPBELL, *Secretary.*

This rare broadside was printed seven days after Brown's execution. BOTH BROADSIDE COPIES COURTESY AMERICAN SOCIAL HISTORY AND SOCIAL MOVEMENTS, PITTSBURGH, PA.

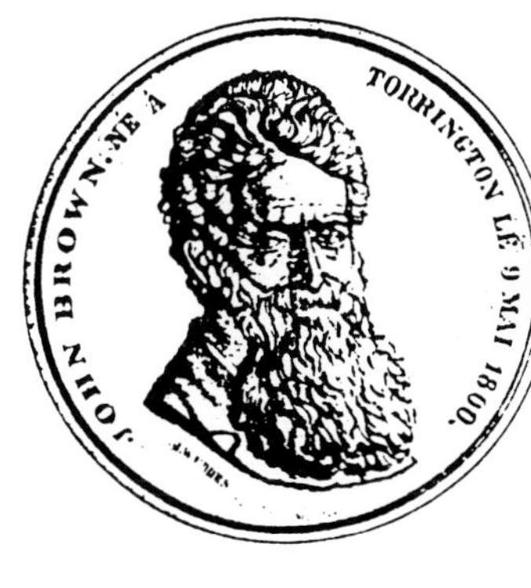

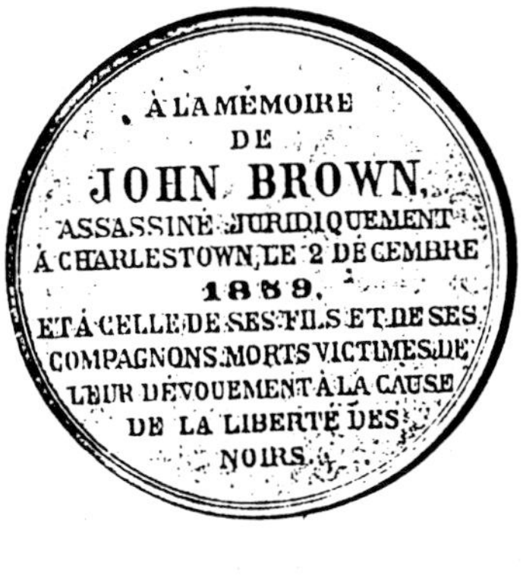

This gold medal was sent to the Brown family in 1867 by Victor Hugo and the citizens of France. The editor of *Paris La Co-Operation* received this letter from Hugo:

"Sir:

"My name belongs to all who would make use of it to serve progress and truth. A medal to Lincoln calls for a medal to John Brown. Let us cancel that debt pending such time as America shall cancel hers. America owes John Brown a statue as tall as Washington's. Washington 'founded' America; John Brown diffussed liberty. I press your hand."

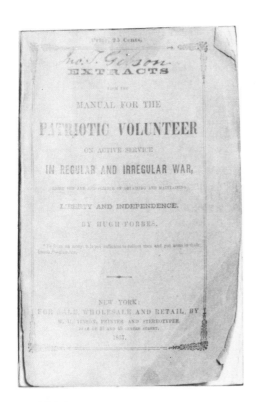

This book, *Extracts from the Manual For The Patriotic Volunteer on Active Service In Regular and Irregular War*, was taken from John Brown after his capture and so noted by Col. John Gibson.

This lithograph was produced by E.B. & E.C. Kellogg of Hartford, Conn., in 1860. This unsigned depiction of Brown was intended for circulation among his supporters. Once initial condemnation of the Harpers Ferry attack changed to support by the Northern press, the brothers signed the lithographs.

John Brown artifacts on display in the Jefferson County Museum at Charles Town, West Virginia.
PHOTOS BY GARY KABLE

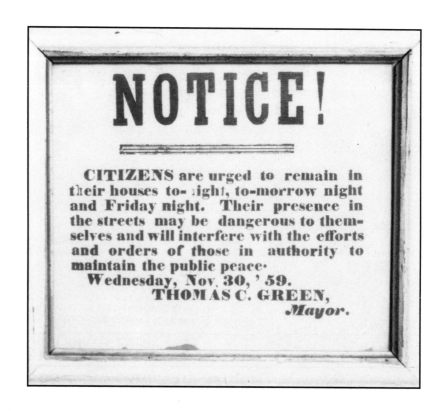

NOTICE!

CITIZENS are urged to remain in their houses to-night, to-morrow night and Friday night. Their presence in the streets may be dangerous to themselves and will interfere with the efforts and orders of those in authority to maintain the public peace.
Wednesday, Nov. 30, '59.
THOMAS C. GREEN,
Mayor.

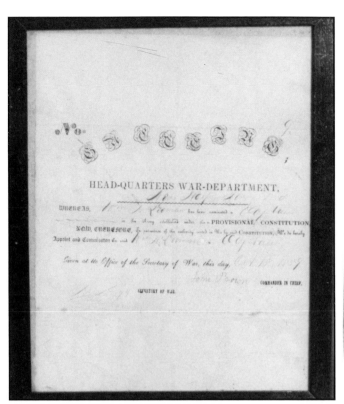

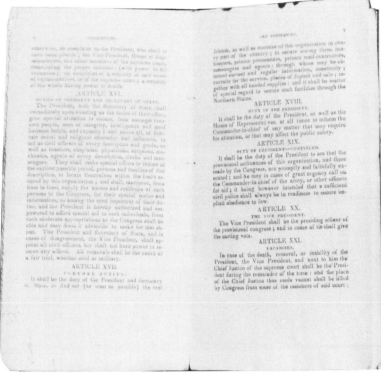

Brown's copy of his Constitution and Ordinances for his proclaimed new non-slave country.

This document was taken from the pocket of William Leeman, who was shot as he swam across the Shenandoah River. Brown signed this commission which made Leeman a "captain" in Brown's army.

During Brown's imprisonment in Charlestown he gave his trunk to a slave named "Billy Hill" who brought his meals to him.

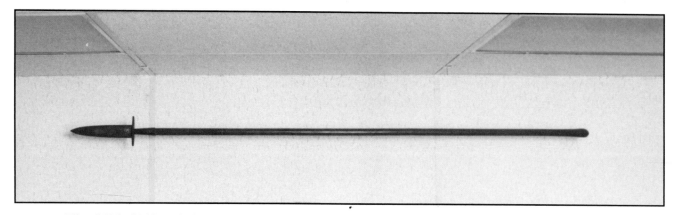

Pike #635 of 954 made for Brown by Charles Blair of the Collinsville section of Canton, Conn. Blair was told that these pikes were to be sent to Kansas but Brown was actually going to hand them out to the slaves at Harpers Ferry. This is one of two on display at the museum and is six feet long with a six- to seven-inch long knife at its end. This pike was acquired by Col. John Gibson after the raid. The Canton Historical Museum also has a pike on display.

This is the actual wagon used to transport John Brown to the gallows on Dec. 2, 1859, at Charlestown, Virginia. The wagon was drawn by two white horses. Jailor John Avis sat next to Brown in the wagon along with George W. Sadler, the undertaker, and several other men. Sheriff Campbell followed behind in a buggy. The wagon was flanked by three companies of infantry. After the execution, the coffin, upon which Brown had sat, and now containing his body, was taken in this wagon to the Baltimore & Ohio station in Charlestown for shipment to his burial site in North Elba, New York. The wagon was donated to the museum by Melvin T. Strider and Frank L. Ronemous in 1965.

The key on the left was to
the U.S. Armory at
Harpers Ferry. The key
on the right is believed to
be from the jail at
Charlestown, circa. 1859

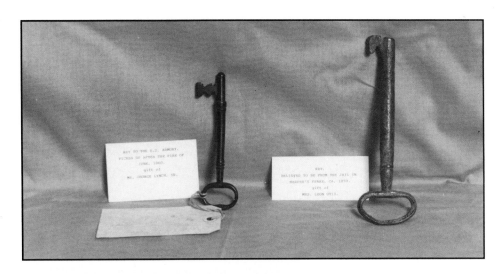

A piece of the scaffold
used to hang John Brown.
It was acquired by Col.
John Gibson. After the
execution, the scaffold
was disassembled and
made into a porch on a
residence at the corner of
Liberty and Lawrence
streets in Charlestown.

Handcuffs used on John
Brown.

This hammer was used to
nail up the notice in the
Charlestown Courthouse
yard for the hanging of
John Brown.

The Saga of John Brown's Bell

Since the 1960s a bell, supposedly from the enginehouse at Harpers Ferry has hung in the John Brown Bell Tower at Union Common in Marlboro, Mass. How it got there is a strange and interesting story that has been involved in some controversy since then.

In August 1861 members of Co. I of the 13th Massachusetts Regiment from the Marlboro area entered Harpers Ferry to remove equipment to send to Washington, D.C. They wanted to take a souvenir from the historic enginehouse, scene of Brown's raid two years before.

They noticed that the bell in the cupola was still in its original position. Brown was going to ring it to call the slaves in the area to rebellion. Some of the troops took it down and along with some assorted bricks and pieces of wood took it across the Potomac River.

They transported it to Williamsport, Maryland, along the Chesapeake and Ohio Canal. There it was deemed too heavy to continue man-handling it so they persuaded an area farm woman to care for it while the troops were campaigning. The woman feared for the bell's safety so she ordered a slave to bury it in a field, where it stayed for seven years. After the war, she had it unearthed and kept it for 30 years.

In 1892 some of the surviving troops from Co. I were attending a reunion near Williamsport. They wondered if the bell was still on the farm and went to inquire. They found the woman and the bell and returned it to Marlboro.

The bell was placed on the front of the John A. Rawlins Post 43 G.A.R. building on Main Street where it remained for over 60 years. In the 1960s the bell was moved to the tower at Union Common.

There was a movement in 1987 to bring the bell back to its original home in Harpers Ferry but no action was taken.

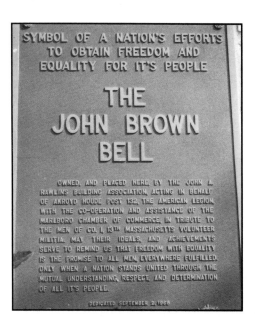

The plaque on the bell tower.

The John Brown Bell Tower at Union Common in Marlboro, Mass.

The John Brown Bell,
Marlboro, Mass.

Mrs. Elizabeth William Snyder of
Williamsport, MD, kept the bell
for 30 years. WVSA

The bell hung on the outside of the
John A. Rawlins Post Grand Army
of the Republic (GAR) building,
formerly on Main Street in
Marlboro, from 1892 to the 1960s.
USAMHI

James M. Gleason of Marlboro,
Mass., recovered the bell in 1892.
WVSA

Published by Thomson, Stationer.

John Brown's Pikes *

Of the artifacts still in existence that were associated with John Brown, his pikes are perhaps the most interesting. They are also the most well-known of all the American polearms manufactured in the United States.

Ordered originally by Brown for use in his Kansas adventures, they were delivered too late for that battle zone. The pikes were manufactured under the supervision of Charles Blair of Collinsville, Connecticut, at the Collins Cutlery Company. The company was, and still is, well-known for its axes.

Brown met Blair the morning after he had given a speech in a public hall in Collinsville about the situation in Kansas. He was soliciting money and supplies for the settlers in the territory. In a local drugstore Brown was showing some men, including Blair, some of the weapons that he had captured from Capt. Henry Clay Pate at Black Jack, Kansas. One of the weapons was a double-edged dirk with an eight-inch blade. With these Brown said, the Free-State settlers could defend themselves.

When Brown found out that Blair was in the edged-tool business, he asked him how much it would cost to produce them. Blair replied that he could make 500 pikes for $1.25 each or 1,000 for $1.00 each. Brown thought the price high, but asked that 12 sample pikes be sent to him at Springfield, Massachusetts, for his approval.

The samples were slightly different than the later ones made under contract. The type of handle was altered so that it fastened to the ferrule (cap placed on the end to prevent splitting and add strength) by a screw instead of by a single rivet. This made shipment, and concealment of the pikes easier. A foot was also added to each handle. Ash had been chosen by Blair for the shafts, or handles, because it was the wood commonly used for hayfork handles; and when he shipped the pikes to Brown he even labeled them fork-handles.

A contract was given to Blair to produce 1,000 pikes with a time limit of 90 days or to be finished by July 1, 1857. Only 954 were eventually delivered. There was no explanation for the missing 46. Brown, however, ran out of money at the time when the blades had been roughly forged and to avoid losing money on the deal, Blair stopped work and considered the contract abrogated.

A year later Brown showed up at the factory, apologized and offered the final payment. By this time Blair was busy with other work and offered to give Brown all the unfinished parts. Under pressure Blair accepted the remaining $450 from Brown and found a sub-contractor to finish the job. So Charles Hart of Unionville, Connecticut, actually finished the job and delivered the 954 pikes.

It was now the summer of 1859 and the pikes were no longer needed in Kansas, but Brown had another plan anyway. They were shipped to Chambersburg, Pennsylvania, and eventually to the Kennedy farm to be used in the infamous raid on the Harpers Ferry arsenal.

This weapon was to be one of the crucial weapons used to arm the expected liberated slaves. However, no more than 50 were taken on the raid, the remaining ones remained at the Kennedy farm.

After the raid, Col. Robert E. Lee sent Lt. J.E.B. Stuart and Lt. Israel Greene to the Kennedy farm to recover the remaining arms. They found the bulk of the pikes in the loft of a nearby cabin and threw them out of a window. Neighbors had gathered at the farm to see what was going on and Lieutenant Greene began giving the pikes to anyone who wanted one. He even offered them 50 apiece or more. More than 400 were given away before the rest were transported to the Harpers Ferry arsenal for storage.

The pikes became prized relics very soon after the raid and Gov. Henry Wise of Virginia startled a group of clergymen by presenting one at the Episcopal Church Convention in Richmond to Rev. Dr. Wiley of Waterbury, Connecticut.

In April 1861 the Confederate Army occupied Harpers Ferry and shipped everything usable south to Richmond, including 483 pikes and possibly another 175 with broken shafts. It is thought that some of these pikes found their way to some Confederate cavalry units in 1862 when a shortage of arms was acute. It is likely that they were of little use for a man on horseback and were soon turned in.

In the 1870s, they were burned in an arsenal fire and eventually were shipped to the Rock Island Arsenal where they rusted in a heap of condemned scrap iron. A Mr. Witherell rescued them, purchased them from the government, and sold them as souvenirs.

This is not the end of the pike story however. The Harpers Ferry Raid became so notorious that passengers passing through town would buy reproduction pikes for two to three dollars from unscrupulous vendors by the tracks. The *Cincinnati Penny Press* on Nov. 26, 1859, reported that the traffic in fake pikes was becoming such an annoyance that the railroad finally had to interdict their sale and drive the pike vendors off the platform. The bogus pikes were of much poorer workmanship and were easily spotted and discarded years ago, as nearly all the major newspapers carried accurate steel engravings of the original ones. Many fakes were still on hand at the outbreak of the Civil War.

*Excerpts of this article were taken from *American Polearms*, 1526-1865 by Rodney Hilton Brown, published by N. Floyderman & Co., New Milford, Conn., 1967.

Charles Blair

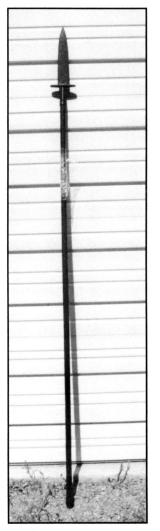

This John Brown pike, serial number 484, was sent by Mr. F.M. Gibson to his wife in 1859 as a souvenir of the raid. Gibson was the clerk to arsenal superintendent Col. Henry K. Craig. Through the years the Gibson family migrated west and eventually settled in Missoula, Montana. Hayes Otoupalik, a Missoula militaria dealer, now owns it.

Hatchet used to cut the gallow's rope at John Brown's execution. WVSA

John Brown's Song & The Battle Hymn of the Republic

Julia Ward Howe (1819-1910) was a writer, lecturer and social reformer and one of the most remarkable American women of her time. She was born into a prominent New York City family and married Dr. Samuel Gridley Howe in 1843. She wrote poems and plays and helped edit her husband's *The Commonwealth*. In 1861, she visited a military camp near Washington, D.C. There she heard the tune "John Brown's Body" and wrote a hymn to its tune – "The Battle Hymn of the Republic," which became the major war song of the Union. It was published in the *Atlantic Monthly* in 1862. The tune was a camp-meeting song written by William Steffe to the words, "Say, brothers, will you meet us on Canaan's happy shore?" Howe became a noted suffragette and lecturer on women's rights. Mrs. Howe had known the original John Brown through her husband who was one of Brown's "Secret Six" financial backers.

The Massachusetts John Brown Song

Old John Brown's body is a-mouldering in the dust,
Old John Brown's rifle's red with blood-spots turned to rust,
Old John Brown's pike has made its last, unflinching thrust,
    His soul is marching on!

Glory! Glory! Hallelujah!
"Forward!" calls the Lord, our Captain:
Glory! Glory! Hallelujah!
    With him we're marching on.

For treason hung because he struck at treason's root,
When soon palmetto-tree had ripened treason's fruit,
His dust, disquieted, stirred at Sumter's last salute –
    His soul is marching on!

Who rides before the army of martyrs to the word?
The heavens grow bright as He makes bare his flaming sword,
The glory fills the earth of the coming of the Lord –
    His soul is marching on!....

Like so many other tales involving John Brown's life, the song about him has an unusual irony.

John Brown's song was not written about the abolitionist John Brown. Shortly after the war began the 2nd Battalion Boston Light Infantry, Massachusetts Volunteer Militia was formed and stationed in Boston Harbor. Among the recruits was a young Scotsman named John Brown.

Because of his name he became the butt of jokes by his comrades. The soldiers formed a singing group, including Brown, and sang various tunes including the chorus of "Glory, Glory Hallelujah." One of the group added a new line: "John Brown's Body Lies a Mouldering in the Grave," and others added "His Soul is Marching On." Other troops started singing the song thinking it was about the abolitionist John Brown. The soldier John Brown drowned in the Shenandoah River at Front Royal, Virginia, during the war and did not live to see the song originally written about him become an inspiration to so many others. After the war the song Promotional poster for *"Battle Hymn,"* a play in three acts by Michael Blankfort and Michael Gold. It was presented by the Federal Theatre Project of the Works Progress Administration. (WPA). "Battle Hymn of the Republic" became so well-known that many thought it should be the song for all Americans to sing on patriotic occasions. President Theodore Roosevelt even started a movement to have it replace the "Star Spangled Banner" as the country's national anthem.

Sgt. Henry J. Hallgreen of the 2nd Battalion Boston Light Infantry of the Massachusetts Volunteer Militia was a member of the Battalion's singing group. WVSA

The Battle Hymn of the Republic*

Circumstances under which it was written.

In the first year of the Civil War Mrs. Julia Ward Howe visited the city of Washington. During the journey a feeling of discouragement came over her as she thought of the women of her acquaintance whose sons or husbands were fighting for the preservation of the Union. Something seemed to say to her, "You would be glad to serve, but you cannot help anyone; you have nothing to give, there is nothing for you to do."

While at Washington Mrs. Howe was one day invited with her husband and others to attend a review of troops near the city. During the manoeuvers [sic], a sudden movement of the enemy broke up the review and a detachment of soldiers galloped to the assistance of a small body of Union troops who were in danger of being surrounded and cut off from retreat. On the return to the city by a road thronged with soldiers, Mrs. Howe and her party sang snatches of war songs then popular, including "John Brown's body lies a-mouldering in the ground; His soul is marching on."

The singing of this song seemed to please the soldiers greatly. Rev. James Freeman Clarke, a member of the party, said, "Mrs. Howe, why do you not write some good words for this stirring tune?" Mrs. Howe replied that she had often wished to do so, but as yet had found nothing in her mind leading toward it. That night she wrote the Battle Hymn of the Republic, and in "Reminiscences," from which the foregoing has been adapted, she tells the story in the following words:

"I went to bed that night as usual and slept ac-

cording to my wont, quite soundly. I awoke in the gray of the morning twilight; and as I lay waiting for the dawn, the long lines of the desired poem began to twine themselves in my mind. Having thought out all the stanzas, I said to myself, 'I must get up and write these verses down, lest I fall asleep again and forget them.' So with a sudden effort, I sprang out of bed, and found in the dimness an old stump of a pencil which I remembered to have used the day before. I scrawled the verses almost without looking at the paper. I was obliged to decipher my scrawl before another night should intervene, as it was only legible while the matter was fresh in my mind. At this time having completed my writing, I returned to bed and fell asleep, saying to myself, 'I like this better than most things I have written.'"

The song was soon after published in the "Atlantic Monthly." It cheered on to victory the Union armies and has been sung by countless thousands since the war.

At its commencement last year, Brown University conferred upon Mrs. Howe, who had passed her ninetieth birthday, the honorary degree of Doctor of Letters. When she was assisted to the platform to receive the degree, the whole audience rose while the orchestra played "The Battle Hymn of the Republic." In the presentation she was addressed as "Author, Philanthropist, Mother, Friend of the Slave, a personal friend of all who suffer, Singer of the Battle Hymn of the Republic, allied with all educators through her faith."

*Excerpted from *Wisconsin Memorial Day Annual, 1910*

-153-

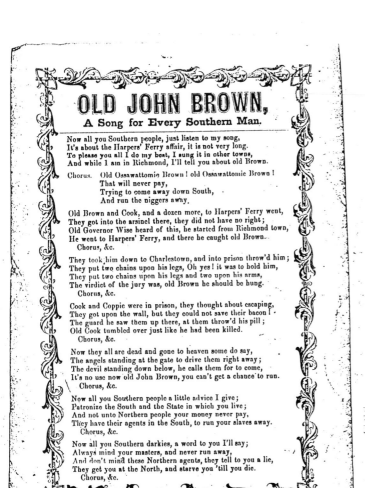

OLD JOHN BROWN,
A Song for Every Southern Man.

Now all you Southern people, just listen to my song,
It's about the Harpers' Ferry affair, it is not very long.
To please you all I do my best, I sung it in other towns,
And while I am in Richmond, I'll tell you about old Brown.

Chorus. Old Ossawattomie Brown! old Ossawattomie Brown!
    That will never pay,
    Trying to come away down South,
    And run the niggers away.

Old Brown and Cook, and a dozen more, to Harpers' Ferry went,
They got into the arsinel there, they did not have no right;
Old Governor Wise heard of this, he started from Richmond town,
He went to Harpers' Ferry, and there he caught old Brown.
    Chorus, &c.

They took him down to Charlestown, and into prison throw'd him;
They put two chains upon his legs, Oh yes! it was to hold him,
They put two chains upon his legs and two upon his arms,
The virdict of the jury was, old Brown he should be hung.
    Chorus, &c.

Cook and Coppie were in prison, they thought about escaping,
They got upon the wall, but they could not save their bacon!
The guard he saw them up there, at them throw'd his pill;
Old Cook tumbled over just like he had been killed.
    Chorus, &c.

Now they all are dead and gone to heaven some do say,
The angels standing at the gate to drive them right away;
The devil standing down below, he calls them for to come,
It's no use now old John Brown, you can't get a chance to run.
    Chorus, &c.

Now all you Southern people a little advice I give;
Patronize the South and the State in which you live;
And not unto Northern people your money never pay,
They have their agents in the South, to run your slaves away.
    Chorus, &c.

Now all you Southern darkies, a word to you I'll say;
Always mind your masters, and never run away,
And don't mind these Northern agents, they tell to you a lie,
They get you at the North, and starve you 'till you die.
    Chorus, &c.

John Brown

Respectfully dedicated to THE YOUNG MONKEY CRAZY ASSOCIATION, and the public in general,
BY C. A. BOGGS.
Published for the diffusion of facts as they are, and to let people know what they aint.

AIR.—"The other side of Jordan."

In Harper's Ferry section, they have had an insurrection,
Old Brown thought the niggas would sustain him;
But old Gov'nor Wise, put spectacles on his eyes,
To show him the happy land of Canaan.
    Clear the way—clear the way for old John Brown,
    Don't you see the old man coming,
    And give me your attention, &c.

The Abolitionists are kicking up a dust,
The people of Virginia they are blaming;
Gov'nor Wise would hang them freely, Gerrit Smith and Horace Greely,
If he catches them in the happy land of Canaan.
    Clear the way, &c.

Now old Brown is hung, and the last words he did say,
Was "Don't keep me long remaining;"
They walked him up a slope, where they swung him on a rope,
And dropped him through the happy land of Canaan.
    Clear the way, &c.

The nigger people, they, held a meeting for to pray,
And with hymns their voices were a straining;
To pray is very well, but old Brown is now in ___,
And he will never see the happy land of Canaan.
    Clear the way, &c.

The druggists now-a-days, have got such funny ways,
The principal business they do am slaying,
If you ask for epecac, they give you something black,
Which will send you to the happy land of Canaan.
Chorus.—Oh, ah, don't you see the people running,
    Give me your attention and some funny things I'll mention,
    As I travel to the happy land of Canaan.

The "Y. M. C. A." are getting mighty gay,
The things in the Big Book they are explaining;
That's the business they follow, they'll sell tickets for a dollar,
That will take you to the happy land of Canaan.
    Oh, ah, &c.

Way down in Market Street, where the butchers sold their meat,
They have now commenced to make an alteration;
They have torn the markets down to beautify the town,
And make it like the happy land of Canaan.
    Oh, ah, &c.

Queen Victoria laid a plan, for the Isle of San Juan,
To have more territory there for to reign in;
She will find it mighty bad, if she makes old Scotty mad,
For he'll blow her to the happy land of Canaan.
    Oh, ah, &c.

The ladies' hoops will soon, be as large as Low's Ballon,
Every day, in size, they are gaining;
They soon will be so big, they will use them for a brig.
To smuggle you to the happy land of Canaan.
    Oh, ah, &c.

I have sung about old Brown; the ladies. and this town,
But I have some ideas still remaining,
But this song is done, and I'll write the other one,
When I arrive in the happy land of Canaan.
    Oh, ah, &c.

These songs show the resentment to Brown's abortive insurrection in a southern state.

"JOHN BROWN'S BODY LIES MOULDERING IN THE GRAVE, BUT HIS SOUL GOES MARCHING ON"

An Acrostic by Hon. Nathan Ward Fitz-Gerald, Tacoma, Wash., U. S. A.

J oin all ye people, small and great,
O n "Battlefield" we dedicate,
H ere in this TOWN where John Brown's fame
N ow helps immortalize ITS NAME.

B rave, noble soul, with courage grand!
R aised here HIS standard, "FREE THE LAND."
O n Kansas plains his work begun
W hich freedom gained for "Afric's" son,
N or feared to meet impending strife,
S tood for state's "FREE-SOIL" with his life.

B ody and soul, this hero brave,
O n his convictions, freely gave,
D earest of all life could command,
Y earning to FREE this virgin land.

L ived, fought, on this great Kansas plain
I n days when slavery sought to gain
E xtension of its bounds, far wide,
S tood here and freedom's foes DEFIED.

M an of great purpose, iron will,
O f deeds, which hist'ry's pages fill;
U ndaunted in THAT PURPOSE great,
L ived! died! to help perpetuate,
D ecree, which God had surely wrought,
E ven if with OWN BLOOD 'twas bought.
R ighteous and just, the cause he led;
I t marches on, he is not dead,
N or ere shall be—let freedom ring!
G randly his praise, which millions sing.

I n dust, his "body" soon was gone;
N ot so his "soul!" "It marches on."

T rue Patriots! Nation, town and state,
H old sacred, dear, his mem'ry great;
E ach, HIS GRAND DEEDS, they venerate.

G rave cannot hide great deeds of men,
R are, honored, grand, they live again,
A nd greater grow with passing time—
V iewed ages after:—deeds sublime,
E 'er speak in prose, and poets' rhyme.

B righter his name and fame will shine,
U nsullied in "GREAT MARTYR'S" line,
T hat noble soul, with grand design.

H ARPER'S FERRY! with JOHN BROWN'S name,
I s linked, for all time, with his fame;
S o! "OS-SA-WAT-O-MIE," too, can claim.

S ons! daughters! yea! now freemen all,
O nce, enslaved millions! heard his call;
U nion then torn, by slaverys hand,
L ives! re-united, FREEDOM'S LAND.

G reat! through the years of endless time,
O n hist'ry's page, HIS NAME, sublime,
E ver in undimmed lustre bright,
S hall stand AS FREEDOM'S SHINING LIGHT!

M arching on! ages yet to be!
A ttuned—HIS NAME—WITH LIBERTY!
R aised arm and voice to give men hope,
C ared not for self, feared not the rope:—
H eard cries of millions, gave his all
I n their behalf; DID DUTY'S CALL:—
N e'er shall his FAME in glory's line
G row DIM; but BRIGHT THRO' AGES shine.

O n FAME'S ETERNAL TABLET FAIR,
N ame of JOHN BROWN is written there.

John Brown's desk and safe, used by him while residing in Springfield, Mass., are in the collections of the Connecticut Valley Historical Museum. COURTESY CONNECTICUT VALLEY HISTORICAL MUSEUM, SPRINGFIELD, MASS.

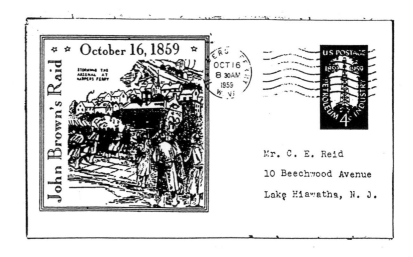

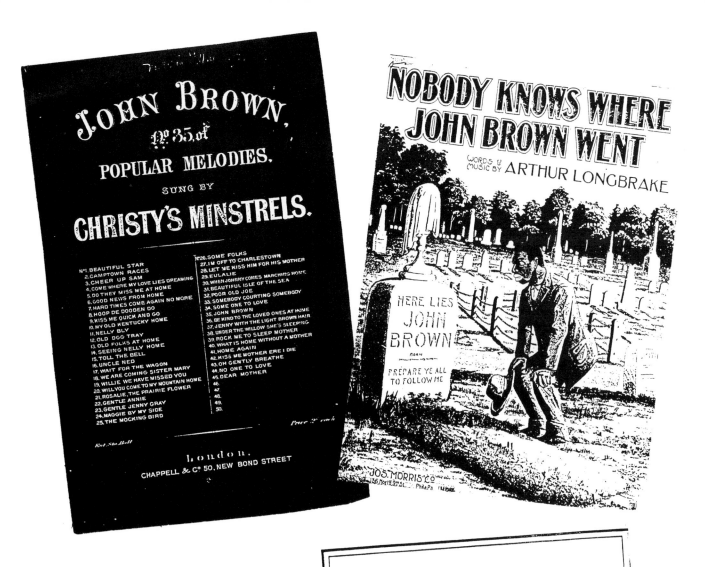

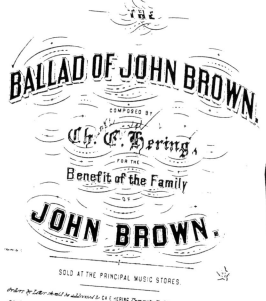

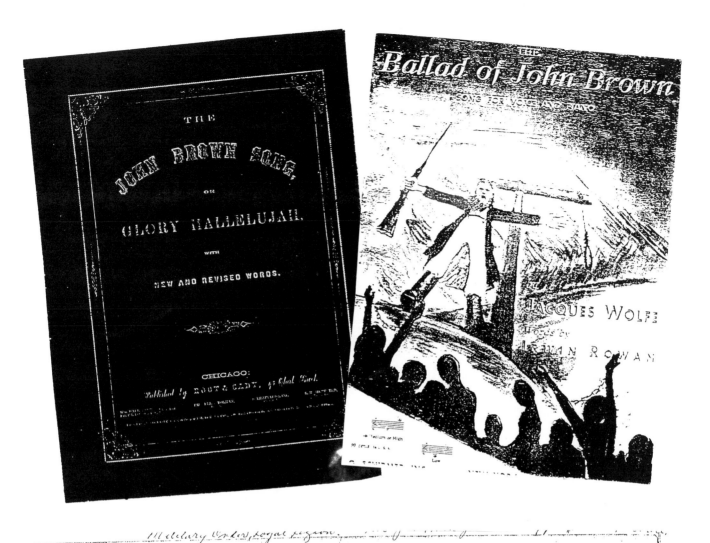

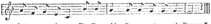

OSSAWATOMIE BROWN.

Music from memory by Companion J. R. Saville,

Colorado Commandery.

Old John Brown to Har-per's Fer - ry went, And

there he looked all round, Said he: "Guv'ner Wise you must

let my peo - ple go, For I'm old Os - sa - wat - o - mie

Brown,(says he) I'm old Os - sa - wat - o - mie Brown, I'm

old Os - sa - wat - o - mie Brown," Said he:"Gov-n'r Wise you must

let my people go, For I'm old Os - sa - wat - o - mie Brown."

His soul went straight to Peter's gate
  With a sudden bound ;
As he winged his way, he still exclaimed,
  "I'm old Ossawatomie Brown."

Chorus—I'm old Ossawatomie Brown, etc.

They opened wide the pearly gates,
  And, with a joyful sound,
The angel host rang out a cheer
  For old Ossawatomie Brown.

Chorus—For old Ossawatomie Brown,
    For old Ossawatomie Brown,
  The angel host rang out a cheer
    For old Ossawatomie Brown.

The deed was done ; the war begun ;
  And thus it came around,
That Uncle Abe set all the darkeys free
  For old Ossawatomie Brown.

Chorus—That Uncle Abe set all the darkeys free
    For old Ossawatomie Brown.

His faith was great, and to relate
  His deeds of great renown,
Our voices raise in loudest praise
  Of old Ossawatomie Brown.

Chorus—Our voices raise in loudest praise
    Of old Ossawatomie Brown.

His cause was just, in God his trust ;
  To ages shall go down
The glorious name and deathless fame
  Of old Ossawatomie Brown.

Chorus—The glorious name and deathless fame
    Of old Ossawatomie Brown.

Major Elliott, Denver Commandery.

88

89

EXTRACTS FROM SPEECH.

"I say, I am yet too young to understand that God is a respecter of persons. I believe to have interfered as I have done—as I have always freely admitted I have done—in behalf of his despised poor, was not wrong but right. Now if it is deemed necessary that I should forfeit my life for the furtherance of the ends of justice, and mingle my blood further with the blood of my children * * * I submit; so let it be done!"

TRIBUTE TO A MARTYR.

"Not any spot six feet by two
    Will hold a man like thee;
John Brown will tramp the shaking earth
    From Blue Ridge to the sea,
Till the strong angel comes, at last,
    And opens the dungeon door,
And God's Great Charter holds and waves
    O'er all his humble poor.

And then the humble poor will come,
    In that far distant day,
And from the felon's nameless grave
    They'll brush a tear away;
And gray old men will point the spot
    Beneath the pine tree shade,
As children ask, with streaming eyes,
    Where Old John Brown is laid.

MEMORIAL OF

HIS APPEARANCE.

He was lean, strong and sinewy; of the best New England mould; built for times of trouble, fitted to grapple with the most stone-like hardships; clad in plain American wool, shod in boots of cow-hide leather, and wearing a cravat of very substantial material. He stood about six feet high and weighed about 150 pounds. His age was 59 years. He presented a figure straight and symmetrical as a mountain pine. His bearing was singularly impressive; his head was of medium size, firm and high. His hair was coarse, strong, slightly gray. He wore a full beard and had a strong, square mouth, supported by a broad, firm chin; his eyes were blueish gray, and in conversation they seemed full of light and fire.

BORN:

MAY 9TH, 1800.
At Torrington, Conn.

JOHN BROWN.

EXTRACTS.

Said he: "Time and the honest decision of posterity will approve every act of mine to prevent slavery from being established in Kansas.

"The blood of a fellow man has never been shed by me except in self defense, or in promotion of a righteous cause. * * * I have always been in favor of the idea that all men are created equal; and to my mind it is like our Saviour's command, "Thou shalt love thy neighbor as thyself." Friends, how can we do that unless our neighbor is equal to ourselves? This is the doctrine! and rather than have that fail in this world, or in these States, it would be better that a whole generation die a violent death.—Yea, better that heaven and earth pass away than that one jot or title of this be not fulfilled.

EXECUTED:

DECEMBER 2ND, 1859.
Charlestown, Va.

Sketch of the Life of John Brown.

JOHN BROWN, the celebrated champion of liberty, was born in Torrington, Conn., May 9th, 1800, of poor, but respectable parents. He was the fifth descendent from Peter Brown, who landed at Plymouth, in 1620. At the age of five his father emigrated to Ohio; at eight he suffered a great loss in the death of his mother. He early in life became ambitious to excel in anything he undertook to perform. During 1812 he visited several camps of American troops, and became disgusted with soldiery and resolved never to take part in any war which was not for liberty. About this time he conceived that detestation of slavery which became the master passion of his life. He received a strict religious education and intended to enter the christian ministry, but a chronic disease of the eyes made this impossible. He then resumed a tanner's business, which he had previously carried on with his father. He was afterwards engaged in different lines of business until through speculation he was ruined. In 1855 he emigrated to Kansas, where his son had preceded him. Here he became a daring and most resolute partisan leader of the Free State Party during the civil war in Kansas, in 1856-57. In May, 1859, he organized an invasion into Virginia, for the purpose of liberating the slaves. On October 16th, aided by about 20 men, he took possession of the Arsenal and Armory at Harper's Ferry, but he was attacked the following day by the Virginia Militia. Two of his sons and almost all of his men were killed; and himself being captured was tried for treason and murder, and sentenced to be hung, December 2nd, 1859. In the speech which he addressed to the Court on this occasion, he disavowed any intention of committing murder or treason, or the willful destruction of property. His prime object, he said, was to liberate the slaves, not to excite them to insurrection, and he therefore felt no consciousness of guilt. On the day appointed for his execution he left the jail, an eye-witness said, "with the radiant countenance and the step of a conqueror." "Shall I give you a handkerchief," asked the Sheriff, "and let you drop it as a signal?" "No; I am ready at any time; but do not keep me needlessly waiting," he answered. On the scaffold he was calm, gentle and resigned, and warmly thanked all who had been kind to him during his imprisonment. Let it be remembered that when John Brown came out of jail at Charlestown, in the last moments of his life, and saw a poor colored woman sitting on the steps with two little children, he took up one of them and kissed it, which seemed to show to the nation that there was yet a spark of affection that could never be blotted out. And that spark lit up the world never to go out while the Nation stands. He met his death with perfect composure, and was apparently the least concerned of all present over the tragic event of the day. John Brown died as he had lived, a resolute, unyielding zealot. His piety was as sincere as it was severe. No doubt from his acts came the great civil war which resulted in the freedom of a great race of cruelly wronged people. The name of John Brown will ever be held in reverence by the grateful colored people.

PROVISIONAL CONSTITUTION AND ORDINANCES

FOR THE

PEOPLE OF THE UNITED STATES.

PREAMBLE.

Whereas, Slavery, throughout its entire existence in the United States, is none other than a most barbarous, unprovoked, and unjustifiable War of one portion of its citizens upon another portion; the only conditions of which are perpetual imprisonment, and hopeless servitude or absolute extermination; in utter disregard and violation of those eternal and self-evident truths set forth in our Declaration of Independence: Therefore,

WE, CITIZENS OF THE UNITED STATES, AND THE OPPRESSED PEOPLE, WHO, BY A RECENT DECISION OF THE SUPREME COURT ARE DECLARED TO HAVE NO RIGHTS WHICH THE WHITE MAN IS BOUND TO RESPECT; TOGETHER WITH ALL OTHER PEOPLE DEGRADED BY THE LAWS THEREOF, DO, FOR THE TIME BEING ORDAIN AND ESTABLISH FOR OURSELVES, THE FOLLOWING PROVISIONAL CONSTITUTION AND ORDINANCES, THE BETTER TO PROTECT OUR PERSONS, PROPERTY, LIVES, AND LIBERTIES; AND TO GOVERN OUR ACTIONS:

ARTICLE I.

QUALIFICATIONS FOR MEMBERSHIP.

ALL persons of mature age, whether Proscribed, oppressed and enslaved Citizens, or of the Proscribed

A

Brown in Chatham, Ontario, Canada

In May 1858 Brown journied to Chatham, Ontario, Canada, for a meeting of 46 white and black delegates. At the meeting his "Provisional Constitution and Ordinances for the People of the United States" was adopted.

The main purpose of this document was to provide an instrument for the government of a nation of liberated slaves by "amendment and reform" of the federal government. The ordinances called for a kind of military dictatorship under the commander-in-chief of the army. John Brown was expected to fill this position when his new nation was established. Brown's government would exist side-by-side with the United States government while his army was liberating the slaves.

The printer of this document was a free Black man living in St. Catherine's, Ontario, by the name of William Howard Day. Day helped to organize Canadian Blacks for Brown's cause, several of them joined him on the Harpers Ferry Raid. CONSTITUTION COPY FROM JEFFERSON COUNTY MUSEUM

2   CONSTITUTION

and oppressed races of the United States, who shall agree to sustain and enforce the Provisional Constitution and Ordinances of this organization, together with all minor children of such persons, shall be held to be fully entitled to protection under the same.

ARTICLE II.

BRANCHES OF GOVERNMENT.

The provisional government of this organization shall consist of three branches, viz: Legislative, Executive, and Judicial.

ARTICLE III.

LEGISLATIVE.

The legislative branch shall be a Congress or House of Representatives, composed of not less than five, nor more than ten members, who shall be elected by all citizens of mature age and of sound mind, connected with this organization; and who shall remain in office for three years, unless sooner removed for misconduct, inability, or by death. A majority of such members shall constitute a quorum.

ARTICLE IV.

EXECUTIVE.

The executive branch of this organization shall consist of a President and Vice President, who shall be chosen by the citizens or members of this organization, and each of whom shall hold his office for three years, unless sooner removed by death, or for inability or misconduct.

ARTICLE V.

JUDICIAL.

The judicial branch of this organization shall consist of one Chief Justice of the Supreme Court, and of four Associate Judges of said court; each constituting a Circuit Court. They shall each be chosen in the same manner as the President, and shall continue in office until their places have been filled in the same manner by election of the citizens. Said court shall

AND ORDINANCES.   3

have jurisdiction in all civil or criminal causes, arising under this constitution, except breaches of the Rules of War.

ARTICLE VI.

VALIDITY OF ENACTMENTS.

All enactments of the legislative branch shall, to become valid, during the first three years, have the approbation of the President, and of the Commander-in-Chief of the Army.

ARTICLE VII.

COMMANDER-IN-CHIEF.

A Commander-in-Chief of the army shall be chosen by the President, Vice President, a majority of the provisional congress, and of the supreme court, and he shall receive his commission from the President, signed by the Vice President, the Chief Justice of the supreme court, and the Secretary of War: and he shall hold his office for three years, unless removed by death, or on proof of incapacity or misbehavior. He shall, unless under arrest, (and until his place is actually filled as provided for by this constitution) direct all movements of the army, and advise with any allies. He shall however, be tried, removed or punished, on complaint to the President, by, at least, three general officers, or a majority of the House of Representatives, or of the supreme court; which House of Representatives, (the President presiding,) the Vice President, and the members of the supreme court, shall constitute a court-martial, for his trial; with power to remove or punish, as the case may require; and to fill his place as above provided.

ARTICLE VIII.

OFFICERS.

A Treasurer, Secretary of State, Secretary of War and Secretary of the Treasury, shall each be chosen for the first three years, in the same way and manner as the Commander-in-chief; subject to trial or removal on complaint of the President, Vice President, or Commander-in-chief, to the Chief Justice of the supreme court ; or on complaint of the majority of the members of said court, or the provisional congress. The supreme court shall have power to try or punish either of those officers ; and their places shall be filled as before.

ARTICLE IX.
SECRETARY OF WAR.

The Secretary of War shall be under the immediate direction of the Commander-in-chief ; who may temporarily fill his place, in case of arrest, or of any inability to serve.

ARTICLE X.
CONGRESS OR HOUSE OF REPRESENTATIVES.

The House of Representatives shall make ordinances providing for the appointment (by the President or otherwise) of all civil officers, excepting those already named ; and shall have power to make all laws and ordinances for the general good, not inconsistent with this constitution and these ordinances.

ARTICLE XI.
APPROPRIATION OF MONEY, &c.

The provisional congress shall have power to appropriate money or other property actually in the hands of the Treasurer, to any object calculated to promote the general good, so far as may be consistent with the provisions of this constitution ; and may in certain cases, appropriate, for a moderate compensation of agents, or persons not members of this organization, for important service they are known to have rendered.

ARTICLE XII.
SPECIAL DUTIES.

It shall be the duty of Congress to provide for the instant removal of any civil officer or policeman, who becomes habitually intoxicated, or who is addicted to other immoral conduct, or to any neglect or unfaithfulness in the discharge of his official duties. Congress shall also be a standing Committee of Safety, for the

purpose of obtaining important information ; and shall be in constant communication with the Commander-in-chief ; the members of which shall each, as also the President, Vice President, members of the supreme court, and Secretary of State, have full power to issue warrants returnable as Congress shall ordain, (naming witnesses, &c.,) upon their own information, without the formality of a complaint. Complaint shall be immediately made after arrest, and before trial ; the party arrested to be served with a copy at once.

ARTICLE XIII.
TRIAL OF PRESIDENT AND OTHER OFFICERS.

The President and Vice President may either of them be tried, removed or punished, on complaint made to the Chief Justice of the supreme court, by a majority of the House of Representatives ; which house, together with the Associate Judges of the Supreme Court, the whole to be presided over by the Chief Justice in cases of the trial of the Vice President, shall have full power to try such officers, to remove, or punish as the case may require ; and to fill any vacancy so occurring, the same as in case of the Commander-in-chief.

ARTICLE XIV.
TRIAL OF MEMBERS OF CONGRESS.

The members of the House of Representatives may any and all of them be tried, and on conviction, removed or punished on complaint before the Chief Justice of the supreme court, made by any number of the members of said house, exceeding one-third ; which house, with the Vice President and Associate Judges of the supreme court, shall constitute the proper tribunal, with power to fill such vacancies.

ARTICLE XV.
IMPEACHMENT OF JUDGES.

Any member of the supreme court may also be impeached, tried, convicted or punished by removal or

otherwise, on complaint to the President, who shall in such case, preside ; the Vice President, House of Representatives, and other members of the supreme court, constituting the proper tribunal : (with power to fill vacancies ;) on complaint of a majority of said house of representatives, or of the supreme court ; a majority of the whole having power to decide.

ARTICLE XVI.
DUTIES OF PRESIDENT AND SECRETARY OF STATE.

The President, with the Secretary of State, shall immediately upon entering on the duties of their office, give special attention to secure, from amongst their own people, men of integrity, intelligence and good business habits, and capacity ; and above all, of first-rate moral and religious character and influence, to act as civil officers of every description and grade, as well as teachers, chaplains, physicians, surgeons, mechanics, agents of every description, clerks and messengers. They shall make special efforts to induce at the earliest possible period, persons and families of that description, to locate themselves within the limits secured by this organization ; and shall, moreover, from time to time, supply the names and residence of such persons to the Congress, for their special notice and information, as among the most important of their duties, and the President is hereby authorized and empowered to afford special aid to such individuals, from such moderate appropriations as the Congress shall be able and may deem it advisable to make for that object. The President and Secretary of State, and in cases of disagreement, the Vice President, shall appoint all civil officers, but shall not have power to remove any officer. All removals shall be the result of a fair trial, whether civil or military.

ARTICLE XVII.
FURTHER DUTIES.

It shall be the duty of the President and Secretary of State, to find out (as soon as possible) the real

friends, as well as enemies of this organization in every part of the country ; to secure among them, innkeepers, private postmasters, private mail-contractors, messengers and agents : through whom may be obtained correct and regular information, constantly ; recruits for the service, places of deposit and sale ; together with all needed supplies : and it shall be matter of special regard to secure such facilities through the Northern States.

ARTICLE XVIII.
DUTY OF THE PRESIDENT.

It shall be the duty of the President, as well as the House of Representatives, at all times to inform the Commander-in-chief of any matter that may require his attention, or that may affect the public safety.

ARTICLE XIX.
DUTY OF PRESIDENT—CONTINUED.

It shall be the duty of the President to see that the provisional ordinances of this organization, and those made by the Congress, are promptly and faithfully executed ; and he may in cases of great urgency call on the Commander-in-chief of the army, or other officers for aid ; it being however intended that a sufficient civil police shall always be in readiness to secure implicit obedience to law.

ARTICLE XX.
THE VICE PRESIDENT.

The Vice President shall be the presiding officer of the provisional congress ; and in cases of tie shall give the casting vote.

ARTICLE XXI.
VACANCIES.

In case of the death, removal, or inability of the President, the Vice President, and next to him the Chief Justice of the supreme court shall be the President during the remainder of the term : and the place of the Chief Justice thus made vacant shall be filled by Congress from some of the members of said court :

and the places of the Vice President and Associate Justice thus made vacant, filled by an election by the united action of the Provisional Congress and members of the supreme court. All other vacancies, not heretofore specially provided for, shall during the first three years, be filled by the united action of the President, Vice President, Supreme Court and Commander-in-chief of the Army.

ARTICLE XXII.
PUNISHMENT OF CRIMES.

The punishment of crimes not capital, except in case of insubordinate convicts or other prisoners, shall be, (so far as may be,) by hard labor on the public works, roads, &c.

ARTICLE XXIII.
ARMY APPOINTMENTS.

It shall be the duty of all commissioned officers of the army, to name candidates of merit for office or elevation to the Commander-in-chief, who, with the Secretary of War, and, in cases of disagreement, the President shall be the appointing power of the army: and all commissions of military officers shall bear the signatures of the Commander-in-chief and the Secretary of War. And it shall be the special duty of the Secretary of War to keep for constant reference of the Commander-in-chief a full list of names of persons nominated for office, or elevation, by the officers of the army, with the name and rank of the officer nominating, stating distinctly but briefly the grounds for such notice or nomination. The Commander-in-chief shall not have power to remove or punish any officer or soldier; but he may order their arrest and trial at any time, by court-martial.

ARTICLE XXIV.
COURTS MARTIAL.

Courts-martial for Companies, Regiments, Brigades &c., shall be called by the chief officer of each com-

mand, on complaint, to him by any officer, or any five privates, in such command, and shall consist of not less than five nor more than nine officers, non-commissioned officers and privates, one-half of whom shall not be lower in rank than the person on trial, to be chosen by the three highest officers in the command, which officers shall not be a part of such court. The chief officer of any command shall of course be tried by a court martial of the command above his own. All decisions affecting the lives of persons, or office of persons holding commission must, before taking full effect have the signature of the Commander-in-chief, who may also, on the recommendation of at least one-third of the members of the court martial finding any sentence, grant a reprieve or commutation of the same.

ARTICLE XXV.
SALARIES.

No person connected with this organization shall be entitled to any salary, pay or emolument, other than a competent support of himself and family, unless it be from an equal dividend, made of public property, on the establishment of peace, or of special provision by treaty; which provision shall be made for all persons who may have been in any active civil or military service at any time previous to any hostile action for Liberty and Equality.

ARTICLE XXVI.
TREATIES OF PEACE.

Before any treaty of peace shall take full effect, it shall be signed by the President and Vice President, the Commander-in-chief, a majority of the House of Representatives, a majority of the supreme court, and majority of all the general officers of the army.

ARTICLE XXVII.
DUTY OF THE MILITARY.

It shall be the duty of the Commander-in-chief, and all officers and soldiers of the army, to afford special

protection when needed, to Congress, or any member thereof; to the supreme court, or any member thereof; to the President, Vice President, Treasurer, Secretary of State, Secretary of the Treasury, and Secretary of War; and to afford general protection to all civil officers, or other persons having right to the same.

ARTICLE XXVIII.
PROPERTY.

All captured or confiscated property, and all property the product of the labor of those belonging to this organization and of their families, shall be held as the property of the whole, equally, without distinction; and may be used for the common benefit, or disposed of for the same object; and any person, officer or otherwise, who shall improperly retain, secrete, use, or needlessly destroy such property, or property found, captured or confiscated, belonging to the enemy, or shall wilfully neglect to render a full and fair statement of such property by him so taken or held, shall be deemed guilty of a misdemeanor, and on conviction, shall be punished accordingly.

ARTICLE XXIX.
SAFETY OR INTELLIGENCE FUND.

All money, plate, watches or jewelry, captured by honorable warfare, found, taken, or confiscated, belonging to the enemy, shall be held sacred, to constitute a liberal safety or intelligence fund; and any person who shall improperly retain, dispose of, hide, use, or destroy such money or other article above named, contrary to the provisions and spirit of this article, shall be deemed guilty of theft; and on conviction thereof, shall be punished accordingly. The Treasurer shall furnish the Commander-in-chief at all times with a full statement of the condition of such fund, and its nature.

ARTICLE XXX.
THE COMMANDER-IN-CHIEF AND THE TREASURY.

The Commander-in-chief shall have power to draw

from the treasury, the money and other property of the fund provided for in Article twenty-ninth, but his orders shall be signed also by the Secretary of War, who shall keep strict account of the same; subject to examination by any member of Congress, or general officer.

ARTICLE XXXI.
SURPLUS OF THE SAFETY OR INTELLIGENCE FUND.

It shall be the duty of the Commander-in-chief to advise the President of any Surplus of the Safety and Intelligence Fund; who shall have power to draw such Surplus, (his order being also signed by the Secretary of State,) to enable him to carry out the provisions of Article Seventeenth.

ARTICLE XXXII.
PRISONERS.

No person, after having surrendered himself or herself a prisoner, and who shall properly demean himself or herself as such, to any officer or private connected with this organization, shall afterward be put to death, or be subjected to any corporeal punishment, without first having had the benefit of a fair and impartial trial: nor shall any prisoner be treated with any kind of cruelty, disrespect, insult, or needless severity: but it shall be the duty of all persons, male and female, connected herewith, at all times and under all circumstances, to treat all such prisoners with every degree of respect and kindness the nature of the circumstances will admit of; and to insist on a like course of conduct from all others, as in the fear of Almighty God, to whose care and keeping we commit our cause.

ARTICLE XXXIII.
VOLUNTARIES.

All persons who may come forward and shall voluntarily deliver up their slaves, and have their names registered on the Books of the organization, shall, so long as they continue at peace, be entitled to the fullest protection of person and property, though not connected with this organization, and shall be treated as friends, and not merely as persons neutral.

ARTICLE XXXIV.
NEUTRALS.

The persons and property of all non-slaveholders who shall remain absolutely neutral, shall be respected so far as the circumstances can allow of it ; but they shall not be entitled to any active protection.

ARTICLE XXXV.
NO NEEDLESS WASTE.

The needless waste or destruction of any useful property or article, by fire, throwing open of fences, fields, buildings, or needless killing of animals, or injury of either, shall not be tolerated at any time or place, but shall be promptly and properly punished.

ARTICLE XXXVI.
PROPERTY CONFISCATED.

The entire personal and real property of all persons known to be acting either directly or indirectly with or for the enemy, or found in arms with them, or found wilfully holding slaves, shall be confiscated and taken, whenever and wherever it may be found, in either Free or Slave States.

ARTICLE XXXVII.
DESERTION.

Persons convicted, on impartial trial, of desertion to the enemy after becoming members, acting as spies, or of treacherous surrender of property, arms, ammunition, provisions, or supplies of any kind, roads, bridges, persons, or fortifications, shall be put to death and their entire property confiscated.

ARTICLE XXXVIII.
VIOLATION OF PAROLE OF HONOR.

Persons proven to be guilty of taking up arms after having been set at liberty on parole of honor, or after the same, to have taken any active part with or for the

enemy, direct or indirect, shall be put to death and their entire property confiscated.

ARTICLE XXXIX.
ALL MUST LABOR.

All persons connected in any way with this organization, and who may be entitled to full protection under it : shall be held as under obligation to labor in some way for the general good ; and persons refusing, or neglecting so to do, shall on conviction receive a suitable and appropriate punishment.

ARTICLE XL.
IRREGULARITIES.

Profane swearing, filthy conversation, indecent behavior, or indecent exposure of the person, or intoxication, or quarreling, shall not be allowed, or tolerated ; neither unlawful intercourse of the sexes.

ARTICLE XLI.
CRIMES.

Persons convicted of the forcible violation of any female prisoner, shall be put to death.

ARTICLE XLII.
THE MARRIAGE RELATION—SCHOOLS—THE SABBATH.

The marriage relation shall be at all times respected ; and families kept together as far as possible ; and broken families encouraged to re-unite, and intelligence offices established for that purpose, schools and churches established as soon as may be ; for the purpose of religious and other instructions ; and the first day of the week regarded as a day of rest, and appropriated to moral and religious instruction and improvement ; relief of the suffering, instruction of the young and ignorant, and the encouragement of personal cleanliness ; nor shall any persons be required on that day to perform ordinary manual labor, unless in extremely urgent cases.

ARTICLE XLIII.
CARRY ARMS OPENLY.

All persons known to be of good character, and of sound mind, and suitable age, who are connected with this organization, whether male or female, shall be encouraged to carry arms openly.

ARTICLE XLIV.
NO PERSON TO CARRY CONCEALED WEAPONS.

No person within the limits of the conquered territory, except regularly appointed policemen, express-officers of the army, mail carriers, or other fully accredited messengers of the Congress, President, Vice President, members of the supreme court, or commissioned officer of the army—and those only under peculiar circumstances—shall be allowed, at any time, to carry concealed weapons ; and any person not specially authorized so to do, who shall be found so doing, shall be deemed a suspicious person, and may at once be arrested by any officer, soldier, or citizen, without the formality of a Complaint or Warrant, and may, at once be subjected to thorough search, and shall have his or her case thoroughly investigated ; and be dealt with as circumstances, on proof, shall require.

ARTICLE XLV.
PERSONS TO BE SEIZED.

Persons within the limits of the territory holden by this organization, not connected with this organization, having arms at all, concealed or otherwise, shall be seized at once ; or be taken in charge of some vigilant officer ; and their case thoroughly investigated : and it shall be the duty of all citizens and soldiers, as well as officers, to arrest such parties as are named in this and the preceding Section or Article, without the formality of Complaint or Warrant ; and they shall be placed in charge of some proper officer for examination, or for safe keeping.

ARTICLE XLVI.
THESE ARTICLES NOT FOR THE OVERTHROW OF GOV'MT.

The foregoing Articles shall not be construed so as in any way to encourage the overthrow of any State Government, or of the General Government of the United States: and look to no dissolution of the Union, but simply to Amendment and Repeal. And our Flag shall be the same that our Fathers fought under in the Revolution.

ARTICLE XLVII.
NO PLURALITY OF OFFICES.

No two of the offices specially provided for, by this Instrument, shall be filled by the same person, at the same time.

ARTICLE XLVIII.
OATH.

Every officer, civil or military, connected with this organization, shall, before entering upon the duties of his office, make solemn oath or affirmation, to abide by and support this Provisional Constitution and these Ordinances. Also, every Citizen and Soldier, before being fully recognized as such, shall do the same.

SCHEDULE.

The President of this Convention shall convene, immediately, on the adoption of this instrument, a convention of all such persons as shall have given their adherence, by signature, to the constitution ; who shall proceed to fill by election all offices specially named in said constitution, the President of this convention presiding, and issuing commissions to such officers elect : all such officers being thereafter elected in the manner provided in the body of this instrument.

THE NEW YEAR MESSAGE

OF THE

NEWSMEN OF THE NEW YORK HERALD,

TO THEIR SUBSCRIBERS AND READERS,

January 1, A. D. 1860.

NEW YEAR! NEW YEAR'S!—Welcome the day—champagne or
    lager bier,
Or schnapps, or punch, or lemonade, or water cool and clear—
Good morning, fellow-citizens. To all a good NEW YEAR,
Indeed they say we are a day behind the time ; but who
That had one New Year yesterday will now object to two?
The Old Year gone—the New Year on, again the minstrel sings,
Thus bears Old Time our lives away, upon his rushing wings.
Thanks to a bounteous Providence, for all His mercies, and
May He continue still to shower His blessings on our land.

Brown! Old Brown! Ossawatomie Brown!
Border ruffian, free State Kansas Captain John Brown.
    What a terrible story
      His last plunge for glory!
What a dare-devil dash—what a bloody break down!
But the ladies are waiting. We hasten—we fly
To receive their commands and fulfil them, or die.

The Ladies! yes, we must confess, they rule by grace divine—
Not only Queen Victoria, with her sons and daughters nine,
And Eugenie, who, throughout the world, is recognized the queen
Who reigns in all that appertains to the laws of crinoline, [won,
But our own feminines (bless their souls), by whom all hearts are
And whom we hail this festive day as the Persian hails the sun,
What'er the sweet relation which they hold to us—their charms,
From the old grandmother by the hearth, to "baby" in our arms,
Are still our weakness or our strength, whereby we fall or rise ;
So a New Year toast to woman, for the welcome in her eyes—
Or whether at the bounteous board, or at the humble door
Where she can but her welcome give, her wish, and nothing more.

Brown ! Brown !
That hard-headed Puritan crusader, Brown.
A cast-iron man, was this fanatic Brown ;
His followers, his children, he led to the slaughter
As coolly as if to a sail on the water ;
Such, such, the extremes of that dreadful sedition,
Preached for years by our teachers of black abolition.
And to see in the North the bold traitor extoll'd
As a saint,—as a hero of freedom enroll'd
With Washington, Hampden, and Sydney and Tell,
What does all this mean? we may ask :—Who can tell
The drift of this fierce agitation?—We fear
That the crisis of strife and disunion is near.
Or upward to peace, or to anarchy down,
We must go from these crusades of Helper and Brown.

We fly the track—we hurry back. We hear the joyous chimes
Which bring to us again the scenes, and friends of other times,
And sad yet blessed memories of some who have passed away
To the happier band of a better land, even since last New Year's day.
Peace—peace. We look around—we see this is a day of fun,
Yet, judging from the tipping and the sipping thus begun—
Some boys will find it otherwise before the day is done.

The Atlantic Cable—"mum's the word"—De Sauty, where is he?
Down, down among the dead men, at the bottom of the sea.
But never fear, he'll reappear as soon as he is able
To telegraph a sound or sign from the Atlantic Cable.
And when he shall do so, look out, good people, one and all,
For another bonfire of the dome that crowns our City Hall.

Can anyone show—or does anyone know
What became of the four hundred niggers, or so.
Of the merry yacht, Wanderer, landed hard by
The port of Savannah? Oh ! where did they fly?
'Tis reported that from this aforesaid Savannah,
They were strewn all the way down to Louisiana ;
That the traveller along the Tombigbee to-day,
Without going very much out of his way,
May meet here and there with a specimen clod
Of the gang which the Wanderer brought from the sod.
Did the enterprise pay? Let that question remain
Till the merry yacht Wanderer has tried it again.

Time ! time ! we must roll on the panorama—
Ah ! what is this ! A bloody melo-drama—
The very queerest of the last half dozen years :
A gay young wife in unavailing tears—
Her lover slaughtered and her lord insane—
You know the rest—why tell it o'er again ?

Pass we to Italy—That field of Mars,
That theatre of armies and of wars,
And lo ! "the nephew of his uncle," proves, we see,
Himself another "child of Destiny,"
Giving to France the Uncle's deeds again,
In five great victories in a brief campaign,—
When, mixed up "in the elbows of the Mincio," he
The "nephew of his uncle" claimed to be
The liberator of all Italy,
Found that "the quadrilateral" was no joke,
And over a mild segar with Austria, broke
The "dream of Italy" in a cloud of smoke.
Indignant were her sons to find, next day,
Her hopes of liberty thus whiff'd away,
The "word of promise broken to her hope,"
In the "King Log" awarded in the Pope.

Nor can the keenest statesman comprehend,
Even yet where this pacification will extend ;
But we maintain that peace is well nigh won,
That Italy's liberation's half way done,
Where the good work has been so well begun,
As by the Italian people, since the fray
Of Solferino's memorable day,
And "by the margin of fair Zurich's waters," say
Is it not so, good Monsieur Bourquenay ?"

On Africa's shores,
The piratical Moors,
From a truce of three hundred long years, are again
Call'd to arms to repel
The bold "infidel,"
Who drove their ancestors in blood out of Spain.
And of this war, whate'er the cause, we may predict the advance
Of "the annexation" policy of young imperial France.
The Moors, descendants of that race, renowned in song and story,
As the heroes of Grenada, whose deeds of love and glory,
Will never die ! Alas ! that now that people should be found
A nest of buccaneers pursued into their native ground,
By the same hostile race from whom the fallen Moor must know,
His fathers seized "Alhambra's" site a thousand years ago.

The Chinese, John Bull, and Johnny Crapeau,
Have had some hot work away up the Peiho,
Brother Jonathan towing a gun-boat or so.
The allies were smart, but the pigtails were smarter,
And the "outside barbarians" for once caught a Tartar,
For in choosing their own way to go to Pekin,
They had to step out, for they could not go in.
Not so the American minister, who
Appeared to know better what route to pursue,
And thus reached the city to tender his bow,
To the "Son of the Sun," who demanded "ko-tow !"
A form which our minister could not get round,
Three kneels and nine bumps of the head on the ground ;
Nor would the great Emperor, nor could he, back down,
So without kneeling, or bumping his head on the floor.
    And without even a sight of the Chinese Blue
    Beard, our distinguished fellow-citizen left, getting
    His treaty signed for what it is worth,
    Some miles out of town.

En passant, we must say,
'Twas a great thing, that squadron to wild Paraguay,
Proving Lopez the prince of good boys, and quite willing
To admit he had bought too much pork for a shilling.
Ah ! me, could such a fleet be sent to our neighbors just below,
How soon could we dictate the fate of wretched Mexico.

But, hark ! what news is this we hear from the Pacific coast ?
A small disputed island seized, and Harney rules the roast,
And mark, the news from England, this act has raised the ire,
Of the fierce old British lion whose eyes are flashing fire,
But, then, brave Gen. Scott, you know, has been to Puget's sound,
To place the island as it was, until the owner's found.

Enough ! what of the Mormons, that loose, ungodly set ?
I calculate we'll have to abate that horrid nuisance yet.
From Brigham with his forty wives, down to the saintly brother,
Whose harem is an Indian squaw and a white one and her mother.
"Can such things be" in a Christian land, and recognized by law ?
Yes, such is Squatter Sovereignty out yonder in Utah ;
Our politicians have no time to attend to aught just now
Except the "almighty nigger," to whom we all must bow.

Brown ! done brown !
Laid low in the mud. Yea, the "wigwam" is down—
For the man she has labored to crush, bones and all,
Has just turned the tables on Tammany Hall.
The people were with him. Well done Mayor Wood,
And all but poor Tammany say it is good.

Good morning !
We have lingered too long ; and without further warning ;
Without even touching the church or the stage ;
Or the last prima donna, who proved "all the rage :"
Or the fashions, or fine arts, or talk of the town ;
Or the noise raised in Congress by Helper and Brown ;
Or the President's message ; or the contest for Speaker ;
Or whether the Union grows stronger or weaker ;
Or the steamship Great Eastern at low-water mark ;
Or that pet of the people our great Central Park ;
Or fast men or fast nags, or fast yachts on the sea,
Or the next great sensation or what it will be,
Or the sad fate of Franklin ; for many years sealed,
But at last by bold Captain McClintock revealed ;
Or the highwayman's seizure (quite enough sir to vex us,
Of Brownsville, a place on the outskirts of Texas ;
Or the late abolitionist orgies to Brown ;
Or our great Union meetings, or how they go down ;
Long, long, live the Union, and a health to old Buck,
Like the man in the play, he "was born to good luck."
Long, long, live the HERALD, "EXCELSIOR," and now
Dear reader, the Newsman, in making his bow,
Pleads his claim to some kind recognition just here,
And would say of this day that each bright souvenir
Is the cake and the wine of his happy NEW YEAR.

John Brown's Legacy

John Brown figures prominently in the 1930s art phenomenon that has been termed Regionalism. The movement's three most important artists were Thomas Hart Benton of Missouri, Grant Wood of Iowa and John Steuart Curry of Kansas. They were also known, at that time, as the "Midwestern Triumviate of American Regionalism."

By the late 1930s, the art movement was in decline. But one of the most representative Regionalism art forms was the mural painting which was done by Curry for the Kansas statehouse in Topeka from 1937 to 1941.

Curry was a magazine illustrator, an artist in Westport, Conn., and finally an artist-in-residence at the University of Wisconsin. A campaign was waged in Kansas to bring the artist back to his home state to produce murals for the statehouse.

A Kansas Murals Commission was established in July 1937 and Curry was hired to paint scenes depicting Kansas history for the statehouse. There was much controversy as to subjects picked by Curry for his murals. One of the subjects was John Brown, which Curry expressed in these words, "the fratricidal fury that first flamed on the plains of Kansas, the tragic prelude to the last bloody feud of the English-speaking people."

Curry named this large mural *The Tragic Prelude* and John Brown's part, as shown here, covers the north wall of the East Corridor. Brown is the central character with many figures of the Civil War surrounding him. There was such an uproar over Curry's paintings that he was not allowed to complete the entire murals and was let out of his contract in 1941.

Curry died of a heart attack in Madison, Wisc., in 1946 at the age of 48. His widow thought the mural controversy "shattering, absolutely shattering. I think it really contributed toward his death."

Curry painted this oil and tempera on canvas, *Freeing of the Slaves* in 1942. The mural is in the Law School library of the University of Wisconsin in Madison.

This was a preliminary study for *The Tragic Prelude*, an oil on canvas done in 1938

John Steuart Curry's John Brown painting was featured on the 1974 album cover of the nationally known band--Kansas.

This was Curry's facial study, done in red chalk, of John Brown for the Kansas statehouse murals. This was one of several portraits sketches made just after he returned from Europe in the fall of 1938

John Steuart Curry painting his canvas *John Brown* at his Madison, Wisc., studio in 1939. This figure study for the Kansas statehouse mural was published in an edition of 250 by the Associated American Artists in 1940.

John Brown Commerative Plaques

A plaque on the outside wall of the old Ashtabula County courthouse in Jefferson, Ohio, reads as follows:

"Owen Brown, son of John Brown, protected by the Black Strings, a secret society of over 1,000 armed men, here described the battle of Harper's Ferry, Va. The night after his father was hung at Charleston, Owen Brown, Barclay Coccic, Francis Meriam, Osborne Anderson, Refugees, and James Redpath, came to this section for protection.

Capt. John Brown, Jr., of the Kansas Border Warfare then lived on the Dorset Road.

Dangerfield P. Newby of Dorset was killed at Harper's Ferry.

Several of Brown's men left this country in 1859 directly from the Maryland Rendezvous. The Federal Government made little effort to arrest any person in Ashtabula County as a conspirator or witness for fear of invoking civil war." [sic.]

The John Brown Plaque at the entrance to the Howard University School Law Library was a gift from the noted sculptor Jacob Lipkin. It is a bas-relief done in mahogany wood, eight feet high and four feet wide, of John Brown holding one child on his shoulder, a large book (supposedly the Bible) in the other hand and another older, naked child, standing beside Brown, holding a sword. The inscription reads "A Naked Child Shall Lead Them."

This mural was painted by Eitaro Ishigaki about 1935 as a Works Progress Administration (WPA) art project and was temporarily placed in the Harlem Magistrate Court in New York City. The mural was the subject of much controversy because some critics viewed the portrait of Lincoln as possessing certain Negro characteristics. Brown stands between Lincoln and Frederick Douglass; other figures are symbolic. Brown is shown holding a rifle, alluding to his violent nature. The black mother and child came from Whittier's poem of the baby kissing incident.

Well-known American poet John Greenleaf Whittier wrote his poem "Brown of Osawatomie" soon after Brown's execution. It first appeared in the *New York Tribune* on Dec. 5, 1859. The poem was widely reprinted, and popularized the legend that Brown stopped to kiss a slave child held by its mother on his descent down the stairs from his jail cell on the way to the gallows. The poem reads at follows:

> John Bown of Osawatomie spake on his dying day:
> 'I will not have to shrive my soul a priest in Slavery's pay.
> But let some poor slave-mother whom I have striven to free,
> With her children, from the gallows-stair put up a prayer for me!'
> John Brown of Osawatomie, they led him out to die;
> And lo! a poor slave-mother with her little child pressed nigh.
> Then the bold, blue eye grew tender, and the old, harsh face grew mild,
> As he stopped between the jeering ranks and kissed the Negro's child!
> The shadows of his stormy life that moment fell apart;
> And they who blamed the bloody hand forgave the loving heart.
> That kiss from all its guilty means redeemed the good intent,
> And round the grisly fighter's hair the martyr's aureole bent!

This incident never happened but several artists translated the poem onto canvas in 1860, thus perpetuating the legend for years. Louis L. Ransom was the first artist to bring the legend to life. His painting was exhibited by P.T. Barnum at his New York City Museum in 1863 where it created a sensation. Currier & Ives issued two versions of it. Thomas Noble painted a life-sized version of the now famous incident in 1867.

JOHN BROWN — THE MARTYR.

The man who made the effort to abolish Slavery. The man who made the effort to prohibit the sale of the Black man. The man who made the effort to loosen and bury the handcuffs, and to establish Freedom throughout the land, with God...

Top left: Another rendition of Whittier's baby kissing incident, with some soldiers dressed more like pirates than military men. This lithograph was painted by Thomas Noble in 1867 and titled, *John Brown's Blessing*.
USAMHI

Top right: The most famous rendition was painted by Thomas Hovenden (1840-1895). His "The Last Moments of John Brown" was an oil on canvas, 46" x 38". It was paid for by Robins Battell of Norfolk, Conn., at an agreed upon price of $4,000. Battell was so pleased with Hovenden's painting and its reception by the public that he increased his check by $12,500, making his total payment $16,500. The painting was donated by Mr. and Mrs. Carl Stoeckel (Battell's daughter) to the Metropolitan Museum of Art in New York City in 1897, where it is still on display.

Bottom: Currier & Ives produced this lithograph in 1870. It was a take-off from their 1863 colored lithograph entitled, *John Brown Meeting the Slave-mother and her Child on the steps of Charlestown jail on his way to execution*, which had four more characters and other art works.

This cenopath is in the Oberlin, Ohio, cemetery. The Inscription reads:

S. GREEN
Died at Charleston, Va., Dec. 2, 1859
Aged 23 years
J.A. COPELAND
Died at Charleston, Va., Dec. 2, 1859
Aged 25 years
L.S. LEARY
Died at Harper's Ferry, Oct. 20, 1859
Aged 24 years
These colored citizens of Oberlin,
The heroic assoicates of the immortal
JOHN BROWN
Gave their lives for the slaves.
Et nunc servitudo etiam mortua est, laus Deo.
OBERLIN HISTORICAL AND IMPROVEMENT
ORGANIZATION.

This life-sized carrera marble statue of John Brown was dedicated on June 1, 1911, on the campus of the former Western University near Kansas City, Kansas, at the corner of 27th and Sewell Avenue, near the Quindaro ruins (an underground railroad stop). WVSA

Monument dedicated on Sept. 25, 1938, by the Negro 25 Year Club of Akron, Ohio. The monument is in a deteriorated condition today. WVSA

John Brown's Cave and Historical Village

This log cabin was built about 1854 in Nebraska City, Nebraska, by Allen B. Mayhew and his father-in-law, Abraham Kagi. It housed the Mayhews and their six sons until 1864 and is one of the oldest structures in Nebraska. Mrs. Mayhew's brother was John Henry Kagi, one of John Brown's closest confidantes. Kagi made this his home for a time in the 1850s. Nebraska City's location on the edge of free territory, and near the site of the Missouri River crossing, made it an integral part of the Underground Railroad. Fugitive slaves were hidden in the hand-dug cave underneath the cabin. It has been known as John Brown's Cave as early as 1874. Brown was in Nebraska City at least five times: Aug. 9 and Oct. 5, 1856; twice in November 1857 and Feb. 4, 1859. The site is now owned by Larry and Linda Shepard.

The restored John Brown's Cave about 1938.

Stephen Vincent Benét (1898-1943) was a famous American writer from a family of writers. Benét's interest in American history and folklore, and his interest in the ballad form, influenced his major work, *John Brown's Body*, written in 1928. His book-length poem received a Pulitzer prize in 1929. In his poem, he tried to give a complete picture of the Civil War. He dramatized battles and portrayed the political events that led to the war. Benét also traced the history of slavery in America starting in th 1600s. The war itself is seen through the eyes of several characters, including a Southern Belle, a runaway slave, an abolitionist from New England and a Pennsylvania farmer who takes part in the Gettysburg battle. The poem has often been presented on the stage as a dramatic reading.

Benét also wrote novels and short stories, including "The Devil and Daniel Webster" in 1937. He received his second Pulitzer prize for his 1943 poem *Western Star*.

A new commemorative stamp was issued on July 22, 1998, at Harpers Ferry National Historical Park to honor Stephen Vincent Benét. The stamp is the 15th in the U.S. Postal Service's Literary Arts Series. It was designed by Michael Deas and depicts a detail of the Robert Gould Shaw Memorial, a bas-relief by Augustus Saint-Gaudeus that depicts the black 54th Massachusetts Infantry.

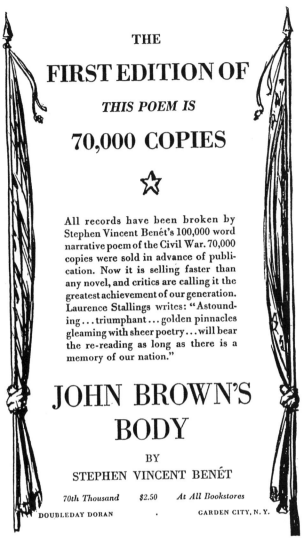

THE

FIRST EDITION OF

THIS POEM IS

70,000 COPIES

☆

All records have been broken by Stephen Vincent Benét's 100,000 word narrative poem of the Civil War. 70,000 copies were sold in advance of publication. Now it is selling faster than any novel, and critics are calling it the greatest achievement of our generation. Laurence Stallings writes: "Astounding...triumphant...golden pinnacles gleaming with sheer poetry...will bear the re-reading as long as there is a memory of our nation."

JOHN BROWN'S BODY

BY

STEPHEN VINCENT BENÉT

70th Thousand $2.50   *At All Bookstores*

DOUBLEDAY DORAN   •   GARDEN CITY, N. Y.

WVSA

When the Township of Torrington, Conn., became a city in 1923, they adopted this seal with John Brown's birthplace on it. COURTESY ERNEST CEDAR, TORRINGTON CITY HISTORIAN.

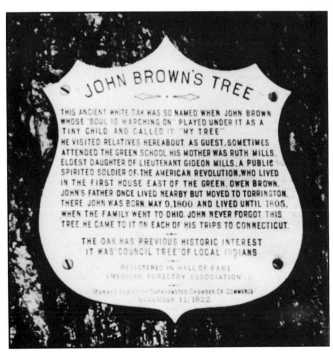

Miscellaneous Facts or Fiction

♦ Congressman Frank Reid said of Gen. "Billy" Mitchell upon his court-martial conviction in 1925. "Col. William Mitchell is a 1925 John Brown. They may think they have silenced him, but his ideas will go marching on and those who crucified him will be the first to put his aviation suggestions into use."

♦ Robert Buffum served with John Brown in the Kansas action. He gained fame as one of the Andrews Raiders on their famous raid in Georgia to destroy the railroad between Atlanta and Chattanooga. Buffum was mustered into the Union Army in September 1861 and volunteered for the famous raid in April 1862. He was captured following the raid and exchanged about a year later. He was awarded, along with the other 19 raiders, the Medal of Honor. These were the first medals of honor awarded. Due to a drinking problem, he resigned from the army in April 1864 and committed suicide at his home in Auburn, New York in 1871.

♦ About 1916 a story appeared in Part 63 of a booklet series titled, *The History of Our Country*. It concerned Joseph R. Winter, known during the Civil War as "Indian Jack." He was born in Leesburg, Va., in 1816. He had lived in Chambersburg, Pa., since 1830, and was the author of the war song, "Ten Days After the Battle of Gettysburg." He supposedly served as John Brown's orderly during the Harpers Ferry raid but no mention of his name could be found in the literature on the raid.

♦ The Socialist's party's leader Eugene Debs announced to the press in 1908, "the Socialist Party is carrying on the work begun by John Brown."

♦ There have been reports of a 23rd man included in the Harpers Ferry raid. A Mr. Jacob Wildner of New Lisbon, Wisc., claimed in 1901 to be the last survivor of the raid. He supposedly was in the enginehouse just before the attack and claimed that a black woman suggested that he blacken his hands and face, wear one of her dresses and escape. He jumped out a rear window and made his way to a cave nearby where he remained for 17 days and then passed into history until 1901. While the story is mostly implausible, it is typical of other famous events in history.

John Brown Historical Groups

The John Brown Heritage Association can be reached at 291 Park Avenue, Meadville, PA 16335. Its goals are:

> **Searching, preserving and documenting** historical information and landmarks relating to the life and times of John Brown.
>
> **Maintaining** the John Brown Tannery Site for public visitation.
>
> Maintaining a living history of the expansion of human freedom through holding periodic Pilgrimages in New Richmond.
>
> **Studying and interpreting** early 19th Century United States' social, economic and political history, particularly as it relates to the events of John Brown's life.

The John Brown Society can be reached at P.O. Box 1046, Canal Street Station, New York, NY 10013. Its goals are:

> **To encourage and promote** the preservation of historical sites associated with John Brown and his comrades-in-arms.
>
> **To recognize and encourage** outstanding scholarship in the history of abolitionism
>
> **To provide recognition and honor** to those today who emulate the spirit of John Brown.

Opposite page, top left: The John Brown Statue is located in the John Brown Memorial Park on West Main Street in Osawatomie. The 20-acre park was donated to the State of Kansas by the Women's Relief Corps of the Grand Army of the Republic and dedicated in 1910 by former President Theodore Roosevelt. At the time he gave his famous New Nationalism speech. A short distance north of the park entrance is a life-size statue of John Brown, dedicated in 1935. The bronze statue was cast in the foundry of Monsieur F. Bardedienne of Paris, France. This foundry also cast the Statue of Liberty. WVSA

Opposite page, top right and bottom: Dedication of the Soldiers Monument at Osawatomie on Aug. 30, 1877. It was erected 21 years to the day to commemorate the Battle of Osawatomie fought between 400 Border Ruffians and 38 Free State Men under the command of John Brown. Fourteen of Brown's men were at the dedication: S.A. Stonebraker; E.W. Robinson; S.C. Woolard; F.G. Adams; S.L. Adair; Jas. Hanway; Dr. Updegraft; D.C. Cook; Samuel Walker; William Kralman; H.H. Williams; S.H. Howser; S.H. Bundy; and Capt. J.M. Anthony. It was erected to honor the five men killed in the battle. Buried beneath the monument are Frederick Brown, George W. Partridge, David Garrison and Theron Parker Powers. The body of Charles Kaiser was never found but his name appears on the stone. John Brown's name also appears on the monument. The monument was paid for by friends and relatives of those buried beneath it. It was planned and erected by "The Monument Association," which later disbanded, and gave the ground at Ninth and Main streets to the city. WVSA

CELEBRATION

The Colored Citizens of Pasadena and Los Angeles
will celebrate

JOHN BROWN'S BIRTHDAY.

—AT—

Raymond Hill, South Pasadena,

—ON—

MAY 9, 1900.

A splendid Program has been arranged.

The following gentlemen will address the audience:

REV. R. H. HERRING, J. C. JACKSON, Pasadena.
REV. F. L. DONOHOO, ATTY E. H. CASSY, Los Angeles.
REV. CLARENCE TRUE WILSON, Santa Monica.
MAJOR H. N. RUST, South Pasadena.
    Subject:—"The Causes that Led John Brown to make th[e]
        Sacrifices he made at Harper's Ferry."
J. L. EDMUNDS, South Pasadena.
    Subject: "How to prove Ourselves worthy of John Bro[wn's]
        Sacrifices."

Splendid Singing

by the School Children.

All are invited to bring their LUNCHES.
Exercises begin at 2 o'clock sharp.

The Raymond Hill is one of the most picturesque hills in Sou[thern]
California, commanding a fine view of the
entire San Gabriel Valley.

Come early and spend the day

COMMITTEE:

J. C. Williams, Wm. Prince, A. C. Hall, Thos. Pillow, Geo. [
Mrs. M. Weatherton, Mrs. G. M. Warner, Mrs. Ida For[
Wallis, Mrs. W. C. Dent, Mrs. J. I. Harding, Mrs. Harp[i
Wm. Prince, Mrs. Samuel Prince, Mrs. J. E. Iverson, Mrs [
Herring.
    People from Los Angeles will take Pasadena Cars.

The Liberator Print, 620 S. Broadway.

JOHN BROWN

MEMORIAL ASSOCIATION

PICNIC

SATURDAY, JUNE 30, 1928

PROGRAM

ADDRESS—

Mr. Boyd B. Stutler

Charleston, W. Va.

STUNTS
GAMES
MUSIC

Ladies Aid Will Furnish Dinner

MENU

Roast Beef, Brown Gravy
Mashed Potatoes   Cottage Cheese
        Corn
    Lettuce Salad
    Jam   Jelly   Pickles
Pie   Cheese   Coffee
    Brown Bread   White Bread

Seventy-five Cents Plate

Contribute to

STORER
COLLEGE

In Memory of
JOHN BROWN

-174-

John Brown Picnic
New Richmond, Pa.
August 3rd, 1929
2:00 P. M.

Music by Orchestra.
Greetings by Chairman .... Wm. R. Lingo
Reading—Ode to John Brown.
Business Meeting.
In Memoriam.
Violin Solo .... Mr. Lingo

TABLEAUX

Depicting Scenes from the Life of John Brown.
Arranged by Bess Heath Olmstead.

CAST OF CHARACTERS

John Brown .... Jas. H. Wright
Mary Day Brown .... Elizabeth Olmstead
Owen Brown .... Children of John Brown ... Georgia Olmstead
Ruth Brown .... Mary Loveland
Overseer .... Floyd Hotchkiss

Slaves, Carpet-baggers, Slave Traders, Soldiers and others.
Plantation Singers

SCENE 1—Plantation Life
a—In the Cotton Fields.
b—The Whip.
SCENE 2—The Slave Block
a—Traffic in Slaves.
b—Enter John Brown.
SCENE 3—John Brown, the Tanner
a—New Richmond.
b—The Underground.
Battle Cry of Freedom
John Brown's Body ....

SCENE 4—Bleeding Kansas
a—John Brown at Bay.
b—The First Bloodshed.
SCENE 5—Harper's Ferry
a—Capture of John Brown.
b—Defeated.
SCENE 6—The Execution
a—On the Way to the Gallows.
b—The Last Farewell.

Address of the Day .... Hon. Lew R. Rodgers, of Erie, Penna.
Finale—Post War Music by Plantation Singers.
1—Jubilo
2—Uncle Joe's Dream .... Solo by Merrill Lilli
Plantation Dance:
By Marian Sullivan, Virginia Sullivan, Ruth Stanford, Olive Hixson, Rut
Kinney, Elizabeth Lanston, Virginia Kamps, Helen Grace Merrick.
Audience will join with the Plantation Singers in singing
1—John Brown's Body.
2—America.

JOHN BROWN
CENTENNIAL
PICNIC and CELEBRATION
In the John Brown Grove
New Richmond, Pa.
AUG. 2, 1930

MID DAY PICNIC
Business Meeting of John Brown Memorial Ass'n at 2:00 P. M.
PROGRAM AT 2:30

THE SPEAKER OF THE DAY
DR. JOHN STEELE DUNCAN
OF MERCER, PA.
Will tell us about John Brown's history-making career

A ONE ACT PLAY
"An Evening in New Richmond 100 Years Ago"
To be presented by a cast of 16.   Costumes of 1830.   Old time songs

EXHIBITION OF RELICS 100 YEARS OLD
OLD CHINA, TOOLS, BOOKS, FURNITURE—COLLECTED FROM 3 COUNTIES

COME and see the John Brown properties and hear about John Brown
COME and picnic in the John Brown grove and listen to the band
COME and see the play. Old time costumes. Old time songs
COME and see the violin 335 years old; the gun 303 years old, and dozens of
articles made and used by our pioneer ancestors
COME   John Brown Grove, New Richmond, Pa.   COME

John Brown Day
AUGUST 23rd, 1916

PROGRAM
OF
EXERCISES

Morning Exercises at 10:30

At Happy Hour Theatre
M. E. Church bell will toll ten minutes previous to commencing of exercises.

SPEAKERS
HON. FRANK B. SANBORN
Friend and Biographer of John Brown
DEAN KELLY MILLER
Howard University, Washington, D. C.
Collection will be taken to defray expenses of tablet and exercises
Special arrangements have been made with auto bus drivers to carry passengers to and from the grave at the uniform price of 25 cents each way.

Afternoon Exercises at 3 p. m.

At the Grave of John Brown
Music By Lake Placid Band
Prayer—Rev. E. A. Braman
UNVEILING THE TABLET
Wendell Phillips' Oration at the Burial of John Brown
Read by Prof. Riggs
SPEAKERS
HON. JOHN E. MILHOLLAND
HON. FRANK B. SANBORN
DEAN KELLY MILLER
RABBI STEPHEN S. WISE
Collection
Music by the Band, B. R. Brewster Presiding

Forty-three years after the Harpers Ferry raid John Brown artifacts
were of interest to collectors.

At the 1893 World's Columbian Exposition in Chicago F.G.
Logan, a wealthy grain merchant showed his collection of
John Brown artifacts. He had obtained these from Horatio
Rust, an Indian agent in California. Included in the
collection were Brown's field glasses, various letters, a pike,
a saber presented to him and a receipt for money given to
him at Collinsville, Conn. Logan also had Owen Brown's
gun and Bowie knife.

STORER COLLEGE CAMPUS

2:00 CONCERT — Shepherd College Band
                              Mr. William Stewart, *Announcer*

3:00 ARRIVAL OF DISTINGUISHED GUESTS

        GREETINGS.....................Mrs. John Newcomer, *President*
                              Harpers Ferry Centennial Association
                              Presenting Mrs. Cyrus Cavalier, *Chairman,*
                              John Brown Raid Centennial

        INTRODUCTION OF DISTINGUISHED GUESTS
                                            Mr. Lee Bushong

        SPEAKER OF THE AFTERNOON
                              Senator Jennings Randolph
                Introduced by Mr. W. P. C. Perry

        FASHION SHOW OF 1859

        BEARD GROWING CONTEST
        Sponsored by The Junior Women's Club of Charles Town,
              W. Va., Mrs. James Gore and Mrs. Donald Engle,
                                            Co-Chairmen

                              Mrs. Donald Engle, *Announcer*

Representative Jennings Randolph of West Virginia
introduced a bill in Congress in 1935 to establish an
historical park at Harpers Ferry. It took until 1944
to establish a national monument and until 1963 to
establish a national historical park.

Centennial Observance

John Brown Raid

Harpers Ferry, West Virginia

Historians' Day

October 16, 1959

Hill Top Hotel   12:30 P.M.

Chicago Ill Feb. 16th 1888
Headquaters John Brown No 50
GAR Department of Illinois

To the Surviving Members
and Relatives of the Family of the
Late John Brown Sr.

We The officers and comrades of this Post 50 GAR Dept Ill City of
Chicago
Do herby Express our Sincere Love and appreciation of the Noble Deades of our late
friend and advocate of the Colerd Race the Late John Brown Sr. Recognising that in as
much as he gave his life in the attempt to stripe the shackeles from Our Race that in
token of this act We The Colerd Survivors of the Late Rebellion Did on the 12 Day of
Janury 1878 organnise a Grand army Post in this City to Be knowen as the John
Brown Post No 50 Dept Ill Duley Charterd under the GAR of the State of Ill. Said
Post was named in memory of the heroe of Harpers Ferry. Said Post was organised with
12 charter members and now has a membership of 86 attached to wich is the Womens
Relief Corp No 14 With 40 members as an auxilery. In Behalf of these 2 organnisations
We herby extend a cordial invitation to aney and all Survivors of the late John Brown Sr
to visite us at aney and all times. Our doors will allwayes be found wide openen and our
hearts will allwayes be in Readiness to Welcome you and Rest assured the noble sacafise
given by John Brown at Harpers Ferry will dwell ever in our minds his Sacred Love will
Dwell Ever in our hearts and his memory and name shall be handed down to our Childrens
Chrildrens While time shall last on the 16th Day of this month it was the priviledge of 21
members of this Post and 2 Representatives of the Ladies Corp No 14 to welcome within
its doors one of the Survivors of this illustirous Friend and father of our Race the Son of
John Brown Sr John Brown Jr had we of knowen the Distingushed gentelman and
Comrad was in 5 hours sooner the Colerd Citicens would of ben out in masses to welcome so
Illustirous a Son of So noble a Sire permit us to hope for a long and prosperes Life to all
the Surviving members of the Family and hoping to see any and all at any time
Respectfully yours in the Blessings of Fredome
Barney Moore Commander
Post 50 2834 Butterfield St
James F. Burton S.V.C. 1333 State St
John H Taylor 397 Dearbourn St
on Behalf of Post 50

Endorsed and approved By John Brown
Womens Relief Corp No 14 Depot Ill
Mrs Frances Powell President
Mrs. Henett L. Burton Post SV Presdet
on Behalf of Corp 14

Bibliography

This short list of books includes a few of the standard reference works on John Brown, his life, Bleeding Kansas and the attack on Harpers Ferry. Also included are a few contemporary works used as research for this book. Since 1859, hundreds of books, newspaper and magazine articles, and pamphlets have been written about John Brown. These books should give the reader interested in pursuing the subject further an adequate base. Many articles and newspaper accounts not listed here were also used by the author for basic research.

Abels, Jules, *Man on Fire: John Brown and the Cause of Liberty*, Oxford University Press, New York, 1971.

Boyer, Richard O., *The Legend of John Brown: A Biography and a History*, Alfred A. Knopf, New York, 1973.

Conway, Martin, *Harpers Ferry Time Remembered,* Carabelle Books, Reston, Va. 1981.

Everhart, William C., and Arthur L. Sullivan, *John Brown's Raid*, National Park Service, Washington, D.C., 1974.

Furnas, J.C., *The Road to Harpers Ferry*, William Sloane Associates, New York, 1959.

Hearn, Chester G., *Companions in Conspiracy: John Brown & Gerrit Smith*, Thomas Publications, Gettysburg, Pa., 1996.

Hinton, Richard J., *John Brown and His Men,* Funk and Wagnalls, New York, 1894.

Junker, Patricia, *John Steuart Curry, Inventing The Middle West*, Hudson Hills Press, New York, 1998.

Keller, Allan, *Thunder at Harper's Ferry*, Prentice-Hall, Inc., Englewood Cliffs, NJ, 1958.

Kendall, M. Sue, *Rethinking Regionalism, John Steuart Curry and the Kansas Mural Controversy*, Smithsonian Institution Press, Washington, D.C., 1986.

Nalty, Damon, *The Browns of Madronia, Family of Abolitionist John Brown Buried in Madronia Cemetery, Saratoga, California*, Saratoga Historical Foundation, 1996.

Oates, Stephen, *To Purge This Land With Blood: A Biography of John Brown*, Harper and Row, New York, 1970.

Redpath, James, *The Life, Trial and Execution of Capt. John Brown*, Robert M. Dewitt, New York, 1859.

_____, *The Public Life of Captain John Brown,* Thickbroom and Stapelton, London, 1860.

Renehan, Edward J. Jr., *The Secret Six, The True Tales of the Men Who Conspired with John Brown,* University of South Carolina Press, Columbia, S.C., 1997.

Sanborn, Franklin B., *The Life and Letters of John Brown*, Roberts Brothers, Boston, 1885.

Scott, John Anthony & Robert Alan, *John Brown of Harper's Ferry, With Contemporary Prints, Photographs and Maps*, Facts on File, New York, 1988.

Southern Revenge! Civil War History of Chambersburg, Pennsylvania, Greater Chambersburg Chamber of Commerce, 1989.

Stake, Virginia Ott, *John Brown in Chambersburg*, Franklin County Heritage, Inc., Chambersburg, Pa., 1977.

Stone, Edward, *Incident At Harper's Ferry*, Prentice-Hall, Inc., Englewood Cliffs, NJ, 1956.

Villard, Oswald Garrison, *John Brown: 1800-1859; a Biography Fifty Years After*, Houghton Mifflin Co., New York, 1910.

Warren, Robert Penn, *John Brown: The Making of a Martyr,* Payson and Clarke Ltd., New York, 1929.

Zittle, John Henry, *A Correct History of the John Brown Invasion*, Mail Publishing Co., Hagerstown, MD, 1905.

Index

The author, holding an original John Brown pike from the collection of Hays Otoupalik, Missoula, Mont.

Boyd Stutler is shown at the foundation walls of Brown's tannery in New Richmond, Pa., 1949. wvsa

About the Author

Stan Cohen is a native of Charleston, West Virginia, and a graduate of West Virginia University with a BS degree in geology. He established Pictorial Histories Publishing Company in 1976 with his first book, *The Civil War in West Virginia, A Pictorial History*. Since then he has authored or co-authored 70 books and published over 300. He moved to Missoula, Montana, in 1961 to work for the U.S. Forest Service and has been a full-time author/publisher since 1980. He lives in Missoula with his wife, Anne, but maintains an office in Charleston and travels extensively throughout the state, selling and researching new books.

Boyd Stutler

One of the most noted John Brown scholars of this century was Boyd Stutler. He was born in 1889 in Gilmer County, West Virginia. He was member of the 80th Division in France during WWI and a war correspondent in WWII. He was managing editor of the *American Legion Magazine* from 1936-54 and a director of the Education Foundation, Inc., in Charleston. He was a noted historian of West Virginia's Civil War history and amassed a large John Brown collection of documents, objects and photographs which is now part of the West Virginia State Archives. Stutler died in 1970 before he was able to complete his biography of John Brown.

The Back Cover Artist

The back cover artist is Col. Charles Waterhouse USMCR ret. of Edison, New Jersey. His first tour of duty with the Marine Corps was in 1943-46 with the 5th Marine Division FMF in the Pacific. His second tour was from 1972-92 as artist-in-residence USMC. He has been an artist and illustrator for major book and magazine publishers, advertising and private clients, and as official or combat artist for all services. His paintings hang in virtually every Marine Corps post in the world.

John Brown's Fort, Harpers Ferry

Modern-day views of John Brown's Fort in lower town, Harpers Ferry. It was moved from Storer College in 1968 by the National Park Service.

PHOTOS BY NOAH MEHRKAM

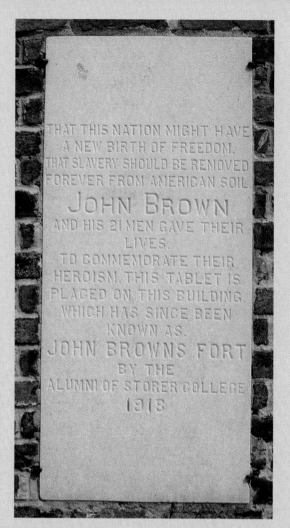

THAT THIS NATION MIGHT HAVE
A NEW BIRTH OF FREEDOM,
THAT SLAVERY SHOULD BE REMOVED
FOREVER FROM AMERICAN SOIL.
JOHN BROWN
AND HIS 21 MEN GAVE THEIR
LIVES,
TO COMMEMORATE THEIR
HEROISM, THIS TABLET IS
PLACED ON THIS BUILDING,
WHICH HAS SINCE BEEN
KNOWN AS,
JOHN BROWNS FORT
BY THE
ALUMNI OF STORER COLLEGE
1918

Left (top and bottom) and above: Interior views of John Brown's Fort. The fire apparatus is similar to equipment in use in 1859. PHOTOS BY NOAH MEHRKAM

ON THE NIGHT OF OCTOBER 16, 1859,
HEYWARD SHEPHERD, AN INDUSTRIOUS
AND RESPECTED COLORED FREEMAN,
WAS MORTALLY WOUNDED BY JOHN
BROWN'S RAIDERS, IN PURSUANCE
OF HIS DUTIES AS AN EMPLOYEE OF
THE BALTIMORE AND OHIO RAILROAD
COMPANY, HE BECAME THE FIRST
VICTIM OF THIS ATTEMPTED
INSURRECTION.
    THIS BOULDER IS ERECTED BY
THE UNITED DAUGHTERS OF THE
CONFEDERACY AND THE SONS OF
CONFEDERATE VETERANS AS A
MEMORIAL TO HEYWARD SHEPHERD,
EXEMPLIFYING THE CHARACTER AND
FAITHFULNESS OF THOUSANDS OF
NEGROES WHO, UNDER MANY
TEMPTATIONS THROUGHOUT
SUBSEQUENT YEARS OF WAR, SO
CONDUCTED THEMSELVES THAT
NO STAIN WAS LEFT UPON A RECORD
WHICH IS THE PECULIAR HERITAGE
OF THE AMERICAN PEOPLE, AND AN
EVERLASTING TRIBUTE TO THE BEST
IN BOTH RACES.

Heyward Sheperd Monument.

Items located in the John Brown exhibit at the Harpers Ferry Historical Park. *Top left:* Pieces of the hanging scaffold from Charlestown. *Top right:* One of the original gates at the entrance to the U.S. Government arsenal. *Bottom right:* A door from the Charlestown jail. *Below:* John Brown's personal bible. PHOTOS BY NOAH MEHRKAM AND NPS

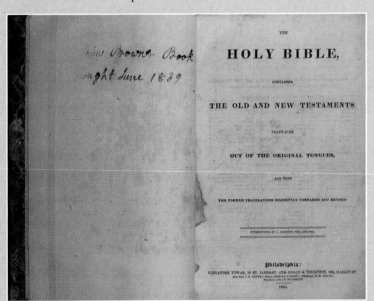

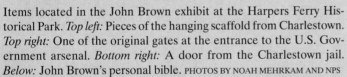

Kennedy Farm

Front, back and side views of the restored Kennedy farmhouse, a National Historic Landmark, located between the Harpers Ferry Road and the Chestnut Grove Road, four miles north of Harpers Ferry in Maryland. It is owned by Capt. South and Sprigg Lynn. PHOTOS BY NOAH MEHRKAM

Historical figures inside the Kennedy farmhouse.
PHOTOS BY NOAH MEHRKAM

Osawatomie, Kansas

The Adair Cabin in the John Brown Memorial Park. The cabin, built in 1854, was enclosed within a huge stone pergola in the 1920s. In 1995, the cabin was broken into, looted and burned by an arsonist. Money was raised from local and federal funds to restore the cabin. The cabin was rededicated on Aug. 30, 1998, with several descendants of the Adair's present. PHOTOS BY DEAN BROWN

Top: John Brown Memorial Park located at Tenth and Main streets. *Above left:* John Brown statue. *Above right:* Soldier's Monument located at Ninth and Main Streets.

Kansas

Tragic Prelude—John Brown, 11'6"×31', oil and tempera on canvas, Kansas State Capitol, Topeka, 1937–42.

POTTAWATOMIE MASSACRE
On the night of May 24-25, 1856, a small band of abolitionists led by John Brown murdered five pro-slavery men just north of here along Pottawatomie Creek. This massacre in "Bleeding Kansas" was one of the most famous events leading up to the American Civil War. Brown was later captured, tried and hanged for his unsuccessful raid on Harper's Ferry, (West) Virginia in 1859.

FRANKLIN COUNTY HISTORICAL SOCIETY

PHOTOS BY DEAN BROWN, OSAWATOMIE, KANSAS

On the morning of August 30, 1856, John Brown led about 30 antislavery men into battle against 250 proslavery Missourians. This Battle of Osawatomie raged on the site of John Brown Memorial Park.

Local tradition maintains that the statue of John Brown is located where the mounted proslavery men fired their first shots. Brown positioned his men about four hundred yards to the north in the timber lining the south bank of the Marais des Cygnes River. The Missourians charged down the hill toward Brown's men with their guns blazing. The free-state force held firm, checking the first charge. The attackers dismounted, outflanked Brown's force, and brought their cannon into action.

Finally Brown and his men bolted from their hiding places and fled across the river. The Missourians swarmed into Osawatomie, where they sacked and burned the town. Both sides sustained about a half-dozen casualties, the most of any battle during the Bleeding Kansas period. Among the dead was John Brown's son Frederick.

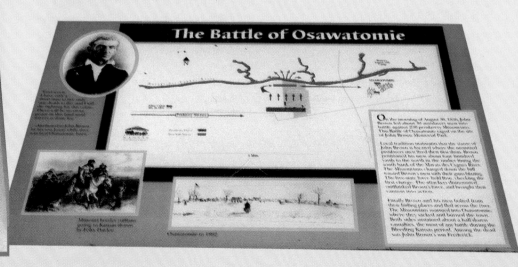

The Battle of Osawatomie

John Brown rented this house in Akron on the corner of Diagonal and Copley roads. It is across the street from the Perkins stone mansion, currently the headquarters of the Summit County Historical Society.

John Brown's son Jason is buried in the Glendale Cemetery, Akron, Ohio.

PHOTOS BY THOMAS VINCE, HUDSON, OHIO.

John Brown's house in Hudson, Ohio, has been greatly modified through the years.

Monument in downtown Hudson, Ohio.

John Brown preached at the Free Congressional Church in Hudson, Ohio, in 1859.

New Richmond, Pennsylvania

Scenes at the John Brown Tannery Site, New
Richmond, Crawford County, Pennsylvania.
The site was placed in the National Register of
Historic Places in December 1978. PHOTOS ON
BOTH PAGES BY BRUCE NOBLE, JR., HARPERS FERRY
NATIONAL HISTORICAL PARK

Ross Prather is on the right, Rev. Arthur Crawford on the left.

The informational sign reads:

A Tanner Comes to the Township

The tannery in 1885, then being used as a corn-grinding mill

Near Collapse

Mary Day Brown, year unknown

A Community Presence

His Household's Provider

Crawford County

Western Reserve

The gravesite of John Brown's first wife, Dianthe (left) and their son, Frederick I (right). Dianthe died on Aug. 10, 1832, and Frederick I on March 31, 1831. Now open on the property is the Historic John Brown Museum. Contact: Donna Coburn, 17620 John Brown Road, Guise Mills, PA 16327, Tel: (814) 967-2099.

John Brown marker near the tannery site. Patricia Noble (left) and Mark Peaster.

Scenes at the John Brown Farm State Historic Park, North Elba, New York. PHOTOS BY ED COTTER JR., LAKE PLACID, NY

Lake Placid, New York